S0-CBC-848

SPELLBOUND
Studies on Mesmerism
and Literature

SPELLBOUND

Studies on Mesmerism and Literature

Maria M. Tatar

PRINCETON UNIVERSITY PRESS
Princeton, New Jersey

Published by Princeton University Press, Princeton, N.J.
In the United Kingdom: Princeton University Press,
Guildford, Surrey

Library of Congress Cataloging in Publication Data will be found on the last printed page of this book

Publication of this book has been aided by a grant from The Andrew W. Mellon Foundation

This book has been composed in linotype Baskerville
Clothbound editions of Princeton University Press books are printed on acid-free paper, and binding materials are chosen for strength and durability.

Designed by Laury A. Egan

Printed in the United States of America by
Princeton University Press,
Princeton, New Jersey

To my parents

Contents

List of Illustrations viii

Preface ix

1 From Mesmer to Freud: Animal Magnetism, Hypnosis, and Suggestion 3

2 Salvation by Electricity: Science, Poetry, and *Naturphilosophie* 45

3 Thunder, Lightning, and Electricity: Moments of Recognition in Heinrich von Kleist's Dramas 82

4 Blindness and Insight: Visionary Experience in the Tales of E.T.A. Hoffmann 121

5 The Metaphysics of the Will: Voyeurs and Visionaries in Balzac's *Comédie humaine* 152

6 Masters and Slaves: The Creative Process in Hawthorne's Fiction 189

7 From Science Fiction to Psychoanalysis: Henry James's *Bostonians*, D. H. Lawrence's *Women in Love*, and Thomas Mann's *Mario and the Magician* 230

Appendix: Mesmer's Propositions 273

Index 277

List of Illustrations

(following page 80)

Mesmer
An eighteenth-century engraving of Mesmer's salon
A mesmerist session in full swing
A literalist's view of animal magnetism
Chodowiecki's *Magnetiseur*
A satirical view of mesmerist phenomena
Samuel Collings's "Magnetic Dispensary"
The "magnetized elm" of Buzancy
Fragonard's *Au génie de Franklin*
Charcot lecturing at the Salpêtrière

Preface

Few approaches to literature have promised more and delivered less than the psychoanalytic. Freud's theories have, however, opened new avenues of interpretation for critics of all persuasions. The difference between the critic who searches for Oedipal situations and obsessional neuroses and the critic who speaks of ambivalence and forbidden wishes is primarily one of degree. Both have assimilated the world view of psychoanalysis. One recent apologist for the Freudian critical method contends that psychoanalysis is "the only psychology to have seriously altered our way of reading literature."[1] Psychoanalysis did not, however, rush into a vacuum. Freud himself was the first to admit that philosophers and psychologists of past generations had anticipated many essential features of his system. To discredit the vast literature on psychology that existed before Freud and to forget that the authors of this literature shaped the views of their contemporaries (in much the same way as Freud changed our perspective on the world) is to shut one's eyes to the insights that the past can offer.

The nineteenth-century version of psychology is by no means alien to the spirit of psychoanalysis. All the same, Freud developed his theories using a frame of reference radically different from the one employed by his precursors. This study aims principally to demonstrate that the writings of both Romantics and Romantic Realists were informed by contemporary psychological sources and that the very ideas in their works that strike us as "modern" are firmly anchored in nineteenth-century thought.[2]

[1] Frederick Crews, *Out of My System: Psychoanalysis, Ideology and Critical Method* (New York: Oxford University Press, 1975), p. 4.

[2] I borrow the term "Romantic Realism" from Donald Fanger. See

The reader who finds an undertaking of such dimensions suspect will appreciate the complex problems raised by any study of psychology in the first half of the nineteenth century. Psychologists of that epoch were for the most part physicians, scientists, or philosophers with a special interest in nervous disorders or mental aberrations. Psychology itself had not yet secured a fixed position in the hierarchy of academic disciplines. Faced with the formidable task of collecting and analyzing the rich and varied material on this branch of knowledge, I have limited the scope of my subject by singling out one aspect of nineteenth-century psychology —animal magnetism, or mesmerism—for closer scrutiny. In addressing such a topic, this work aims less to pay tribute to the revival of the occult sciences in our own day than to understand the preoccupations of an earlier age. Mesmerism was, to be sure, espoused by countless mountebanks, magicians, and false prophets (the names of Cagliostro and Svengali come immediately to mind), but it also captured the attention of the literary elite in Europe and America— E.T.A. Hoffmann, Balzac, Dickens, and Poe, to mention only a few of the most distinguished devotees. Mesmerist doctrines, in part because of their eclectic nature, also furnish an ideal index of psychological, scientific, and philosophical issues of the nineteenth century. An understanding of such a seemingly alien topic can provide some insight into the patterns of thought prevailing in another age.

The vocabulary of mesmerism has assimilated itself into our own speech. Unless we deliberately avoid the now hackneyed expressions bequeathed to us by the mesmerists, we find ourselves talking without a second thought of "magnetic" personalities that exert an irresistible influence and "mesmerizing" gazes that weave a magical spell. It is easy to forget that these colorless, now nearly dead, metaphors

---

Dostoevsky and Romantic Realism: A Study of Dostoevsky in Relation to Balzac, Dickens, and Gogol (Cambridge, Mass.: Harvard University Press, 1965).

were once alive with meaning. When such figures of speech occur in a literary text, most critics dismiss them as tired clichés or unimaginative borrowings from the language of the Gothic thriller. If we examine the linguistic texture of literary works using the eye of a twentieth-century reader, then these phrases, it is true, can only be perceived as flat. But if we seek out the natural connections that link them with contemporary ideas, it is often possible to enlarge our understanding of a text. Nabokov once noted that the text of *Eugene Onegin* contains "a conspiracy of words signalling to one another."[3] Such conspiracies infiltrate every literary text, and it is the task of the critic to expose them and lay bare their meaning.

While the language of mesmerism has eluded the grasp of many readers by its deceptive familiarity, it has escaped the attention of others as a result of its recondite nature. What is one to make of the electrical energy vibrating through Kleist's dramas, the "streams of magnetic fluid" coursing through Balzac's novels, the "electrical heat" radiating from figures in E.T.A. Hoffmann's tales, and the "magnetic chain of humanity" joining together the characters in Hawthorne's novels? And why is it that Rodolphe woos Emma Bovary by entertaining her with "dreams, forebodings, magnetism"?[4] Why does Charles Bovary, distraught by his wife's death, recall stories about the "miracles of animal magnetism" and imagine that, by "straining his will," he can resuscitate his wife?[5] By taking the reader on a mesmerist tour of German, French, and American literature, this book attempts to answer such questions.

Franz Anton Mesmer, a physician armed with a medical degree from the University of Vienna, had never claimed

[3] Vladimir Nabokov, trans., *Eugene Onegin*, by Aleksandr Pushkin, 4 vols. with a Commentary, rev. ed. (Princeton, N.J.: Princeton University Press, Bollingen Series, 1975), III, 59.

[4] Flaubert, *Oeuvres*, ed. A. Thibaudet and R. Dumesnil, 2 vols. (Paris: Gallimard, 1951), I, 460.

[5] Ibid., p. 627.

to offer mankind anything more than a panacea for physical ailments. The key to health, he maintained, lay in recovering the wholly harmonious relationship that had once existed between man and nature. But Mesmer could hardly expect his French pupils (many of them raised on Rousseau) to disregard the spiritual and moral implications of his pronouncements. If animal magnetism promised to regenerate man's physical constitution, could it not also, by returning him to the wellsprings of his being, purify his moral faculties? Whether speaking of the progress of science and medicine or the improvement of human nature, magnetizers adopted a tone of millennial expectation that was to become a distinguishing characteristic of nineteenth-century mesmerist creeds.

Although the outcome of the French Revolution to some extent dissipated the vitality of the mesmerist movement in France, it by no means prevented mesmerist ideas from filtering through France to Germany and the United States. The twists and turns taken by the mesmerist movement in each of these countries is too complex a subject for extended discussion in a study that explores literary questions. I have tried, however, to give the reader a general sense of the way in which nineteenth-century mesmerists reinterpreted and redefined the precepts of their teacher.

The author of *Madame Bovary* furnishes perhaps the most concise and comprehensive introduction to the various phases of the mesmerist movement. The eighth chapter of *Bouvard et Pécuchet* depicts the titular heroes of Flaubert's encyclopedic narrative alternately testing and pronouncing judgment on nearly every version of animal magnetism with the same hierophantic enthusiasm that they bring to the entire range of human learning. The two bachelors collect iron filings and clean scores of bottles for a "magnetic tub" with which they intend to restore the health of invalids; they set up benches around a magnetized pear tree in their orchard for further mesmerist therapy; they hunt buried treasure with a divining rod, attempt to harness the energy of ethereal fluids, and finally host séances at which their guests hearken to cryptic messages rapped out by emissaries from a spiritual world.

Mesmer himself would hardly have recognized the many new interpretations of his teachings that emerged during the nineteenth century. In the decades following the French Revolution, mesmerism escaped the control of its founder to become enmeshed with a wide range of mystical, spiritual, and metaphysical doctrines. The magnetic fluid that had once streamed so abundantly through Mesmer's clinic was transformed by mystics into a divine afflatus, by spiritualists into ethereal specters, and by metaphysicians into an impalpable force designated as the will. The trances induced by these latter-day mesmerists represented a state in which the medium's body remained fixed on earth while his soul escaped its corporeal prison to roam through another world. No longer merely a palliative for physical ills or a remedy for moral degeneration, mesmerism now promised to endow man with a sixth sense that would expand his cognitive consciousness.

To move from the occult applications of mesmerism to the psychoanalytic use of hypnosis requires no great leap of the imagination. If one grants that mental activity under hypnosis can reveal thought processes normally hidden from view, then it hardly comes as a surprise that Freud regarded modern psychiatrists as the "legitimate heirs" to the hypnotists and their forebears. Indeed, Freud himself used hypnosis in the early years of his practice.

Although this work focuses on the literary implications of mesmerist theories, its introductory chapter offers a portrait of Mesmer, identifies his contributions, and seeks to establish connections between mesmerism, hypnotism, and psychoanalysis. It makes no attempt to rescue Mesmer's name from obloquy by honoring him as a neglected prophet of psychoanalysis, but aims at presenting a balanced appraisal of his historical significance. The chapter that follows places mesmerism within the context of scientific thought, psychological theory, and philosophical speculation in the eighteenth and nineteenth centuries. It examines the remarkable congruity between theories of magnetism and electricity—a congruity that led many literary figures to blur the lines distinguishing the two phenomena several decades before scientists began speaking of electromagnetism. The next four chapters trace the impact of mesmerist ideas on literature, giving special attention to the works of Heinrich von Kleist, E.T.A. Hoffmann, Honoré de Balzac, and Nathaniel Hawthorne. A final chapter describes the way in which twentieth-century writers absorbed and subsequently reshaped the mesmerist tradition that they had inherited from an earlier generation.

Although many of the texts discussed in this book have been rendered into English, I have chosen in most cases to provide my own translations of passages cited from those texts. I have sought to avoid pedantry, but occasionally the reader will find that I sacrifice elegance for precision of expression. Kleist's dramas in verse pose a special problem for a writer accustomed to thinking in prose. For this reason, I have relied on two highly readable English versions of the German texts: *The Prince of Homburg,* trans. Charles E. Passage (Indianapolis and New York: Bobbs-Merrill, 1956), and *Penthesilea,* in *Five German Tragedies,* trans. F. J. Lamport (Baltimore: Penguin Books, 1969). For Mann's *Mario und der Zauberer,* I have drawn on *Mario and the Magician,* in *Death in Venice and Seven Other Stories,* trans. H. T. Lowe-Porter (New York: Random House, 1930). Finally, the quotations from *Aurélia* come from *Gérard de Nerval: Selected Writings,* trans. Geoffrey Wagner (Ann Arbor: University of Michigan Press, 1970). For the sake of complete accuracy, I have at times changed a word or phrase in these translations. Passages from Freud's works are, unless otherwise noted, cited from James Strachey's *Standard Edition of the Complete Psychological Works,* 24 vols. (London: Hogarth, 1953-74). All other bibliographical notes refer the reader to the untranslated source of the quotation. In order to meet the needs of specialists, I have included the original versions of key passages either in parentheses within the text or in notes at the bottom of the page.

A number of friends and colleagues have followed the course of this book from inception to completion. Like so many other students trained in the German department at Princeton University, I owe much to Theodore Ziolkowski. He awakened my interest in German Romanticism and patiently guided my initial research in that field. This study has profited greatly from the example of his scholarship and from his careful criticism of my ideas. My colleagues at Harvard University have each in a unique way contributed to a congenial environment for scholarly enterprise. To Henry Hatfield I owe a special debt of gratitude. Setting aside his own work, he read every chapter with an expert eye and always managed to temper his suggestions for improvement with just the right measure of encouragement. Dorrit Cohn's warm support of this study proved especially valuable because of my admiration for her contributions to literary criticism. For advice, philosophy, and friendship, I am much indebted to the late Jack M. Stein. During his years as chairman of the German department at Harvard, he selflessly promoted the research of his younger colleagues by lightening their teaching duties, easing their administrative burdens, and providing a generous measure of personal encouragement.

Many other friends, students, and colleagues have listened to my ideas in their various stages of formulation, challenged my interpretations, and helped to sharpen my arguments. They will no doubt find here many tangible signs of their efforts, but also certain monuments to my own stubbornness. Theodore Andersson, Ernst Behler, Rudolph Binion, Ellen Chances, and John Neubauer graciously agreed to read the manuscript. Each made useful suggestions for improvement. Jerrold Levine, as a student of both science and literature, brought an invaluable perspective to his reading of the introductory chapters. I also benefited from the close attention that Gerald Geison gave to the sections on science and mesmerism. The students in my seminar on mesmerism and literature, who served as a captive but by no means unresponsive audience, deserve special thanks for their fresh insights and unflagging enthusiasm. To Stephen Schuker, who took an interest in my preoccupations even when they diverged from his own, spent countless disagreeable hours editing my prose, and stood by during the agony of checking footnotes, I offer a special word of appreciation. Finally, it is a pleasure to express my gratitude to Jerry Sherwood, who guided my manuscript to publication, and to Barbara Westergaard, whose tact and editorial precision sustained my interest in mesmerism and literature through the final stages of production.

I wish to record here my obligation to the staffs of Firestone Library at Princeton University, of Widener Library and the Countway Library of Medicine at Harvard University, of the Medical Library at Yale University, and of the National Library of Medicine in Bethesda, Maryland. I am also grateful to the National Endowment for the Humanities and the Committee for Faculty Research Support at Harvard University for their financial assistance.

Cambridge, Massachusetts *Maria M. Tatar*
July 1977

SPELLBOUND
Studies on Mesmerism and Literature

CHAPTER 1

From Mesmer to Freud: Animal Magnetism, Hypnosis, and Suggestion

"Go to France," Monsieur de Metternich told Gall, "and if they laugh at your bumps, you will be famous."
—Balzac, *Ursule Mirouët*

Franz Anton Mesmer was a man of mediocre talents and dubious ideals, but he came to occupy a pivotal position in the history of medicine and psychology. Because mesmerism serves as the principal link connecting primitive rites of exorcism with modern psychoanalysis, Mesmer himself has assumed the role of a transitional figure in the development of therapeutic procedures for functional disorders. Yet his actual contributions to psychological theory and medical knowledge have been largely forgotten. In the lexicon of psychology, "hypnotism," a word coined by the Scottish physician James Braid, has supplanted the term "mesmerism," and psychoanalysis has substituted the couch and the attentive analyst for the magnetic trance and the spellbinding hypnotist. Although "mesmerism" and "animal magnetism" (Mesmer's own name for his discovery) linger on in our language today, both terms are used in a strictly metaphorical sense. They have become near equivalents for hypnotism but have taken on—for reasons that will become clear in this chapter—distinct erotic overtones which are absent from their synonymous relative.

Mesmer's theories find a place somewhere near the middle of the spectrum where primitive psychotherapy shades off into psychoanalysis, faith healing merges with Christian Science, and ancient superstition blends with spiritualism and parapsychology. The royal commission appointed by Louis XVI in 1784 to investigate Mesmer's claims reported that the doctrine of animal magnetism was an "ancient fallacy."[1] Opponents of animal magnetism had always been eager to point out that Mesmer's precursors were legion and that, far from introducing a unique therapeutic procedure, Mesmer had borrowed his magnets, fluids, and occult forces from a variety of disreputable sources. Although historians of science have documented the ancestry of animal magnetism in detail, it will be instructive to review the precedents they cite for Mesmer's precepts and techniques.[2]

Mesmer drew largely on two traditions to formulate the central tenets of his teachings. He capitalized first of all on the age-old view that certain individuals are endowed with healing powers which they can turn to account by focusing their gaze on others or by touching them. Centuries before Mesmer performed his cures in the French capital, medicine men and shamans had taken advantage of hypnosis and suggestion to achieve effects rivaling those of modern psychologists and psychoanalysts. The venerable history of healing by touch can be traced back to Pyrrhus of Epirus, who cured his patients of colic by touching them with his big toe. When Jesus of Nazareth placed his hands on the afflicted areas of persons possessing "great faith," he miraculously restored their health. Secular rulers in Western Europe later revived this art by specializing in a "royal touch," which they used to cure scrofula, a disease of the neck com-

1 *Rapport des commissaires chargés par le Roi de l'examen du magnétisme animal* (Paris, 1784), in *Histoire académique du magnétisme animal*, ed. C. Burdin and F. Dubois (Paris: Baillière, 1841), pp. 26-91.

2 See especially Henri F. Ellenberger, *The Discovery of the Unconscious: The History and Evolution of Dynamic Psychiatry* (New York: Basic Books, 1970), pp. 3-52; Emil Schneider, *Der animale Magnetismus: Seine Geschichte und seine Beziehungen zur Heilkunst* (Zurich: Lampert, 1950), pp. 25-92; and Margaret Goldsmith, *Franz Anton Mesmer: The History of an Idea* (London: Arthur Baker, 1934), pp. 1-37.

monly known as the "King's Evil."[3] The extraordinary success attending measures taken by saints and sorcerers throughout the ages to heal the sick no doubt stemmed from the development of a psychological situation closely resembling hypnotic rapport—a situation that fostered responsiveness to suggestion.

The cosmological underpinnings of Mesmer's theories derived from the concept of an imponderable fluid permeating the entire universe and infusing both matter and spirit with its vital force. This fluid, Mesmer reasoned, could be pressed into the service of medicine with the aid of magnets. As early as the sixteenth century, Paracelsus had taught that an ethereal fluid issues from the earth and the stars to converge upon the human body, which, like a magnet, attracts effluvia of both a good and evil nature. By placing a magnet at the source of his patient's pain, Paracelsus hoped to draw out the baneful qualities of astral and terrestrial fluids and to send them swirling through the atmosphere until they returned to their point of origin. Eighteenth-century scientists brought these fluids back down to earth by identifying them as the sources of light, heat, magnetism, electricity, and gravity. Mesmer at first entertained the notion of endorsing gravity and electricity as universal agents of health, but he ultimately gave his support to the magnetic fluid backed by Paracelsus and his disciples Johann Baptist van Helmont, William Maxwell, and Robert Fludd.

How heavily Mesmer relied on these antecedents in developing his theories is not clear. His own writings reveal that he was not a learned man and that he acquired his scientific knowledge from a small number of secondhand sources. Furthermore, his decision to postulate the existence of a subtle magnetic fluid and to extol its therapeutic benefits was not shaped by a combination of extensive reading and painstaking experimentation, but emerged in the course

[3] On such royal miracles, see Marc Bloch, *The Royal Touch: Sacred Monarchy and Scrofula in England and France*, trans. J. E. Anderson (London: Routledge & Kegan Paul; Montreal: McGill-Queen's University Press, 1973).

of polemical arguments advanced to defend the originality of his discovery. Mesmer, however, repeatedly stressed the empirical basis of animal magnetism in much the same way that Christian Science and spiritualism, lineal descendants of mesmerism, persistently underscore the scientific foundations of their persuasions.

By furnishing a scientific explanation for his cures, Mesmer had hoped to liberate medicine from the mystical and religious constraints imposed upon it during previous centuries. Yet the flavor of the occult that permeated the tenets of animal magnetism allowed mesmerists of a later generation to dispense with the physical fluids invoked by Mesmer and to embrace metaphysical and theological solutions to the riddles posed by the magnetic trance. In Europe, Mesmer exercised a pervasive and widespread influence on his own epoch, and animal magnetism stimulated interest not only in faith healing and in the spiritual world, but also in the laws governing the human psyche. Mesmerism deserves serious consideration, if only for the reason that for several decades it aroused enormous excitement throughout Europe and captured the imagination of physicians, scientists, politicians, philosophers, and poets. While many of these men recognized the fraudulent dimensions of animal magnetism, they also perceived that this new art of healing was more than a sophisticated form of hocus-pocus. An investigation of the direct line of influence extending from Mesmer through Bernheim and Charcot to Freud can set the mesmerist movement in its historical perspective and elucidate the tremendous appeal that Mesmer's views possessed for his contemporaries.

I

Franz Anton Mesmer was born in the village of Iznang just north of Lake Constance in 1734.[4] He studied medicine at

[4] Sober accounts of Mesmer's life and judicious evaluations of his achievements are rare. Biographers generally hail the man as a misun-

the University of Vienna and received his degree in 1766 after seven years of undistinguished academic work and the publication of a highly derivative study entitled *De planetarum influxu.*[5] A line cited from Horace's *Ars poetica* served as the epigraph for this dissertation: "Many things that have fallen out of use will be born again, and those things that are now held in esteem will fall."[6] Unhappily for

---

derstood genius—thus F. Schürer-Waldheim, *Anton Mesmer: Ein Naturforscher ersten Ranges* (Vienna: privately printed, 1930); Margaret Goldsmith, *Franz Anton Mesmer*; Emil Schneider, *Der animale Magnetismus*; and D. M. Walmsley, *Anton Mesmer* (London: Robert Hale, 1967)—or they denounce him as an impostor—thus Eugen Sierke, *Schwärmer und Schwindler zu Ende des achtzehnten Jahrhunderts* (Leipzig: S. Hirzel, 1874), pp. 70-221, and Stefan Zweig, *Die Heilung durch den Geist: Mesmer, Mary Baker-Eddy, Freud* (Vienna: Reichner, 1936), pp. 27-141. For balanced and informative studies of Mesmer, see Rudolf Tischner, *Franz Anton Mesmer: Leben, Werk und Wirkungen* (Munich: Verlag der Münchner Drucke, 1928); Jean Vinchon, *Mesmer et son secret* (Paris: Legrand, 1936); Rudolf Tischner and Karl Bittel, *Mesmer und sein Problem: Magnetismus, Suggestion, Hypnose* (Stuttgart: Hippokrates, 1941); Ilza Veith, *Hysteria: The History of a Disease* (Chicago: University of Chicago Press, 1965), pp. 221-256; Robert Darnton, *Mesmerism and the End of the Enlightenment in France* (Cambridge, Mass.: Harvard University Press, 1968), pp. 46-81; and Vincent Buranelli, *The Wizard from Vienna* (New York: Coward, McCann & Geoghegan, 1975).

[5] For a detailed discussion of Mesmer's first published work, see Frank A. Pattie, "Mesmer's Medical Dissertation and Its Debt to Mead's *De Imperio Solis ac Lunae*," *Journal of the History of Medicine and Allied Sciences*, 11 (1956), 275-287.

[6] By borrowing only the first half of this passage from Horace, Mesmer conveniently transformed a simple declaration about language into a prophetic utterance. The passage in its entirety reads: "Multa renascentur quae iam cecidere, cadentque / quae nunc sunt in honore vocabula, si volet usus, / quem penes arbitrium est et ius et norma loquendi." H. Rushton Fairclough translates it as follows: "Many terms that have fallen out of use shall be born again, and those shall fall that are now in repute, if usage so will it, in whose hands lies the judgment, the right and the rule of speech" (Horace, *Satires, Epistles and Ars poetica*, rev. ed. [Cambridge, Mass.: Harvard University Press, Loeb Classical Library, 1961], p. 456).

Mesmer, both parts of the quotation proved prophetic for his ideas. The nebulously conceived admixture of astrological theories and Newtonian principles that he served up to the faculty of medicine in Vienna claimed to demonstrate that the sun, the moon, and other heavenly bodies exert a vital influence on earth. By means of a force that Mesmer tentatively called "animal gravity," these celestial spheres controlled not only tidal and atmospheric conditions, but also a fluid that animates matter. Disturbances in the ebb and flow of this superfine fluid, Mesmer declared, could give rise to severe nervous disorders and intense physical pain. Shortly after the publication of this treatise, Mesmer turned his attention to less ambitious projects and began—as yet without the aid of his ethereal fluid—to practice medicine in Vienna.

Mesmer's practice did not flourish immediately. His willingness to extend credit to affluent patients and to treat less prosperous patients free of charge rendered his financial situation highly precarious. Determined to resume his earlier scientific investigations, he conducted elaborate experiments that drained his dwindling financial reserves. Marriage to a wealthy Austrian widow in 1768 lifted the disagreeable burden of material cares and enabled him to pursue both his research and his hobbies freely. Mesmer could now indulge his most extravagant fancies. His spacious house on the Landstrasse overlooking the Prater contained a laboratory equipped with the finest and most sophisticated instruments; his drawing rooms and gardens provided elegant surroundings for parties and concerts attended by celebrities no less distinguished than Gluck and Haydn. Mesmer, in fact, earned a footnote in musical history by extending his patronage to the twelve-year-old Wolfgang Amadeus Mozart. When a series of court intrigues prevented the performance of a full-scale comic opera composed by the musical prodigy, Mesmer came to the rescue and graciously offered his own gardens for the production of a less grandiose but more polished composition, *Bastien und Bastienne*. Many years later, Mozart immortalized his former patron (in a not altogether flattering way) by introducing into the libretto of *Così fan tutte* an allusion to Dr. Mesmer, who "became so famous in France."

Life in the Landstrasse was nonetheless relatively uneventful. Mesmer continued his efforts to document the influence of the planets and stars on the human body and tried to define more precisely the fluid described in his dissertation. For a time he speculated that this fluid might have some connection with electricity, but discarded that possibility when he learned of a series of remarkable cures performed with magnets. Father Hell, professor of astronomy at the University of Vienna and court astrologer to Maria Theresa, had manufactured steel magnets of various shapes and sizes which he applied to the diseased areas of his patients' bodies: for the ears he used semicircular magnets, for the breast heart-shaped ones, and for the soles of the feet round, flat magnets. The twenty cures that Hell ascribed to the magnetic force of his steel tractors received extensive coverage in the Viennese press. Intrigued by these reports and apparently somewhat envious of the attention that Hell was receiving, Mesmer ordered a supply of magnets from the miracle worker at the court. After testing them on his own patients, he concluded that the magnets, by removing obstacles placed in the path of his magnetic fluid, allowed that fluid to course freely through the body. With the hope of sharing the publicity accorded to Hell, Mesmer rushed into print with a summary of his studies on magnetism.[7] This report, which took the form of a letter addressed to a colleague, ostensibly reiterated the ideas set forth in his dissertation, but in fact introduced significant changes. Mesmer ingeniously substituted the term "animal magnetism" for animal gravity and modified his original definition of the concept with the result that animal magnetism became a

[7] *Schreiben über die Magnetkur von Herrn A. Mesmer, Doktor der Arzneygelährtheit, an einen auswärtigen Arzt* (Vienna: Kurzböck, 1775).

property of organic matter rather than an extraterrestrial force operating upon it. Health, Mesmer now claimed, depended on the proper distribution of an imponderable magnetic fluid that responds to planetary motion. Using Hell's magnets, he could promote a natural rhythm in the ebb and flow governing the fluid's movement through the human body and thereby restore health, or harmony between man and the universe.

News of the sensational magnetic cures performed by Mesmer met with the same enthusiastic reception that had attended reports of Hell's success. The Viennese press did not hesitate to applaud the heroic feats and pioneering spirit of Dr. Mesmer. But to Mesmer's dismay, Hell then announced that the effectiveness of magnetic treatment was contingent on the size and shape of the magnets. Mesmer shrewdly retaliated by eliminating Hell's magnets from his procedure. The magnetic fluid, he now contended, could be controlled more dexterously with his hands than with Hell's magnets, and he proceeded to demonstrate that mere passes of the hand in no way diminished the salutary effects of magnetic treatment. While Mesmer's private practice thrived as a result of the controversy, the medical world generally remained indifferent, if not openly hostile to his methods. The learned societies of Europe showed little desire to champion his magnetic fluid; they were even reluctant to acknowledge his letters of inquiry. Only the Berlin Academy of Sciences responded to a request for endorsement, and it politely instructed Mesmer to provide more adequate documentation for the existence of his universal fluid.[8] Academic recognition seemed at last within his reach when Max Joseph of Bavaria summoned him to Munich to demonstrate his magnetic powers. Mesmer put on so dazzling a performance for the court and the Bavarian Academy of Sciences that he subsequently won nomination to membership in the academy.

[8] The critic and aesthetician J. G. Sulzer drafted the reply from the Academy of Sciences to Mesmer's letter. For the text of Sulzer's letter, see Sierke, *Schwärmer und Schwindler*, pp. 78-80.

But the medical faculty of Vienna remained singularly unimpressed with the honors bestowed on Mesmer and continued to disparage his discoveries.

In 1777 Mesmer undertook a cure that brought him public notoriety and ultimately precipitated his decision to leave Vienna and seek more fertile terrain for his ideas. Maria-Theresa von Paradies, a young pianist blind from the age of three, suffered from a debilitating nervous condition —no doubt severely aggravated by the three thousand electrical shocks that well-meaning physicians had administered to her over a period of months. Magnetic therapy appeared to relieve the most serious symptoms of her illness and partially restored her sight. The overjoyed parents quickly circulated the news of their daughter's remarkable recovery. Residents of Vienna flocked to Mesmer's palatial residence with the hope of catching a glimpse of the child who had derived such benefit from magnetic treatment. But a number of prominent physicians in the city resented the attention lavished on Mesmer and voiced grave doubts about his claims. Mesmer later charged that they had spoken privately with Herr von Paradies and had intimated that the empress might curtail her financial support were Maria-Theresa to regain her sight. Rumors that his daughter had developed an inordinately strong attachment to her physician finally prompted the father to act. He stormed Mesmer's home to demand the return of his child and removed her from the premises. Shortly thereafter, a commission appointed to investigate Mesmer's procedures reached the conclusion that animal magnetism constituted a public menace and demanded that the doctor put an end to his fraudulent practice. Faced with the choice of withdrawing from the medical profession or leaving Vienna, Mesmer quietly packed his bags and headed for Paris.

Following a brief tour of Bavaria and Switzerland, Mesmer settled into comfortable quarters near the Place Vendôme. During the decade preceding the Revolution, the occult sciences enjoyed a brief golden age in the French capital. Fortune tellers, astrologers, and faith healers catered to the perennial appetite for low-priced miracles among the working classes. Courses on "la physique amusante" and "la haute science" drew crowds to museums and lecture halls. The Freemasons, who prided themselves on the presence of nearly two hundred lodges in France alone and on an impressive membership list including Voltaire, Lafayette, and Benjamin Franklin, gratified the mystical tastes cultivated by the aristocracy and wealthier bourgeoisie. In an age that witnessed the first balloon flights, the harnessing of electrical energy, and a host of wonders ranging from chess-playing robots to talking dogs, it was not always easy to discern the line dividing science from sorcery. Mesmer's own art seems to have occupied a position somewhere between these two extremes.[9] Many of Mesmer's cures were no doubt authentic, but the magnetic fluid he defended until his death was no more effective than the "sympathetic powders" and other magical potions hawked by street vendors in Paris.

Although Mesmer was highly gratified by the large clientele that gathered at the Place Vendôme, he aspired above all to secure some kind of official endorsement for his views. He therefore prudently set about courting the favor of figures influential in France's most prestigious scientific bodies: the faculty of medicine at the University of Paris, the Royal Society of Medicine, and the Academy of Sciences. As a first step toward acceptance by the Establishment, he published his *Mémoire sur la découverte du magnétisme animal,* a brief treatise setting forth the main tenets of his system.[10] Twenty-seven postulates appended to this slim volume defined the magnetic fluid's attributes and made it clear that a physician who understood its properties and laws of opera-

[9] Darnton, *Mesmerism and the End of the Enlightenment in France,* pp. 36-38. Connections between mesmerism and popular science are discussed in detail on pp. 3-45.

[10] *Mémoire sur la découverte du magnétisme animal* (Paris: Didot, 1779).

tion could learn to cure any disease.[11] "There is only one disease and one cure alone for it," Mesmer was later to assert.

Although the bold claims of the *Mémoire* left academicians cold, rumors about the strange proceedings in Mesmer's clinic stimulated enormous curiosity about animal magnetism. Mesmer had hoped to arouse interest in France, but his popularity with Parisian society exceeded even his own expectations. If his magnetic fluid was incapable of insinuating itself into the assemblies of learned societies, it had little difficulty gaining access to the most exclusive Parisian salons. Whether the French were suffering from nervous disorders or indigestion, from gout or ennui, they thronged to Mesmer's clinic. The gentle passes of the hand, the soothing music played in Mesmer's chambers, and the comfortable surroundings for the séances provided a welcome alternative to the potions, purges, and leeches prescribed by more conventional physicians. Not surprisingly Mesmer soon required the services of a second *valet toucheur* to minister to his patients.

For Mesmer and his followers, group therapy proved the most successful (and most lucrative) form of magnetic treatment. Only when a patient resisted the influence of the magnetic currents streaming through the clinic did Mesmer resort to individual therapy. He seated the patient directly across from him and locked the patient's knees between his own. Staring fixedly into his subject's eyes, Mesmer made passes over his limbs searching for the obstacles impeding circulation of the magnetic fluid. By projecting the fluid emanating from his own eyes into those of the patient, Mesmer not only removed these obstacles, but also immunized his client against disease.

For group sessions Mesmer installed in his apartment an apparatus that allowed at least thirty persons to be mesmerized at one sitting. The *baquet*, a round wooden tub about two feet high, was filled with iron filings and bottles of

[11] See the appendix.

magnetized water extending in rows from the center of the tub to its circumference. Jointed iron rods protruded from holes pierced in the lid of the tub. The patients, ranged in rows around the tub, grasped these rods and applied them to the diseased areas of their bodies. In order to avoid loss of the precious fluid, each person held the thumb of his neighbor between his own thumb and index finger to forge a chain of communication. A rope attached to the tub and passed around the patients' bodies linked them together in one great magnetic chain.

Henri Ellenberger has suggested that Mesmer borrowed the terminology of contemporary discussions on electricity to define his magnetic fluid.[12] Like the electrical fluid that fascinated eighteenth-century scientists, Mesmer's fluid could be accumulated, stored in large quantities, and discharged. The *baquet* was also clearly modeled on the recently invented Leyden jar. Since scientists could collect electrical charges using that instrument, Mesmer was confident that he would be able to amass a large supply of magnetic fluid in his *baquet*.

The setting in which Mesmer treated his patients bore little resemblance to the normally austere décor of eighteenth-century clinics. Delicate perfumes floated in the air to mingle with the magnetic fluid pulsing through the atmosphere. Thick carpets, heavy curtains, and ornate furnishings graced the dimly lit chamber in which patients gripped the iron rods extending from the *baquet* and awaited the onset of the pivotal magnetic "crisis." On the walls of the room hung large gleaming mirrors which, according to Mesmer's precepts, reflected the fluid and intensified its strength. Soft music played on the pianoforte or glass harmonica—on occasion by Mesmer himself—kept the fluid in steady circulation. Everything in Mesmer's clinic seemed designed to foster an aura of mystery and magical enchantment. By the time that Mesmer made his dramatic

[12] *The Discovery of the Unconscious*, pp. 186-187.

entrance, the patients had invariably settled into the proper frame of mind. The pundit of animal magnetism appeared in a violet robe of embroidered silk and carried with him a magnetized iron wand. Acting as master of ceremonies, he strode majestically through the room and treated those patients who had not yet succumbed to the powerful currents of magnetic fluid by passing his hands or his magical wand over their bodies. The solemn ritual (occasionally punctuated by muffled screams and loud moans), the exotic paraphernalia in the clinic, and the eagerness of many patients to please their physician by displaying behavior expected of them produced in most cases a cathartic crisis that coincided with the removal of obstacles in the fluid's path and heralded the restoration of health. If the crisis took the form of particularly violent convulsions, Mesmer's *valet toucheur* speedily transported the patient to the *salle des crises* (skeptical Parisians called it the *enfer des convulsions*), a room padded with silk cushions. Persons less susceptible to suggestion often fell under the spell of Mesmer's penetrating gaze and lapsed into a deep sleep resembling what we today call a hypnotic trance.

For Mesmer the crisis constituted both a symptom of disease and the first step toward its cure. He persistently attributed his therapeutic success to the magnetic crisis and was no doubt at least partially justified in making this judgment. Many of the patients who consulted Mesmer were society women suffering from a fashionable ailment of the time known as the *vapeurs*. The disease, which today might be diagnosed as a mild form of hysteria, rendered its victims vulnerable to nervous fits and fainting spells.[13] The crises provoked at the *baquet*, because they allowed patients to release psychic tension, closely resemble a therapeutic de-

[13] Ellenberger briefly discusses this malady in *The Discovery of the Unconscious*, p. 187. For a contemporary description of the disease, see Pierre Pomme, *Traité des affections vaporeuses des deux sexes, ou maladies nerveuses vulgairement appelées maux de nerfs* (Paris: Desaint et Saillant, 1760).

vice that psychoanalysts today term "abreaction." It was therefore not without reason that Mesmer viewed the crisis as the crucial element of magnetic therapy and dismissed "magnetic sleep" as an unessential part of the cure.

Mesmer was soon unable to accommodate the crowds that sought both distraction and relief from their sufferings at the Place Vendôme. He consequently shifted his base of operation to the Hôtel Bullion and installed four *baquets* there, one of which he reserved for those who could not afford his customary high fees. But the additional facilities proved insufficient to meet the demand for mesmerist treatment. Mesmer cleverly solved the problem by declaring that trees constituted a kind of natural *baquet*. After he magnetized a large elm on the rue de Bondy, hundreds of people flocked there to tap the tree's supply of magnetic fluid by attaching ropes extending from its branches to diseased parts of their bodies.

The rage for Mesmer's treatment among citizens of the French capital was matched in intensity only by the fierce hostility toward magnetism of French physicians and scientists. On first arriving in Paris, Mesmer had invited members of the Academy of Sciences to attend a lecture on animal magnetism and to observe his procedures. The representatives from the academy dutifully listened to Mesmer's disquisition and took cognizance of the salutary effects of magnetism on his patients, but unanimously concluded that a single demonstration could not provide them with the competence to make a sound judgment on animal magnetism. They accordingly asked their guest to prepare detailed reports of his experiments and to submit empirical evidence for the existence of a magnetic fluid. Mesmer flew into a rage. He denounced the "childish behavior" of the inspectors and accused them of making "arrogant demands," though eventually he checked his temper and complied with their requests. The academy, however, left his letters unanswered. Nurturing the hope that the Royal Society of Medicine might prove less demanding, Mesmer appealed to this distinguished body of physicians. The Royal Society, while it accepted his invitation to inspect and evaluate an adjunct clinic in the nearby village of Créteil, also imposed rigid conditions on an inquiry, among them the right to examine Mesmer's patients both before and after magnetic treatment. Mesmer found these terms unacceptable, refused to accede to them, and finally abandoned his attempt to gain official recognition from the Royal Society.

Mesmer's last chance for acquiring a passport to respectability rested with the medical faculty of the University of Paris. Having already secured the enthusiastic support of Charles Deslon, a prominent member of the faculty, Mesmer entertained high hopes that his views would finally attract serious consideration. At a luncheon party, Deslon introduced him to three eminent faculty physicians. But these academics gave the doctor from Vienna a cool reception and, as Mesmer bitterly complained, showed greater interest in the food and wine than in the eloquent discourse he had delivered during the meal. A committee of three was later charged by the faculty with the task of examining mesmerism, but, unable to reach unanimity, it refused to pronounce judgment on the subject.[14]

Deslon, Mesmer's first influential convert, persisted in defending his mentor despite the faculty's repeated threats to strike his name from its rolls. He contributed in no small measure to promoting Mesmer's cause by opening his own magnetic practice and by writing a treatise designed to clarify Mesmer's precepts.[15] Using a richly ornamented *baquet* of his own invention, giving free rein to his showmanship, and capitalizing on his irresistible charm and good looks, Deslon had no difficulty establishing a flourishing

[14] For Mesmer's own account of his struggles with the Academy of Sciences, the Royal Society of Medicine, and the medical faculty, see *Précis historique des faits relatifs au magnétisme animal jusques en avril 1781* (London: n.p., 1781), pp. 20-184.

[15] *Observations sur le magnétisme animal* (London and Paris: Didot, 1780).

practice. (Mesmer was later to denounce him as a traitor who had not only stolen his professional secrets, but also robbed him of his clientele.) Still, daily exposure to the magnetic fluid did not provide Deslon with immunity to all diseases; he contracted pneumonia, an illness that seemed to resist magnetic treatment, and died at the *baquet* in 1786.

Confident that the wide following he was acquiring at all social levels would furnish him with awesome leverage, Mesmer mounted a counterattack against the established order. He threatened to leave France immediately and to deprive Parisians of the magnetic fluid that he had so generously bestowed on them. A group of influential aristocrats who feared that Mesmer's absence would have a disastrous effect on their health begged Marie Antoinette to intervene. The queen dispatched an envoy who offered Mesmer a salary of 20,000 livres a year with an additional 10,000 livres to defray the costs of a clinic; the government asked only that Mesmer allow three persons appointed by the minister of state to take courses at the proposed institute for animal magnetism. Mesmer, however, abruptly broke off negotiations. The three "students," he felt, were sure to be investigators, and he resented this thinly disguised form of surveillance. In a long letter to the queen, Mesmer tersely expressed his gratitude for her interest and then dilated at length on the nobility of his principles.[16] He stressed his devotion to science, his concern for humanity, and his utter indifference to monetary reward. Personal and professional ethics would not allow him to accept bribes from a government so patently corrupt as to lend financial support to his discovery with one hand while holding back scientific recognition with the other. But in the end Mesmer revealed his true motives. The queen's offer, he declared, was in any event not attractive enough to keep him in France. What could a few thousand livres more or less matter to Her Majesty when

[16] *Précis historique*, pp. 215-220.

the health of the French people hung in the balance? Mesmer lashed out at his adversaries and announced that he did not intend to squander his talents on so ungrateful a nation. Followed by his most loyal disciples, he left Paris to attend to his own health by bathing in the medicinal waters of Spa.

Reports that Deslon had succeeded him in the business and was now reaping the benefits of his discovery quickly dispelled Mesmer's contempt for the French. In addition, two of Mesmer's wealthiest and shrewdest pupils, Nicolas Bergasse and Guillaume Kornmann, sought to lure him back to Paris by suggesting that he deliver a course of lectures on animal magnetism. The subscription fee of 100 louis would ostensibly cover the cost of establishing organizations to advance the cause of magnetic healing. The rules and rituals of such societies for the dissemination of mesmerist propaganda were to follow the models provided by masonic lodges. Mesmer accepted the proposition and returned to Paris. The prosperity of the *Société de l'Harmonie Universelle* that he founded there stemmed largely from its appeal to two interdependent groups: idle aristocrats who welcomed an exotic hobby to while away their leisure hours and members of the wealthy bourgeoisie who seized the opportunity to hobnob with the well-bred. With a following of more than 400 persons in Paris alone and 340,000 louis in his treasury, Mesmer had secured his fortune. Branches of the Society of Universal Harmony sprang up in Strasbourg, Lyons, Dijon, and a score of other towns. These mesmerist lodges promised to usher in a golden age of healthy and vigorous individuals united in one great magnetic chain of humanity and living in perfect harmony with nature.

Some of Mesmer's pupils, however, sounded discordant notes that threatened to disturb the cosmic harmony the society aimed to establish. Charging that they had been victimized by a hoax, several members of the society complained that the costly lectures at the Hôtel de Coigny had failed to unravel nature's mysteries. The burgeoning dissension within the society mirrored an even more decisive split in public opinion over the merits of animal magnetism. Academics engaged in undignified squabbles about the merits of the magnetic fluid; newspapers published contradictory accounts of magnetic treatment; and on the streets people either sang Mesmer's praises or hummed ballads deriding "le charlatan Mesmer." The government finally decided to intervene, though it showed less interest in determining the value of animal magnetism than in exploring the moral perils of magnetic therapy. The preponderance of attractive young women in mesmerist parlors had long aroused the suspicions of Mesmer's opponents. Nasty rumors and ribald jokes directed attention to the erotic dimension of mesmerist therapy by playing on the sensual atmosphere of the indoor clinics, the strange noises issuing from the *salle des crises*, and the excessive physical contact between physician and patient.

A second equally serious consideration entered into the government's decision to take action. According to the report of one contemporary, Mesmer's house resembled a "temple of health" uniting all classes of society from aristocrats and statesmen to prostitutes and paupers.[17] Even if Mesmer reserved the best seats in his house for those with impressive pedigrees, he betrayed his political sympathies by welcoming all ranks of society into the same residence. A confidential report drawn up by the Paris police also linked a number of radical political figures to the mesmerist movement. Robert Darnton has suggested that many future revolutionaries allied themselves with Mesmer's cause largely because mesmerism appeared to be a force that could not only restore health to individuals, but also regenerate French society by breaking down social barriers

[17] "La maison de M. Mesmer est comme le Temple de la Divinité, qui réunit tous les états; on y voit des Cordons bleus, des Abbés, des Marquises, des Grisettes, des Militaires, des Traitants, des Freluquets" (*Mesmer justifié* [Paris: Gastelier, 1784], pp. 2-3).

and reinstating the harmony of a natural order.[18] These men were all the more ready to rally around Mesmer because his ideas, like their own, had been repudiated by leading academic bodies in France.

In 1784 Louis XVI's advisers appointed a royal commission to investigate animal magnetism. The highly distinguished panel that they assembled included four representatives from the faculty of medicine and five from the Academy of Sciences: Benjamin Franklin, Lavoisier, and Guillotin figured as its most prominent members. J. S. Bailly, an eminent astronomer, presided over the meetings and drafted the final report recording the conclusions reached by the nine physicians and scientists. At their first meeting in March 1784, the members of the commission decided to attend sessions at Deslon's clinic, where over a period of six months they subjected to close scrutiny the convulsions, crises, and cures produced by Mesmer's pupil. Suspecting that the high social standing of Deslon's patients and the provocative atmosphere of his clinic had some bearing on his results, the commissioners elected to conduct experiments on "persons of the lower classes" in the more neutral setting of Franklin's residence in Passy. Not surprisingly they discovered that a significantly smaller percentage of the patients responded to treatment—of the fourteen new patients only five proved susceptible to the magnetic fluid. The commissioners were quick to note, moreover, that these five patients all knew that they had been magnetized or had come in contact with a magnetized object. Further experiments highlighted the importance of this knowledge. One of the patients, a twelve-year-old boy considered exceptionally sensitive to magnetic objects, was informed that the commissioners would accompany him through a grove of magnetized trees. In fact, Deslon had magnetized only a single tree in the orchard. When the child was still at a distance of twenty-four feet from this

[18] See especially his chapter "The Radical Strain in Mesmerism," in *Mesmerism and the End of the Enlightenment in France*, pp. 82-105.

tree, he displayed all the symptoms of a genuine crisis. Similar experiments produced comparable results. The commissioners, however, found that they themselves were unaffected by Deslon's treatment: magnetic therapy failed to improve their own health in any way.

In their official report to the king, the examiners pointed to Deslon's failure to marshal empirical evidence for the existence of a magnetic fluid. They attributed the crises provoked by the doctor principally to the "imagination" or, more accurately, to the suggestibility of his patients, but added that pressure exerted by the mesmerist's hands often brought on a crisis. Patients without much imagination, they observed, simply imitated the behavior of others. "The imagination works wonders; magnetism yields no results," read their final verdict.[19] Fearing that public displays of convulsions might, through the power of suggestion, engender an epidemic of magnetic crises that could taint future generations of Frenchmen, the commissioners alerted His Majesty to the "highly pernicious" influence of animal magnetism.

These experts dealt yet another blow to the mesmerist movement by submitting to the king a second, confidential document in which they expressed concern about the moral implications of mesmerism. After describing in vivid detail the physical contact between magnetizers and their female subjects and expatiating on the power of touch to arouse women sexually, they warned of the temptations to which mesmerist physicians exposed themselves. Anticipating the phenomenon of transference in hypnotic rapport, they noted that female patients often forged a strong emotional bond to their physicians. Deslon, they stressed, was by no means guilty of exploiting his patients' amorous inclinations, but other physicians, they argued, might show less

[19] *Rapport des commissaires chargés par le Roi de l'examen du magnétisme animal* (Paris, 1784), in *Histoire académique*, ed. C. Burdin and F. Dubois, p. 73.

prudence. "And even if the physician possesses superhuman virtues," they added, "he is still responsible for the wrongdoing he may inspire in others."[20]

In the wake of these two reports followed the verdict of the Royal Society of Medicine.[21] This academic body seconded the views of the royal commission and advised physicians who aspired to enter its rolls to refrain from using animal magnetism. One member of the committee, Laurent de Jussieu, issued a dissenting opinion.[22] Although he agreed with his colleagues that neither Mesmer nor his followers had brought forth persuasive evidence for the existence of a magnetic fluid, he believed further research might show that some kind of subtle fluid—"animal heat" was his candidate—played a significant role in maintaining the health of organisms.

The French government mounted a vigorous antimagnetist campaign that had a devastating effect on Mesmer's reputation. In 1784 it printed nearly 12,000 copies of the royal commission's report and distributed them throughout France and in neighboring countries. The same year witnessed the death of Court de Gébelin ("recently cured by animal magnetism," reported one tactless obituary)[23] and the performance of Jean Baptiste Radet's *Les Docteurs modernes*, a play that drew crowds to the Comédie Italienne by mercilessly parodying mesmerist beliefs with mock cere-

[20] *Rapport secret sur le magnétisme animal* (Paris, 1784), in *Histoire académique*, ed. C. Burdin and F. Dubois, pp. 92-101.

[21] *Rapport des commissaires de la Société Royale de Médecine, nommés par le Roi, pour faire l'examen du magnétisme animal* (Paris, 1784), in *Histoire académique*, ed. C. Burdin and F. Dubois, pp. 102-142.

[22] A.-L. de Jussieu, *Rapport de l'un commissaires chargés par le Roi de l'examen du magnétisme animal* (Paris: Veuve Hérrisant, 1784).

[23] "M. Court de Gébelin vient de mourir, guéri par le magnétisme animal." Cited in Dominique Barrucand, *Histoire de l'hypnose en France* (Paris: Presses Universitaires, 1967), p. 16.

monies held around a *baquet* and in a crisis room.[24] By 1785 most Frenchmen were sailing with the prevailing wind. A carnival float of that year carried a clown waving banners inscribed with the word "Harmonia" and a physician wildly gesticulating to people in the streets; onlookers responded by imitating mesmerized patients in the throes of a crisis. The text of one popular satirical song captures the spirit of the times:

> Le magnétisme est aux abois,
> La faculté, l'Académie
> L'ont condamné tout d'une voix
> Et même couvert d'infamie.
> Après ce jugement, bien sage et bien légal,
> Si quelqu'esprit original,
> Persiste encore dans son délire,
> Il sera permis de lui dire:
> Crois au magnétisme . . . animal![25]

Eager to escape the hostile climate of Paris, Mesmer searched in vain throughout France, Switzerland, and Germany for an environment more sympathetic to his views before finally returning to Vienna in 1793. But Viennese officials shortly sent him packing, this time for political reasons.[26] At a garden party, Mesmer had imprudently taken it upon himself to defend the ideals of the French Revolu-

[24] Jean Baptiste Radet, *Les Docteurs modernes, comédie-parade, en un acte et en vaudevilles, suivie du Baquet de santé, divertissement analogue, mêlé de couplets* (Paris: Gastelier, 1784).

[25] Cited in Goldsmith, *Franz Anton Mesmer*, p. 147. The poem may be translated literally as follows: "Magnetism is finally at bay, / The faculty, the Academy / Have unanimously condemned it / And cast aspersions on it. / If after this wise and just opinion, / An eccentric perseveres in his folly, / We can say to him: / Believe in magnetism . . . animal!" For other verse in a similar vein, see *Mesmer justifié*, p. 46.

[26] Ernst Benz discusses Mesmer's political affiliations and elucidates the nature of his difficulties with the Austrian government. See *Franz Anton Mesmer (1734-1815) und seine Ausstrahlung in Europa und Amerika* (Munich: Wilhelm Fink, 1976), pp. 9-18.

tion, and the Austrian government, well aware of the notoriety that Mesmer had acquired in Paris, feared it was harboring a political agitator. After serving two months of a sentence for treason, Mesmer wisely resolved to leave the city—many of his "co-conspirators" were executed—and to abandon an unfaithful continent to its illnesses. He settled in a sequestered village near the place of his birth and lived out his days in such studied seclusion that a number of German physicians spent years poring over his works before discovering that the author was still alive. Mesmer died in 1815 near Meersburg. A small delegation of local villagers attended the funeral.

II

Long before his death Mesmer had relinquished all hope of securing recognition for his doctrines, but his allies and disciples carried on the crusade for official acceptance of mesmerist views. Promoted by Barbarin, Petetin, and Puységur, mesmerism came into vogue in the French provinces. The persuasions of these three converts, however, deviated considerably from the orthodox mesmerist tenets espoused by the so-called fluidists, who insisted that the magnetic fluid constituted the sole agent of health. In Lyons, the Chevalier de Barbarin jettisoned not only the magnetic fluid, but the *baquet* as well, and replaced them with prayer and steadfast purpose. Healing no longer required the assistance of a crude physical substance; spiritual means alone, the faith of a patient and the resolute will of his physician, yielded more impressive results. "Veuillez le bien, allez et guérissez" was the watchword that Barbarin passed on to his disciples. He further proclaimed that cures could be performed only with aid from God, the supreme magnetizer. Members of the Animist Society of Harmony later founded by Barbarin in Ostend subscribed to the view that the magnetic trance represents an exalted state of consciousness in which the patient's soul draws closer to God. By rejecting psychological and scientific explanations for the rapport between physician and patient, by stressing the visionary powers developed in the trance, and by introducing religious elements into mesmerist therapy, Barbarin at once revived the ancient tradition of faith healing and anticipated the teachings of Christian Science.

J.-H. Petetin, president of the Medical Society in Lyons, also aligned himself with the animist faction of the mesmerist movement. His discovery of induced catalepsy, a state of muscular paralysis in which sensory perception was, in his view, transferred to the epigastric region, pointed the way to the use of hypnotic anesthesia in surgical operations. Patients who demonstrated a predisposition to the cataleptic state could look forward to the prospect of painless tooth extractions and surgical operations. In 1787 Petetin published the case history of a patient who, for the duration of the cataleptic trance, could not only hear, see, and smell through the epigastrium, but was also able to perceive her internal organs, diagnose her ailment, predict the course of her illness, and prescribe a remedy for it.[27] Transforming the mesmerist diagnostician into a clairvoyant medium required only a shift in emphasis from the patient's own physical health to the spiritual well-being of mankind, and it was not long before various mystical organizations and theosophic societies began to enlist the services of such mediums to communicate with spirits from another world. Petetin, whose therapeutic discoveries had slipped out of his control to run rampant in regions where he felt they had no place, later transferred his allegiance to the fluidists and advanced an explanation for the trance based on the accumulation of an electrical fluid in the human body.[28]

In an introduction to the third edition of his study on

[27] *Mémoire sur la découverte des phénomènes que présentent la catalepsie et le somnambulisme* (Lyons: n.p., 1787).

[28] *Electricité animale prouvée par la découverte des phénomènes physiques et moraux de la catalepsie hystérique* (Lyons: Reymann, 1808).

the genesis and history of magnetic healing, the Marquis Chastenet de Puységur attempted to resolve the dispute that was developing between Mesmer's disciples and Petetin's followers over the nature of the cosmic fluid pervading all matter. Scientific experiments, he declared, would one day corroborate the existence of both Mesmer's animal magnetism and Petetin's animal electricity. In fact, the authenticity of his own electromagnetic fluid (so named to reconcile Petetin's theory with Mesmer's) would also be verified, for all these terms were merely different labels for a single agent in nature that "preserves health" and that physicians can turn to use through an "act of will."[29]

To Puységur belongs the credit for recognizing the therapeutic value of the hypnotic trance, or what he called "magnetic sleep." Puységur and his brother, descendants of an illustrious French family, first took an interest in animal magnetism while stationed with their regiment in Paris. They both paid the 100-louis initiation fee to become charter members of the Parisian Society of Harmony and, upon retiring from the army in 1784, spent their leisure hours magnetizing peasants on their estate at Buzancy near Soissons. Puységur's star patient, a young man named Victor Race, suffered from an enervating respiratory ailment. After being mesmerized by his master, Victor fell into a profound sleep undisturbed by the violent convulsions that ordinarily followed magnetic therapy. Under normal circumstances, Victor was a "simple peasant incapable of formulating a sentence, a creature who hardly deserves a name," Puységur reported.[30] But in the trance state, the peasant's mental faculties sharpened: he spoke with remarkable clarity, grasped subtle concepts, and even divined his master's thoughts. When interrogated about his illness, he prescribed the appropriate treatment and medication for it. In a matter of days, he was cured.

29 *Mémoires pour servir à l'histoire et à l'établissement du magnétisme animal*, 3rd ed. (Paris: Dentu, 1820), p. xix.

30 Ibid., p. 28.

In order to understand fully the cause of Victor Race's recovery, we must turn to the clinical picture provided in Puységur's study of animal magnetism. Puységur tells us there that an entirely new personality emerged when his patient fell into a deep "magnetic sleep." The normally taciturn youth was able to express his most intimate thoughts and emotions in a highly animated and eloquent fashion. During his waking life, for example, Victor never uttered a word against his sister, but for the duration of the trance he openly discussed the hostile feelings he harbored toward her. The opportunity to articulate his subconscious thoughts clearly contributed to Victor's rapid recovery from what appears to have been a functional rather than an organic disorder. In addition, Victor was no doubt delighted with the attention paid to him by the marquis (a man who figured as head of the household that his family had served for generations) and made every effort to demonstrate his gratitude by cooperating with his physician's suggestions. Since Victor's elegant diction and medical genius so closely resembled that of his physician, it is safe to assume that the origin of these gifts can also be traced to the suggestions introduced by Puységur into his patient's mind. For Freud and Breuer, the power of suggestion was to work similar miracles.

News of Puységur's prodigious healing powers spread so rapidly that hordes of peasants descended on his country estate for treatment. In order to oblige these new patients, Puységur followed Mesmer's example and "magnetized" an elm tree on the village green. Groups of peasants seated themselves on stone benches surrounding the elm and applied ropes wound around the tree's main branches and trunk to their bodies. As soon as they linked thumbs with their neighbors, the magnetic fluid issuing from the sacred elm was pumped into their own bodies. Not surprisingly, sylvan magnets became quite fashionable in the provinces; French aristocrats showed little reluctance to accommodate the medical needs of their servants and peasants by setting aside a few trees on their country estates.

Despite his deferential attitude toward Mesmer, Puységur developed methods that differed radically from those of his teacher. The marquis did not deny the existence of a universal imponderable fluid, but he attached little importance to it and instead, like Barbarin, stressed the role of the magnetizer. "Croyez et veuillez" was the double imperative he delivered to the nearly two hundred men enrolled in the *Société Harmonique des Amis Réunis* that he had founded in Strasbourg. Only this combination of steadfast faith and unwavering purpose could enable the physician to attain his goals. In addition, Puységur discarded the elaborate trappings of Mesmer's clinic and substituted verbal commands for physical contact. While Mesmer had exerted his magnetic influence to provoke crises and convulsions that allowed his patients to abreact the symptoms of their disease, Puységur capitalized on his own commanding personality to induce a profound trance that rendered his patients receptive to suggestion, refreshed their memory of painful events, and allowed them to articulate forbidden thoughts and wishes.

Mesmer's use of the crisis and Puységur's interrogation of patients during magnetic sleep figure as the crude antecedents of the cathartic method and the "talking cure" employed by Breuer and Freud to relieve the symptoms of hysteria. As Clark L. Hull, a pioneer of experimental research in hypnosis, points out, physicians had identified and described nearly all hypnotic phenomena within a few decades after Mesmer's arrival in Paris.[31] But a clear understanding of these phenomena and their therapeutic benefits, it should be added, did not emerge until nearly a century later. Mesmer's unswerving faith in the magnetic fluid blinded him to the true source of his patients' responses, while Puységur's emphasis on the physician's will prevented him from recognizing the significance of his patients' uncanny ability to unearth memories repressed in conscious

31 Clark L. Hull, *Hypnosis and Suggestibility* (New York: Appleton-Century, 1933), p. 18.

life. By rejecting the magnetic crisis and underscoring the importance of the somnambulist trance, however, Puységur set the stage for the work of Liébeault and Bernheim. And it was during a visit to Bernheim's clinic in Nancy that Sigmund Freud, who had recently opened a medical practice in Vienna, was to form "the profoundest impression of the possibility that there could be powerful mental processes which nevertheless remained hidden from the consciousness of men."[32]

Puységur's investigations marked the end of the first major phase in mesmerist research, but at the same time they initiated new developments of far-reaching consequences. Renouncing all attempts at physiological explanations for magnetic sleep and at the same time embracing a highly personalized theory of willpower, Puységur infused mesmerist doctrines with a fresh appreciation for the mysteries of psychological control and thus replaced animal magnetism with personal magnetism. Mesmer's theory of fluidic action had adequately explained his success with patients in Paris and thereby inhibited speculation on the psychological aspects of the magnetic crisis, but Puységur's disclosure of the preternatural powers that surfaced in the trance challenged his contemporaries to frame new hypotheses about the nature of magnetic control. Instead of providing a key for decoding the mysteries of sickness and health, the somnambulist trance rendered the laws of nature more cryptic than ever.

In the eighteenth century, mesmerism had engaged the minds of many amateur scientists whose investigations often matched or at least complemented the research of physicians and professional scientists. But the discovery of visionary trances, induced catalepsy, and magnetic sleep dissipated

[32] Sigmund Freud, *Standard Edition of the Complete Psychological Works*, trans. and ed. James Strachey, 24 vols. (London: Hogarth, 1953-74), XX, 17. Hereafter cited as *Standard Edition*. I deviate from Strachey's text only by replacing British forms with American spellings.

the spirit of cooperation between amateurs and professionals, for few serious physicians and scientists felt comfortable with the occult strain that their former allies had injected into mesmerist doctrines. In addition to the various mystical groups that allied themselves with the new spiritualist form of mesmerism, there appeared a new breed of mesmerists—itinerant magnetizers who made the rounds of carnivals and festivals with their trance maidens in order to cash in on the latest fad sweeping the Continent. The cruel exploitation of an innocent young girl by a shrewd mesmerist wizard was to become a pervasive theme in nineteenth-century European and American literature.

Physicians who continued to view the somnambulist trance as a powerful therapeutic weapon quite naturally desired to sever all ties with the more exotic aspects of the mesmerist movement, and they therefore greeted with warm enthusiasm the proposal of James Braid for renaming the study of artificially induced trances "neurypnology." The new term, which later came into use under its modified form "hypnotism," seasoned the study of trances with just the right flavor of erudition and was clearly more acceptable to the medical profession than "animal magnetism" or "mesmerism." Braid, a Scottish surgeon practicing in Manchester, rejected all theories that attempted to explain trance states through external influences alone. In 1841 he attended a mesmerist demonstration staged by Charles Lafontaine. Convinced that the French magnetizer was deceiving his audience through a combination of "collusion and delusion," Braid returned six days later with the hope of divining the mountebank's secrets. The second demonstration persuaded him that the trances were authentic—although he still saw no evidence for the existence and influence of a magnetic fluid. What especially struck him on this second visit, however, was that Lafontaine's subjects seemed incapable of opening their eyes once they had been mesmerized, and this observation led him to conclude that the nerve centers of their eyes must have become paralyzed.

Since such paralysis temporarily sets in whenever a person stares at a single point in space for a few moments, Braid asked a friend to gaze fixedly at the neck of a wine bottle: within a matter of minutes the man fell into the same profound sleep that Braid had witnessed on the stage. In 1843 Braid presented the first closely reasoned study of hypnosis in a volume entitled *Neurypnology*.[33] In later years he came to recognize the importance of psychological as well as physiological factors and advanced the theory that hypnosis could be induced not only by ocular fixation but also by verbal suggestion.

On the Continent, questions concerning the origin of hypnotic phenomena divided medical opinion into two rival camps. The Nancy school, led by Liébeault and Bernheim, upheld the view that the hypnotic condition could be produced by planting a suggestion in any patient's mind, while Charcot and his students at the Salpêtrière maintained that the hypnotic trance, a physiologically altered condition of the nervous system, could be induced only in patients demonstrating a predisposition to hysteria.[34] The dispute between the two schools recapitulated the quarrel that persistently attended any revival of mesmerist doctrines. In the eighteenth century, imagination and the magnetic fluid had figured as catchwords in debates between the competing parties; nineteenth-century physicians replaced these concepts with suggestion and neurophysiological conditions.

Ambroise Auguste Liébeault, founder of the Nancy school, began his career as a country doctor of modest ambitions. While studying medicine at the University of Nancy, he had come across a handbook on animal magnetism. He decided to test the methods outlined in it as soon as he received his

[33] *Neurypnology; or, The Rationale of Nervous Sleep, Considered in Relation with Animal Magnetism* (London: Churchill, 1843).

[34] On the conflicts between the two schools, see Robert G. Hillman, "A Scientific Study of Mystery: The Role of the Medical and Popular Press in the Nancy-Salpêtrière Controversy on Hypnotism," *Bulletin of the History of Medicine*, 39 (1965), 163-182.

medical degree. A man of conscience, Liébeault offered to treat without charge those patients who consented to participate in his mesmerist experiments. Although his income was reduced considerably by this policy, his practice expanded rapidly—in a single year over a thousand patients took advantage of his offer. Within a few years, he had accumulated enough evidence to publish a five-hundred-page study on his clinical experience.[35] The book proved no more profitable than his magnetic practice: after five years he had succeeded in selling only five copies of the work.[36] Enthusiastic reports of Liébeault's gifts as a healer, however, came to the attention of physicians at the University of Nancy with annoying regularity. These reports eventually prompted Hippolyte Marie Bernheim, a leading member of the faculty, to pay a visit to the country doctor's clinic.

Bernheim was greeted by a man whose unaffected manner and restrained bearing ran counter to all expectations. Far from trying to proselytize the younger physician, Liébeault simply invited him to visit his clinic and draw his own conclusions. Bernheim became an immediate convert. With a degree of passion bordering on missionary zeal, he declared his intention of rescuing Liébeault's work from obscurity and of defending it against those physicians who viewed suggestion as a thinly disguised form of animal magnetism.[37] At the time that he made this decision, Bernheim could not possibly have comprehended the dimensions of the task he had taken upon himself. Jean-Martin Charcot, then a rising luminary in the field of neurology, had only recently mounted the podium at the Academy of Sciences in Paris to expound his own views on hypnosis and hysteria, and it was not until several months later that he emerged as Bernheim's most powerful opponent.

[35] *Du sommeil et des états analogues considérés surtout au point de vue de l'action du moral sur le physique* (Paris: Masson, 1866).

[36] Barrucand, *Histoire de l'hypnose en France*, p. 90.

[37] Hippolyte Bernheim, *De la suggestion dans l'état hypnotique et dans l'état de veille* (Paris: Doin, 1884), p. 3.

Charcot, director of the Salpêtrière, confined his investigation of hypnosis to the physiological mechanisms operating in the trance. From the start he declared that he had no intention of addressing himself to the "esoteric" aspects of hypnotic phenomena; he wished only to identify and describe the physiological characteristics and clinical signs of hypnosis. The paper that he delivered in 1882 to the Academy of Sciences sought to present a rigorously objective picture of the three phases of hypnotism and to delineate the somatic changes accompanying each stage. But, as Bernheim was later to point out, Charcot conducted his experiments under conditions that did not preclude the use of suggestion. Many of the patients at the Salpêtrière were only too happy to perform for the society people, actors, journalists, and writers to whom Charcot had opened his clinic, and they did not fail to take the proper cues from the verbal explanations that introduced their cases, from the assistants who hypnotized them, and from the paintings decorating the lecture halls of the Salpêtrière.[38]

If Charcot misled the medical community by refusing to recognize the role of suggestion, he nonetheless lent dignity to the study of hypnotism and promoted scientific interest in it simply by announcing his decision to study the subject. "The weight of his reputation," as Sigmund Freud was to write in the year of Charcot's death, "put an end once for all to doubts [concerning] the reality of hypnotic manifestations."[39] Charcot's study of the connections between hypnosis and hysteria also challenged traditional views on the origin of hysteria: through the centuries physicians had attributed the disease either to an irritation of the uterus or to a patient's febrile imagination. Charcot, however, insisted that hysteria was a strictly neurological disorder. He demonstrated that its symptoms could be replicated when sug-

[38] Georges Guillain, *J.-M. Charcot, 1825-1893: His Life—His Work*, trans. Pearce Bailey (New York: Hoeber, 1959), pp. 174-176.

[39] Sigmund Freud, *Collected Papers*, trans. Joan Riviere (New York: Basic Books, 1959), I, 23.

gestions were given to hypnotized patients and, conversely, that the symptoms could be removed through suggestion.[40] Finally, although he rigidly adhered to a neurophysiological interpretation of hysteria, his clinical experiments furnished evidence for the psychogenic nature of some hysterical symptoms and suggested that physicians would henceforth have to distinguish between traumatic and organic paralyses.

III

In 1885 Freud arrived in Paris on a traveling scholarship to continue his neurological studies under the "Napoleon of neuroses." Freud visited Charcot's clinic, attended his lectures, and regularly accompanied him on hospital ward tours. During the seventeen weeks that he spent at the Salpêtrière, Freud formed a personal tie with Charcot and offered to translate into German the third volume of the senior physician's lectures on nervous diseases. Ever afterward Freud remained an unqualified admirer of Charcot the man, whose revolutionary influence he likened to that of Philippe Pinel (the pioneer psychologist who in 1794 released the inmates of Bicêtre from their chains). Nevertheless, further exploration of hypnosis and hysteria modulated the Viennese doctor's initial enthusiasm for Charcot's clinical observations and theoretical views.

When Freud embarked on his trip abroad, he fully intended to pursue research on brain anatomy. Ernest Jones has suggested that Freud's decision to interrupt his neurological studies stemmed largely from the encounter with Charcot. The preoccupation with hypnosis and hysteria generated by this meeting, Jones adds, led Freud directly to the development of psychoanalysis.[41] Yet Freud's views on

[40] On this point see Richard Wollheim, *Sigmund Freud* (New York: Viking, 1971), pp. 3-7, and Walter A. Stewart, *Psychoanalysis: The First Ten Years, 1888-1898* (New York: Macmillan, 1967), pp. 11-14.

[41] Ernest Jones, *The Life and Work of Sigmund Freud*, 3 vols. (New York: Basic Books, 1953), I, 75.

hypnosis were ultimately shaped by the doctrine of suggestion as formulated by Liébeault and Bernheim, and his subsequent use of hypnosis as a technique for exploring the mind was informed by Breuer's method of treating hysteria. Charcot's precise clinical descriptions and his recognition that hysterical paralyses were psychogenic in nature no doubt enlarged Freud's understanding of neuropathology, but it was nonetheless Charcot's compelling personality, rather than his scientific research, that seems to have left the most enduring impression on him.

Shortly after returning to Vienna, Freud sent out cards announcing the opening of his medical practice on the Rathausstrasse. The dearth of patients in the first years of his practice allowed him to continue his neuropathological studies and to translate several works into German, among them three books on hypnosis. A significant number of the patients who did come for consultation in those years appeared to suffer from functional rather than organic ailments, and Freud soon turned his attention exclusively to "the crowds of neurotics, whose number seemed further multiplied by the way in which they hurried, with their troubles unsolved, from one physician to another."[42] He had not yet fully realized how limited were the weapons for combating nervous disorders in the therapeutic arsenal stocked by his predecessors; hence he initially referred patients to hydrotherapists or prescribed the rest cure developed by S. Weir Mitchell. But such referrals failed to provide him with an income sufficient to cover his expenses, and he therefore began to attempt curing the patients himself using electrical treatment. "Innocent faith in authority," Freud later explained, had tempted him to follow the instructions outlined in Wilhelm Erb's popular textbook on electrotherapy.[43] He quickly reached the conclusion that electrical stimulation had no effect whatsoever on his patients' symptoms. Feeling "completely helpless," he set aside

[42] *Standard Edition,* XX, 17. [43] Ibid., p. 16.

his electrical apparatus and cast about for more effective measures.

Freud's experiments with hypnosis fared somewhat better. In 1887 he reported to his friend Wilhelm Fliess that he had taken up hypnosis and was achieving "all sorts of small but remarkable successes."[44] Freud's first encounter with hypnosis goes back to his visit as a student to a demonstration given in Vienna by the magnetist Hansen; the performance left him with no doubts about the authenticity of hypnotic trances. But it is more difficult to date precisely Freud's decision to use hypnosis as an instrument for removing the symptoms of nervous disorders. Even before he visited Charcot at the Salpêtrière, Freud had known of the cathartic method, which employed hypnosis; indeed, his friend and colleague Josef Breuer had used that method to treat a patient who later became known to the medical profession as Anna O. On occasion he had tested Breuer's methods on his own patients. But in Vienna, the use of hypnosis met with considerable resistance from the medical faculty: the majority of Freud's colleagues openly expressed their contempt for those who indulged in such dubious practices. It was only at Charcot's clinic that Freud saw hypnosis used on a regular basis by serious physicians. A year after returning from Paris, he read two papers on hypnotism—one before the Psychological Association of Vienna, the other before the Psychiatric Society—and in his own practice he subsequently began to employ this "powerful therapeutic method."[45]

In his *Autobiographical Study*, Freud declared that there was something "positively seductive" about working with hypnosis.[46] This new therapeutic device not only dispelled the feeling of helplessness that had haunted him in his first years of practice, but also bolstered his self-confidence. "It

[44] Sigmund Freud, *Aus den Anfängen der Psychoanalyse: Briefe an Wilhelm Fliess, Abhandlungen und Notizen aus den Jahren 1887-1902* (London: Imago, 1950), p. 61.

[45] *Standard Edition*, I, 75.

[46] Ibid., XX, 17.

was highly flattering," he confessed in later years, "to enjoy the reputation of being a miracle-worker."[47] Nonetheless, Freud grew increasingly irritated by his inability to induce as deep a state of hypnosis as he wished in some patients and by his complete failure to hypnotize others. Suspecting that he had never truly mastered the necessary techniques, he journeyed to Nancy in the summer of 1889 to learn the art of hypnosis from Liébeault and Bernheim. There he witnessed the "moving spectacle" of Liébeault ministering to women and children of the working classes and observed Bernheim's "astonishing" experiments with hospital patients. Making no attempt to conceal the shortcomings of his methods, Bernheim spoke candidly with Freud about the obstacles he had encountered in hypnotizing some patients. On his return to Vienna, Freud no longer lacked confidence in his hypnotic powers—they seemed to match Bernheim's—but he now began to express dissatisfaction with the hazy concept of suggestion itself and with the uneven results of its clinical use.

Freud had also used hypnosis "in *another* manner, apart from hypnotic suggestion,"[48] and that other manner, Breuer's cathartic method, bridged the gap between suggestion, the principal tool of hypnotic therapy, and free association, the central diagnostic technique of psychoanalysis. The "Preliminary Communication" of 1893 that served to introduce *Studies on Hysteria* (published jointly by Freud and Breuer in 1895) defined the etiology of hysterical disorders and outlined the procedure for removing the symptoms of such diseases. That *"hysterics suffer mainly from reminiscences"* was the central lesson derived from the five case histories that constituted the core of *Studies on Hysteria*.[49] If the memory of an event is deliberately repressed as incompatible with normal consciousness or if it is inaccessible to consciousness because it was experienced in a hypnoid state, the affect attending the painful event does

[47] Ibid. [48] Ibid., p. 19. [49] Ibid., II, 7.

not fade or lose its strength through the normal channels of release. It remains instead in a "strangulated" condition because the memory of the distressing event has entered into a chain of associations cut off from normal consciousness. The charge of affective energy attached to the memory of the traumatic episode invariably manifests its existence in the form of a somatic disorder. Breuer's cathartic method aimed to recover this original experience through verbal utterance and thus to release its strangulated affect. When the patient abreacted or discharged the psychic energy that sustained the symptom in this way, the symptom itself disappeared. While the cathartic method was not new to psychotherapy—Victor Race had benefited from it a half century earlier—Breuer's explanation for its effectiveness was far more precise and sophisticated than that supplied by his predecessors.

Breuer first developed his method while treating Anna O., a patient whose case history figures as the first of five clinical pictures in *Studies on Hysteria*. Anna O., an intelligent and imaginative twenty-one-year-old woman, suffered from all the classical symptoms of hysteria: intermittent paralysis, a nervous cough, aversion to food and drink, disturbances of speech and vision, and "double consciousness." The last symptom represented the splitting of consciousness into a normal waking state and a form of consciousness that Breuer connected with hypnoid states and defined as an *absence*. During one of Anna O.'s *absences*, a friend inadvertently eavesdropped on her spoken remarks. When the friend repeated the words that he had distinguished in her monologue, she responded by constructing a story around these words. Shortly after concluding her narrative, she returned to normal consciousness, feeling calm and refreshed. When Breuer repeated this procedure during her next *absence*, he achieved similar results. Anna O.'s "talking cure," which she referred to as "chimney-sweeping," entered a second phase when she began to recite events from the period immediately preceding her father's death. Breuer discovered that each of her symptoms could be traced to an episode that had occurred during the year of her father's illness and that each symptom disappeared as soon as his patient recalled and talked about the events leading to its first appearance. In the artificially induced hypnoid condition, a state of consciousness analogous to that in which she had acquired her symptoms, Anna O. could reproduce material inaccessible to her in waking life and could vividly describe the circumstances under which she had developed the symptoms of her neurosis.

Although Freud's use of both suggestion and catharsis met with no small measure of success, he bitterly complained that failure to induce hypnosis on the first trial inevitably shook a patient's confidence in his physician. It was, in addition, somewhat humiliating to hear a patient say: "But doctor, I'm *not* asleep," shortly after he had issued the command: "You are going to sleep! . . . sleep!"[50] (Mesmer and Puységur had easily avoided such indignities by treating only true believers—those whose confidence in the miracles of animal magnetism was absolute.) Freud's disenchantment with hypnosis and his subsequent adoption of the "concentration" technique stemmed, however, from a far more serious problem. As early as 1891, in a paper on hypnosis, Freud had touched upon the specific limitations of suggestion when he observed that "with hypnotic treatment both physician and patient grow tired . . . as a result of the contrast between the deliberately rosy coloring of the suggestions and the cheerless truth."[51] With catharsis, the "cheerless truth" became evident as soon as the relationship between physician and patient suffered a disturbance of any kind. Neither hypnotic suggestion nor cathartic treatment could permanently cure hysteria; they merely removed the symptoms, and these symptoms tended to reappear with annoying persistency once therapy had been terminated.

If a clash of temperament between physician and patient

[50] Ibid., p. 108.

[51] Ibid., I, 113.

or a patient's decision to discontinue therapy annulled the benefits of cathartic treatment, then the relationship between doctor and patient was clearly more powerful than the cathartic process itself. The erotic nature of this bond, which had not escaped the attention of the royal commission on animal magnetism, disclosed itself to Freud in a highly dramatic fashion. After responding quite normally to hypnosis, one of his more submissive patients suddenly awoke and threw her arms around the doctor's neck. Freud was "modest enough" not to ascribe the patient's impetuous behavior to his own "irresistible personal attraction," and he resolved henceforth to refrain from using hypnotism. Otherwise he would never be able to eliminate or at least control a "mysterious element" operating in the rapport between his patients and himself.[52]

Freud was determined to find a satisfactory substitute for hypnosis. From Bernheim he had learned that patients who had been hypnotized could, with professional help, overcome posthypnotic amnesia. After returning to a waking state, a patient only appeared to have forgotten the events that had occurred under hypnosis; an astute physician could revive these memories by issuing mild commands and applying pressure to his patient's forehead. By analogy, Freud reasoned that the memories attached to a strangulated affect could be brought back to consciousness in similar fashion. He first introduced the "pressure technique" in conjunction with the "concentration method" while treating Elisabeth von R. Working under the assumption that his patient already knew everything essential to her cure, he sought to extract this information from her without resorting to hypnotism. He instructed her to lie down, shut her eyes, concentrate on a particular symptom, and try to recall any past event that might shed light on the origin of the symptom.

The new technique successfully avoided the pitfalls of hypnotic therapy. But the concentration method brought with it a significant change in the structure of Freud's

[52] Ibid., XX, 27.

thought. "Hypnosis," he reported in retrospect, "had screened from view an interplay of forces which now came in sight and the understanding of which gave a solid foundation to my theory."[53] Two essential features of psychoanalysis, resistance and transference, now came to light. By 1896 Freud had completely abandoned the use of hypnosis and had developed the method of free association out of which his major theoretical discoveries were to emerge.

IV

For Freud, hypnosis was only one of many signposts on the "royal road" to the unconscious. Psychoanalysis, as he himself observed, "only begins with the new technique that dispenses with hypnosis."[54] Yet it would be misleading to underestimate the role of hypnosis in the evolution of his theories, for as noted earlier, Freud also insisted that modern psychoanalysts were the "legitimate heirs" to hypnotists. For nearly a decade, he had relied chiefly on the cathartic method and on hypnotic suggestion—techniques used by Mesmer and Puységur in rudimentary form—to relieve the symptoms of patients suffering from functional disorders. Charcot's demonstration of hypnotically induced hysteria, Bernheim's guidance on suggestion, and Breuer's research on the symptomology of hysteria greatly enriched Freud's understanding of psychopathological processes and revealed the existence of powerful mental processes normally hidden from view.[55] Hypnosis also directed Freud's attention to free association, which in turn pointed the way to the analysis of dreams—one of the central tools of psychoanalysis.

Psychoanalysts inherited not only the methods but also the language of mesmerists and hypnotists. Contemporary

[53] Ibid., p. 29.

[54] Paul Roazen, *Freud: Political and Social Thought* (New York: Knopf, 1968), pp. 48-49.

[55] *Standard Edition*, XIV, 16.

theories on laws governing physical forces had inspired Mesmer's physiological explanations for psychological processes: the subtle fluids posited by Newton as the source of electricity, heat, and light, the model of electrical energy provided by the Leyden jar, and Richard Mead's writings on atmospheric tides shaped his views on the science of healing. Although Mesmer flatly rejected hydrotherapy and electrotherapy (the two predominant methods for treating patients with nervous disorders in his day) and turned to magnetism for man's salvation, he consistently described his discovery in hydraulic and electrical terms.

The terminology that Freud used to describe the operation of mental processes—"flows" and "dams," "charges" and "discharges," "excitation" and "cathexis," "currents of energy," "resistance," and "tension"—similarly reflects an inclination to view mental energy as an electrical or hydraulic force, perhaps on more than a metaphorical level.[56] In one section of *Studies on Hysteria,* Breuer felt obliged to apologize for the excessive number of analogies drawn in that work between psychic and electrical action.[57] Yet if one turns to the neurological model of the mind outlined in Freud's "Project for a Scientific Psychology," the striking number of such analogies appears to be more than pure coincidence. Like Mesmer's speculations on animal magnetism, the ideas expressed in that psychological treatise betray a heavy reliance on theoretical developments in the physical sciences. Witness, for example, Freud's assertion that a *"tendency to keep intracerebral excitation constant"*[58] governs every organism. This law, derived from the teachings of Hermann Helmholtz, constituted the cornerstone of his "Project."[59]

[56] H. Stuart Hughes, *Consciousness and Society: The Reconstruction of European Social Thought, 1890-1930* (New York: Vintage, 1961), pp. 134-135.

[57] *Standard Edition,* II, 203.

[58] Ibid., p. 197.

[59] For a discussion of Helmholtz's influence on Freud's early work, see Siegfried Bernfeld, "Freud's Earliest Theories and the School of

The continuity of the development linking animal magnetism with psychoanalysis was thus in part assured by the persistent tendency of nineteenth-century psychologists to draw analogies between physical and psychic forces.[60] For Mesmer and his contemporaries, both the physical and mental world appeared governed by similar laws, and psychologists repeatedly attempted to explain human behavior using a frame of reference developed by physicists and natural scientists. It is for this reason that a brief examination of scientific views in the late eighteenth century can extend our understanding of psychological theories in that era.

Helmholtz," *Psychoanalytic Quarterly*, 13 (1944), 341-362, and "Freud's Scientific Beginnings," *American Imago*, 4 (1949), 163-196.

[60] For other dimensions of this continuity, see Jean Starobinski, *La Relation critique* (Paris: Gallimard, 1970), pp. 196-213, and L. Chertok and R. de Saussure, *Naissance du psychanalyste de Mesmer à Freud* (Paris: Payot, 1973).

CHAPTER 2

Salvation by Electricity: Science, Poetry, and "Naturphilosophie"

"Every science becomes poetry—once it has become philosophy."
—Novalis, *Notebooks*

Mesmer, curiously, never fully appreciated those features of animal magnetism that came to command the attention of his contemporaries. From his self-imposed exile in Switzerland, he attempted to justify this lack of foresight by announcing that he had deliberately confined his investigations to the magnetic crisis and had refrained from exploring occult powers in order to avoid testing the credulity of an already skeptical medical world. In an interview with the German physician Karl Wolfart, Mesmer finally addressed himself to the issue of "magnetic sleep" and acknowledged the existence of a sixth sense (*innerer Sinn*) that promised to account for the uncanny ability of his patients to look into the past and future, to annul spatial limitations, and to enter into a perfect rapport with nature.[1]

1 Friedrich [*sic*] Anton Mesmer, *Mesmerismus oder System der Wechselwirkungen: Theorie und Anwendung des thierischen Magnetismus als die allgemeine Heilkunde zur Erhaltung des Menschen*, ed. Karl Christian Wolfart (Berlin: Nikolaische Buchhandlung, 1814), pp. 137-142. To his pupils, Mesmer had already spoken about this sixth sense: "Il est probable, et il y a de fortes raisons *a priori*, que nous sommes doués d'un sens interne qui est en relation avec l'ensemble de tout l'univers" (Caullet de Veaumorel, *Aphorismes de M. Mesmer* [Paris: n.p., 1785], p. 44).

Less conventional thinkers, however, had displayed little reluctance to enlarge on the powers of a mysterious faculty analogous to Mesmer's sixth sense. Novalis, for example, distinguished between two discrete systems of sensory perception—one responding to external stimuli, the other to impulses from a spiritual world (II, 546).[2] The central organ of this latter system he defined as an "innerer Sinn" that constitutes the medium of cognition. In an essay contrasting the same two systems of perception, Franz Baader advanced the theory that an internal sense, which he regarded as the vehicle of imagination, furnishes the mind with images far more vivid than those mediated by the other five senses.[3] The Romantic physicist Johann Wilhelm Ritter, in an uncharacteristically lucid formulation, suggested that by cultivating this special faculty, man could enrich his understanding of the universe: "We possess an internal sense—as yet undeveloped—for knowledge of the world. It does not see, it does not hear, etc., but it knows."[4] Novalis characterized the activity of that sixth sense in similar fashion: "It is not seeing, hearing, feeling; it is a combination of all three, more than all three" (II, 421). The teacher in his "Novices of Sais" ("Lehrlinge zu Sais") ends his apprenticeship to nature at the moment when he has fully developed this faculty: "His sense perceptions crowded into vast, colorful images: he heard, saw, touched, and thought at once" (I, 180). A firm belief in the existence of an internal sense that does not differentiate among the various modes of perception explains, to some extent, the widespread use of synesthetic effects in Romantic poetry and prose.

[2] Parenthetical volume and page numbers in this chapter refer to the four-volume edition of Novalis's *Schriften*, ed. Paul Kluckhohn, Richard Samuel, et al. (Stuttgart: Kohlhammer, 1960-75).

[3] Franz von Baader, "Über den inneren Sinn im Gegensatz zu den äusseren Sinnen," in *Schriften*, ed. Max Pulver (Leipzig: Insel, 1921), pp. 60-72.

[4] Johann Wilhelm Ritter, *Fragmente aus dem Nachlasse eines jungen Physikers: Ein Taschenbuch für Freunde der Natur* (1810; reprint ed. Heidelberg: Lambert Schneider, 1969), II, 204.

The view that man is endowed with a special sensorium operating independently of the five senses was a commonplace of eighteenth-century philosophy. The moral sense, a concept introduced into ethics by Shaftesbury, and taste, its analogue in the sphere of aesthetics, both admit of cultivation and refinement (just as they may deteriorate "through custom, or by licentiousness of practice"), but they are no less "natural" faculties having their roots in the human constitution.[5] For Hutcheson, a moral sense that intuitively apprehends the difference between good and evil, and a "natural power of perception, or sense of beauty in objects" that is antecedent to custom, education, and example, occupy the highest position in the hierarchy of internal senses.[6]

Hemsterhuis, to whom the Romantics repeatedly paid tribute for his key role in the development of ethics, derived his concept of an *organe moral,* an agent that transmits ethical and religious sentiments to the soul, from the theories set forth by the two English philosophers. This *organe moral* makes an appearance in Novalis's preliminary notes for a Romantic encyclopedia, and there its scope is broadened to include a psychological and cognitive dimension. "The moral sense," he declares, "is the organ of *existence,* . . . the organ of unity— . . . the organ of harmony— . . . the organ for the *Ding an sich*—the genuine organ of prophecy" (III, 250). Novalis's words echo Fichte's judgment that the supersensual world is perceived through an "innerer Sinn," an organ far superior to any of the external senses in that the latter apprehend only appearances, while the former furnishes, in his words, the only possible *An sich.*[7]

[5] Anthony, Earl of Shaftesbury, *Characteristics of Men, Manners, Opinions, Times,* ed. John M. Robertson, 2 vols. (Indianapolis and New York: Bobbs-Merrill, 1964), I, 262.

[6] Frances Hutcheson, *An Inquiry Concerning Beauty, Order, Harmony, Design,* International Archives of the History of Ideas: Series Minor, 9, ed. Peter Kivy (The Hague: Martinus Nijhoff, 1973), p. 82.

[7] Johann Gottlieb Fichte, "Gerichtliche Verantwortung gegen die Anklage des Atheismus," in *Sämmtliche Werke,* ed. J. H. Fichte (Berlin: Veit, 1845), V, 268.

Just as the Romantics extended the meaning of sympathy—a concept developed by eighteenth-century associationists as an ethical principle—to embrace the idea of a panvitalistic force in nature, so they translated the concept of an internal ethical sense into a psychological and cognitive notion.

Despite the many versions of a sixth sense in nineteenth-century thought, the examples cited above show that in each case we are dealing with precisely the same concept, although the mode of thought in which it is cast ranges from the religious to the philosophical to the aesthetic. For some writers, however, the internal sense figured as an actual organ of the human anatomy; for others it was a merely spiritual reality. The former believed that the internal sense engaged in a reciprocal relation with the world of things by establishing contact with a material substance permeating the entire universe; the latter held that it entered into the same relationship, though on a purely metaphysical level.

Evidence for the existence of a substance that sets up a current between an internal sense in man and the life of nature presented itself in investigations of magnetism, electricity, and other vital forces. Nineteenth-century scientists had shown these impalpable fluids to be nearly ubiquitous, and it was therefore quite logical to assign to them a unifying influence. The sixth sense of mesmerists, Ritter's primeval electrical sense (*elektrischer Ur-sinn*), and the sympathetic nervous system of Romantic vitalists established rapport with nature by picking up impulses from a magnetic, electrical, or vital power diffused throughout the universe.

I

From a twentieth-century perspective, the tenets of animal magnetism appear somewhat bizarre, if not entirely preposterous. Although Mesmer cultivated an image of himself as an imaginative and unorthodox thinker, a scientific genius misunderstood by his age, he actually remained well within the bounds of eighteenth-century thought when he formulated his theories. To consider animal magnetism independently of the tradition out of which it emerged is to magnify its distinctively occult characteristics and to diminish in importance those features that mirror the scientific and philosophical temper of the age in which it flourished. The sixth sense of somnambulists, for example, represented not merely a mystical strain in mesmerist ideas, but was intimately bound up with quite down-to-earth questions raised by Mesmer's predecessors and contemporaries. In short, mesmerism was more than an occult doctrine espoused by a coterie of eccentric spirits: the theories invoked to explain its agency fit squarely into the frame of eighteenth-century cosmology.

The attempt to reduce the mysteries of life to one basic principle, to identify a single animating agent that at once sustains life and figures as its chief cause, spurred the investigations of Mesmer's scientific contemporaries. This heroic effort to recover a sense of immanence led even the most respectable scientists to turn their attention from observation and experiment to philosophical speculation on behalf of a metaphysical ideal. Seeking to develop a system of thought that could lay claim to comprehensiveness, they adopted the deductive methods of philosophy and aspired to nothing less than total explanation.

From Newton these scientists had inherited the view that a subtle ethereal medium, penetrating and surrounding matter, can explain all physical and vital phenomena. In the *Opticks*, Newton had posited the existence of a single universal ether which he hoped would explain everything from light, heat, and gravity through electricity and magnetism to nervous impulses and vision.[8] The forebears of Romantic scientists rejected Newton's notion of one universal ether for

[8] I. Bernard Cohen, *Franklin and Newton: An Inquiry into Speculative Newtonian Experimental Science and Franklin's Work in Electricity As an Example Thereof* (Philadelphia: American Philosophical Society, 1956), p. 431.

all such phenomena in favor of a separate fluid (in some cases a pair of fluids) for each phenomenon. Light, for example, was attributed to the agency of one imponderable fluid, gravity to a different fluid. Mesmer's magnetic fluid was in fact no more miraculous than the imposing array of subtle fluids sponsored by eighteenth-century scientists. Although these invisible forces seem in retrospect to have disguised the failures of speculative science, they actually inspired a number of valuable scientific discoveries that in turn eventually compelled scientists to jettison the fluid theory and to develop new paradigms for explaining the action of, say, heat or magnetism.[9]

Of the many subtle fluids that surged through the atmosphere breathed by the Romantics, electricity was perhaps the most intoxicating. Coleridge quite accurately conveyed the sense of excitement aroused by the discovery of the Leyden jar and by Franklin's experiments with atmospheric electricity when he wrote:

> From the time of Kepler to Newton, and from that to Hartley, not only all things in external nature, but the subtlest mysteries of life and organization, even of the intellect and moral being, were conjured within the magic circle of mathematical formality.
>
> But now a light was struck with electricity, and in every sense of the word it may be affirmed to have electrified the whole form of natural philosophy.[10]

In 1745 Ewald Georg von Kleist (a distant relative of the Prussian poet) had constructed a primitive form of the Leyden jar or condenser, a device that allowed scientists to

[9] On the fluid theory and its role in scientific discovery, see Thomas S. Kuhn, *The Structure of Scientific Revolutions*, 2d ed., International Encyclopedia of Unified Science, vol. 2, no. 2 (Chicago: University of Chicago Press, 1970), pp. 61-62.

[10] Samuel Taylor Coleridge, *The Philosophical Lectures*, ed. Kathleen Coburn (London: Pilot, 1949), p. 342.

collect electrical charges from the atmosphere and to store them in nonconductors. A severe electrical shock received while testing his invention discouraged Kleist from further refining it, but Pieter van Musschenbroek, professor of physics at the University of Leyden, proceeded with greater caution and (independently of Kleist) designed a more sophisticated model of the condenser.

In conjunction with electrostatic generators, or "electrical machines" as they were called in the eighteenth century, the Leyden jar enabled scientists to produce electrical effects on a grand scale. A charge from an electrical machine could be stored in the Leyden jar, then released in a quantity sufficient to kill a small animal or jolt a human being. The Leyden jar, Priestley wrote, "gave éclat to electricity" and rendered it "the subject of general conversation."[11] Scores of aspiring scientists, delighted with the opportunity to display their talents, employed Leyden jars to produce miniature bolts of lightning and peals of thunder that did not fail to ignite the imagination of the man in the salon. Wealthy amateur scientists provided entertainment for the masses by discharging Leyden jars through circuits composed of human beings. The victims of these electrical demonstrations formed conducting chains by joining hands, grasping iron rods, or holding long wires threaded around them. A Polish scientist, the first to perform such experiments, delivered shocks to twenty people simultaneously.[12] In France, Abbé Jean-Antoine Nollet administered shocks to 180 soldiers in a single instant. For the amusement of Louis XV, the inhabitants of a Carthusian monastery were convulsed; the conducting chain formed by the monks was

[11] Joseph Priestley, *The History and Present State of Electricity, with Original Experiments* (London: J. Dodsley, J. Johnson and B. Davenport, and T. Cadell, 1767), p. 84.

[12] A. Wolf, *A History of Science, Technology, and Philosophy in the Eighteenth Century*, 2d ed. (London: George Allen & Unwin, 1952), pp. 221-222.

reported to have stretched for more than a mile.[13] In contrast, Benjamin Franklin proposed far less painful electrical diversions. As host to a "party of pleasure" on the banks of the Schuylkill River, he planned to fire spirits "by a spark sent from side to side through the river," to kill a turkey with an electrical shock, roast it "by the *electrical jack*, before a fire kindled by the *electrified bottle*," and finally to crown the festivities by drinking a toast to "all the famous electricians in *England, Holland, France*, and *Germany* . . . in *electrified bumpers*, under the discharge of guns from the *electrical battery*."[14]

The discovery of atmospheric electricity lent further strength to the view that electricity was the prime agent operating in the economy of nature. Because the discharge of Leyden jars offered many convincing analogies to the effects produced by lightning, Franklin determined to investigate the relationship between these two phenomena. When he ventured out into a storm during the summer of 1752 to confirm his conjecture that thunderclouds are electrified, he carried with him not only the celebrated kite and key, but also a Leyden jar which, in the course of his experiment, he charged with electricity from the clouds. By snatching lightning from the skies and showing it to be a product of the same electrical fluid that existed on earth, Franklin took the first step toward demonstrating the omnipresence of electrical energy.

The dramatic electrical experiments of the 1740s and 1750s stimulated widespread speculation on the role of electricity in inorganic matter and organic life. The discovery that the mineral tourmaline became electrically charged when heated pointed to the possibility that an invisible electrical fluid might also reside in plants and ani-

[13] Philip C. Ritterbush, *Overtures to Biology: The Speculations of Eighteenth-Century Naturalists* (New Haven: Yale University Press, 1964), p. 22.

[14] *Benjamin Franklin's Experiments*, ed. I. Bernard Cohen (Cambridge, Mass.: Harvard University Press, 1941), pp. 199-200.

mals. Experiments showing that *Mimosa pudica*, "the sensitive plant," responded visibly to electrical impulses (as well as to light, changes in temperature, and touch) seemed to corroborate this hypothesis.[15] A positive charge caused the leaves of the plant to curl up; a negative charge unrolled them again. The shocks delivered by electric eels and electric torpedoes, which physicians had been using since antiquity to cure disabilities ranging from headaches to paralysis, also aroused considerable interest among scientists. And again the Leyden jar, once the guide to understanding electrical reactions in the heavens, now furnished a model for explaining the physiology of submarine life. Since the torpedo discharged electricity in precisely the same fashion as the Leyden jar, or electrified phial, it came to be known as the animated phial.

Hoping that "natural" sources of electricity might prove effective therapeutically, physicians added electric eels and torpedoes to their arsenal of weapons for curing disease. Frans van der Lott, a Dutch medical practitioner, created a sensation when he cured an eight-year-old boy of paralysis by plunging him into a vat containing a large black eel. (One can only speculate on the damage done to the child's psyche.) An advertisement appearing in a London paper of 1777 offered the public the opportunity to test the powers of the "torporific eel" at a mere two shillings and sixpence a shock.[16] European physicians continued to ascribe curative powers to the shocks received from electric fish and jolted their patients back to health well into the nineteenth century.

[15] For a fascinating discussion of the *Mimosa* in English Romantic literature, see Robert M. Maniquis, "The Puzzling *Mimosa*: Sensitivity and Plant Symbols in Romanticism," *Studies in Romanticism*, 7 (1969), 129-155.

[16] Peter Kellaway, "The Part Played by Electric Fish in the Early History of Bioelectricity and Electrotherapy," *Bulletin of the History of Medicine*, 20 (1946), 112-137. Ritterbush also discusses electrical cures in *Overtures to Biology*, pp. 43-48.

Most of those who used electrical shock therapy, or Franklinism as it was then known, genuinely believed that their patients stood to derive enormous benefits from it. Disease, they reasoned, stemmed from disturbances in the circulation of the electrical fluid through the human body, and a physician, by removing obstacles in the fluid's path, could restore his patient's health. Although belief in the omnipotence of electricity swelled the ranks of electrotherapists, the growing numbers of patients actually cured by shocks from electric eels and Leyden jars served to enlist even more converts. The most obvious quacks achieved a startling measure of success. James Graham, an Englishman who opened a Temple of Healing on the Royal Terrace at Adelphi, where he featured electrical equipment to buffet his patients' senses and celestial beds in which couples were assured of begetting offspring, could take pride in the growing pile of crutches and canes discarded by the beneficiaries of his ministrations.[17]

The striking similarities between magnetic and electrical cures are not entirely fortuitous. Mesmer's *baquet*, as noted in the previous chapter, was modeled on the Leyden jar, and although the magnetic fluid stored in the *baquet* did not operate as swiftly as the electrical charges accumulated in the Leyden jar, it promised the same results. Both magnetic and electrical therapists based their claims on the existence of a universal subtle fluid that insinuates itself into the nervous system of the human body. Advocates of electrotherapy prescribed shocks from natural and artificial sources of electricity; Mesmer and his disciples induced so-called crises, that is, emotional shocks, by directing shafts of magnetic fluid from their own eyes to those of patients or by exposing the diseased to emanations from the *baquet*. Both electrotherapists and mesmerists enjoyed some degree of success, if only for the reason that they treated a large number of illnesses with psychic rather than somatic foundations.

[17] Ritterbush, *Overtures to Biology*, p. 44.

II

Once the presence of electricity had been detected in minerals, plants, and animals, and in the atmosphere, it remained only to define the source of vital power in terms of electrical discharge. As bewitched by Newton's subtle fluids as were their colleagues in neighboring disciplines, eighteenth-century physiologists inclined to the view that nerves stimulated muscles by means of an imponderable fluid variously identified as ether, heat, or electricity. The Swiss poet and scientist Albrecht von Haller, whose *Elementa Physiologiae* prepared the way for modern neurophysiology, suspected that some kind of nervous fluid—less subtle than fire, ether, or electrical and magnetic fluids—caused muscular contractions. His treatise on sensibility and irritability in the human organism divided the activity of muscles and nerves into two distinct and independent categories.[18] Irritability he characterized as the contraction of a muscle in response to an external stimulus; the term sensibility designated the response of a nerve to a stimulus. Haller took pains to distinguish carefully between these two terms: irritability was a characteristic proper to muscle tissue and had no connection with the nervous system, while sensibility resided within the nerve tissue.

Haller's terminology seemed nonetheless to invite misinterpretation, for irritability and sensibility came to be used so loosely in the next decades that they lost virtually all meaning. The Scottish physician John Brown (whose illustrious descendants include the painter Ford Madox Brown and the novelist Ford Madox Ford) displayed a special talent for effacing Haller's carefully drawn distinctions. Claiming that the source of all nervous reactions could be traced to the principle of irritability, Brown outlined in his *Elementa Medicinae* a theory of disease so oversimplified

[18] Albrecht von Haller, "De partibus corporis humani sensilibus et irritabilibus," *Commentarii Societatis Regiae Scientiarum Gottingensis*, 2 (1753), 114-158.

that it rivaled Mesmer's doctrines in crudeness.[19] Brown's therapeutic proposals rested on the premise that excitability, the capacity of an organism to register external stimuli and respond to them, constituted the life force. Working under the assumption that illness was caused by an excess or deficiency of stimulation, Brown divided diseases into two groups. He recommended that physicians treat "sthenic" diseases, the result of overstimulation, with sedatives, and that they halt the course of "asthenic" diseases, the consequence of insufficient stimulation, with animating agents. (For gout, an asthenic debility from which Brown himself suffered, massive doses of opium and red wine were prescribed.) Brown and his followers believed that they could promote health in the human organism by stabilizing the level of excitability; on a scale of eighty degrees, forty represented a state of health.

More than a century after the publication of the *Elementa Medicinae*, Rudolf Virchow wrote that Brown's medical system had shaken the Continent like an earthquake, leaving—it should be added—countless casualties in its path.[20] Brown's ideas gained currency in Germany shortly after M. A. Weikard, physician to Catherine the Great, translated the *Elementa* into German in 1795. The German medical world hailed the Scottish physician's theories with the same blind enthusiasm that German poets, only two decades earlier, had greeted the "discovery" of Ossian's *Fragments of Ancient Poetry* by Brown's compatriot James Macpherson.[21] Brown was heralded by Novalis as *the* physi-

[19] For a concise summary of Brown's ideas, see Günter B. Risse, "The Brownian System of Medicine: Its Theoretical and Practical Implications," *Clio Medica*, 5 (1970), 45-51.

[20] Rudolf Virchow, "Die Stellung der Pathologie unter den biologischen Wissenschaften: Rede gehalten in der Royal Society zu London, am 16. März 1893," *Berliner klinische Wochenschrift*, 10 April 1893, pp. 357-360.

[21] The impact of Brown's medical theories on German Romantic literature receives detailed treatment in two studies by John Neubauer: "Dr. John Brown (1735-88) and Early German Romanticism," *Journal*

cian of the Romantic era (II, 604). His views on disease and nervous action left an indelible mark on Romantic medicine and *Naturphilosophie*, most notably on Schelling's *On the World-Soul* (*Von der Weltseele*) and his *Preliminary Outline of a System for the Philosophy of Nature* (*Erster Entwurf eines Systems der Naturphilosophie*).[22]

The excitement kindled by Brown's philosophical treatment of medicine quickly dissipated, more because of the theoretical shortcomings than the practical limitations of his system. Yet as late as 1802, a dispute between Brunonians and anti-Brunonians at the University of Göttingen developed into a full-scale riot. Troops were called in after two days to put an end to the fighting.[23] A wave of antagonism toward Brown followed in the wake of his popularity. Like mesmerist cures, which lent themselves well to burlesque, Brunonian therapy provided a wealth of topical material for second-rate playwrights. *The New Age* (*Das neue Jahrhundert*), a rather uninspired farce by August von Kotzebue, featured two physicians, Dr. Reiz and Dr. Potenz, who engage in a tedious quarrel about whether their patient has succumbed to a sthenic or asthenic disease. The chief source of humor in the play derives from a series of predictable puns on the double meaning ("irritate" and "excite")

---

of the History of Ideas, 28 (1967), 367-382, and *Bifocal Vision: Novalis' Philosophy of Nature and Disease*, University of North Carolina Studies in the Germanic Languages and Literatures, no. 68 (Chapel Hill: University of North Carolina Press, 1971). On Brown's views and their connections with scientific and medical developments in Germany, see also Werner Leibbrand, *Die spekulative Medizin der Romantik* (Hamburg: Claassen, 1956), pp. 75-166.

22 Schelling traveled to Bamberg in the summer of 1800 to study Brown's medical theories with Röschlaub and Marcus. The death of Auguste Böhmer, Caroline Schlegel's daughter from her first marriage, has been attributed to Schelling's attempt to cure the child using Brown's methods.

23 Fielding H. Garrison, *An Introduction to the History of Medicine*, 4th ed. (Philadelphia and London: W. B. Saunders, 1929), p. 314.

suggested by the verb *reizen*.[24] The Romantics who turned against Brown were far less amiable than Kotzebue in their criticism. They accused Brown of the ultimate sacrilege: mechanistic thinking and failure to apprehend the nature of organic development. Instead of mounting an attack on the reductionist aspects of Brown's system, they took issue with its limited scope and failure to provide an adequate explanation for the cause of life.[25]

A sequence of experiments conducted by Luigi Galvani, professor of anatomy at the University of Bologna, promised a more comprehensive and thus for the Romantics more congenial explanation for the source of vital power. In 1789 Galvani had observed that the thigh muscles of dissected frogs contracted when lightning flashed across the skies or when a spark happened to be drawn from a nearby Leyden jar. He later recognized that neither electrical thunderstorms nor Leyden jars were required to produce these muscular spasms; a freshly prepared frog's leg began twitching as soon as it was touched by two different metals simultaneously. Reasoning that the exterior and interior surfaces of muscles carry different charges, Galvani immediately drew an analogy between the electrical potential of muscular tissue and that of the Leyden jar. The stimulus for artificial movement in dead organic matter, he contended, was a special form of electricity which he designated as "animal electricity." Resisting the notion that contact between the two metals in a moist environment might have generated the electricity causing muscular contractions, he persistently maintained that a subtle electrical fluid, flowing from the brains of animals to their nerves, stimulates muscular action. His findings not only suggested that electricity was the animating agent of organic life, but also furthered

[24] August von Kotzebue, *Das neue Jahrhundert: Eine Posse in einem Akt*, in *Neue Schauspiele*, 8 vols. (Leipzig: Kummer, 1801), V, 1-90.

[25] Note in this context Novalis's view: "Browns allg[emeine] Grundsätze bleiben in gewisser Hinsicht wahr—sobald sie noch viel allg[emeiner] gemacht werden" (III, 371).

the view that this magical substance constituted the very "soul of the universe."

Although Alessandro Volta demonstrated that the electrical currents producing muscular contractions in his compatriot's frogs could by no stretch of the imagination be ascribed to animal electricity, Galvani's views received support well into the nineteenth century. His ideas took a firm hold in Germany largely through the writings of Alexander von Humboldt and Johann Wilhelm Ritter.[26] A pharmacist by training, Ritter had interrupted his lackluster career to study natural science at the University of Jena. Introduced to the circle of Romantic poets and philosophers gathered in and around Jena at the turn of the century, Ritter came to share their conception of nature as an immense living organism. One critic has pointed out that it was actually Ritter who formulated the central metaphor for this eminently Romantic idea: nature as a cosmic animal (*All-Tier*).[27] The metaphor was not chosen arbitrarily; it succinctly expressed an inference that Ritter had drawn from painstaking scientific experiments on the presence of a galvanic force in nature. He adduced evidence to show that galvanism, the principle of life in nature, could be detected in crystals, metals, plants, animals, and even in the human body. A passage from his "Proof That Galvanism Perpetually Attends the Process of Life in the Animal Kingdom" ("Beweis, dass ein beständiger Galvanismus den Lebensprocess in dem Thierreich begleite") shows how his imagination soared at the prospects opened by this discovery:

26 See Alexander von Humboldt, *Versuche über die gereizte Muskel- und Nervenfaser nebst Vermuthungen über den chemischen Process des Lebens in der Thier- und Pflanzenwelt* (Posen: Decker, 1797). On Humboldt's contribution to discussions of galvanism, see Leibbrand, *Die spekulative Medizin der Romantik*, pp. 83-86.

27 Walter D. Wetzels, "Aspects of Natural Science in German Romanticism," *Studies in Romanticism*, 10 (1971), 44-59. For further discussion of the metaphor, see Alexander Gode-von Aesch, *Natural Science in German Romanticism* (New York: Columbia University Press, 1941), pp. 240-267.

> Where is a sun, where is an atom, which is not a part of, which does not belong to this *organic universe, not living in time, yet comprehending all of time within it?* —What has happened to the distinctive features of animals, plants, metals, and stones? —Are they not all parts of *Nature's cosmic animal*?—A universal *law of nature*, hitherto unknown, seems to light up the horizon! —In the course of time it will perhaps be shown that this light is no optical illusion.[28]

III

Although Ritter's views on galvanism failed to enlist the support of his colleagues, they engaged the attention of several fictional scientists. "Whence, I often asked myself, did the principle of life proceed?" reports the hero of Mary Shelley's *Frankenstein* in the retrospective narrative of his life.[29] The answer comes to him in the same flash of light that Ritter predicted would one day dazzle the world:

> A sudden light broke in upon me—a light so brilliant and wondrous, yet so simple, that while I became dizzy with the immensity of the prospect which it illustrated, I was surprised, that among so many men of genius who had directed their enquiries towards the same sci-

[28] "Wo ist eine Sonne, wo ist ein Atom, die nicht Theil wäre, der nicht gehörte zu diesem *Organischen All, lebend in keiner Zeit, jede Zeit fassend in sich?* —Wo bleibt denn der Unterschied zwischen den Theilen des Thieres, der Pflanze, dem Metall und dem Stein? —Sind sie nicht sämmtlich Theile des grossen *All-Thiers* der *Natur*? —Ein allgemeines bisher noch nicht gekanntes *Naturgesetz* scheint uns entgegen zu leuchten! —Doch die Folge wird vielleicht darthun, dass es mehr sey, als Schein." Cited in Walter D. Wetzels, *Johann Wilhelm Ritter: Physik im Wirkungsfeld der deutschen Romantik*, Quellen und Forschungen zur Sprach- und Kulturgeschichte der germanischen Völker, 59 (Berlin: Walter de Gruyter, 1973), p. 23.

[29] Mary W. Shelley, *Frankenstein; or, The Modern Prometheus*, ed. M. K. Joseph (London: Oxford University Press, 1969), p. 51. Parenthetical page references in the text will be to this edition.

> ence, that I alone should be reserved to discover so astonishing a secret. (52)

The "spark of being" that Frankenstein casts into inanimate matter to create his monster is never explicitly defined as electrical in nature. Yet everything the reader learns of Frankenstein's education suggests that electricity guided the scientist to his discovery of life's secret. As a boy, Victor Frankenstein witnessed the destruction of an "old and beautiful oak" by a sudden bolt of lightning. So profound was the effect of this experience that the fifteen-year-old youth at once abandoned his preoccupation with the "natural philosophy" of Cornelius Agrippa, Paracelsus, and Albertus Magnus to dedicate himself to more empirical sciences. Frankenstein repeats the experiments of Benjamin Franklin, a man with whom he shares more than a fascination with electricity—the surnames of the two scientists also have one common syllable.

> The catastrophe of this tree excited my extreme astonishment; and I eagerly inquired of my father the nature and origin of thunder and lightning. He replied, "Electricity"; describing at the same time the various effects of that power. He constructed a small electrical machine, and exhibited a few experiments; he made also a kite, with a wire and string, which drew down that fluid from the clouds.[30] (233)

Victor Frankenstein is understandably reluctant to divulge the exact formula for creating life, though Mary

[30] The passage appears in the first edition of 1818 only. In the edition of 1831, "a man of great research in natural philosophy" explains the laws of electricity and galvanism to Victor Frankenstein. On the philosophical and scientific sources that entered into the general conception of *Frankenstein*, see James Rieger, "Dr. Polidori and the Genesis of *Frankenstein*," *Studies in English Literature*, 3 (1963), 461-472; Burton R. Pollin, "Philosophical and Literary Sources of *Frankenstein*," *Comparative Literature*, 17 (1965), 97-108; and Martin Tropp, *Mary Shelley's Monster: The Story of "Frankenstein"* (Boston: Houghton Mifflin, 1976), pp. 52-65.

Shelley supplies the reader with some hints about how her character hoped to carry out his plans. "The event on which this fiction is founded," she wrote in the preface to her novel's first edition, "has been supposed, by Dr. Darwin, and some of the physiological writers of Germany, as not of impossible occurrence" (13). In 1831, when she furnished a new edition with an introduction describing the genesis of *Frankenstein,* she became more explicit about the role of Dr. Darwin and others:

> Many and long were the conversations between Lord Byron and Shelley, to which I was a devout but nearly silent listener. During one of these, various philosophical doctrines were discussed, and among others the nature of the principle of life, and whether there was any probability of its ever being discovered and communicated. They talked of the experiments of Dr. Darwin, . . . who preserved a piece of vermicelli in a glass case, till by some extraordinary means it began to move with voluntary motion. Not thus, after all, would life be given. Perhaps a corpse would be re-animated; *galvanism had given token of such things*: perhaps the component parts of a creature might be manufactured, brought together, and endued with vital warmth. (8-9; my emphasis)

Like Victor Frankenstein, Mary Shelley's husband pored over the works of alchemists and conducted chemical and electrical experiments in his youth—a habit that often had disastrous consequences. His room at Oxford, furnished with an electrical machine and galvanic trough, looked as if "the young chemist, in order to analyze the mystery of creation, had endeavored first to reconstruct the primeval chaos."[31] In *Prometheus Unbound,* Shelley was to enshrine electricity as a vitalizing force, the modern analogue for the

[31] Thomas Jefferson Hogg's remark is cited in Carl Grabo's *A Newton among Poets: Shelley's Use of Science in "Prometheus Unbound"* (Chapel Hill: University of North Carolina Press, 1930), p. 9.

divine fire of antiquity. Mary Shelley's decision to choose electricity as the agent animating Frankenstein's monster ultimately rested on her husband's enthusiastic reception of ideas promoted by Newton, Franklin, and Galvani. The full title of her novel, *Frankenstein; or, The Modern Prometheus*, suggests the extent of her debt to Shelley.

Similarities between electricity and the divine fire used by Prometheus to create men from clay did not escape the attention of other fictional scientists. "Every man, without knowing it, bears the name Prometheus," declares Thomas Alva Edison, the hero of Villiers de l'Isle-Adam's *L'Eve future* (1886).[32] All men possess and are capable of bestowing the divine spark of life which, as Edison maintains, is electrical. But who, then, could be better qualified to construct a living creature from inanimate matter than the Wizard of Menlo Park himself? Edison's robot Hadaly, the Eve of the future, proves to be—despite her lungs of gold and joints of steel—more lifelike than her human model. Created to serve as a substitute for the beautiful, but crudely frivolous, fiancée of Edison's friend Lord Ewald, Hadaly owes her corporeal existence to the miracles of electricity and her spiritual life to the powers of animal magnetism. In Edison's subterranean laboratory, she is brought to life by a spark of electricity and animated by the soul of a woman deserted by her husband. Edison's experiment fails in the end—but only because Hadaly perishes while crossing the Atlantic to Lord Ewald's home in Scotland.

For Mary Shelley and Villiers de l'Isle-Adam, the power of galvanism and electricity represented only a means of giving the illusion of plausibility to the fantastic. Frankenstein and Edison occupy center stage in the two novels: both are modern Faustian figures, one creating a monster, the other an ideal woman. For Novalis, however, the investigation of galvanism possessed far-reaching significance. For him galvanism was more than a means to an end; it repre-

[32] Villiers de l'Isle-Adam, *L'Eve future* (Paris: Jean-Jacques Pauvert, 1960), p. 119.

sented a "higher consciousness—of Nature—of the soul of Nature" (III, 603). The *Märchen* narrated by the master poet Klingsohr in the ninth chapter of *Heinrich von Ofterdingen* translates this philosophical statement into poetic allegory: currents of galvanic energy come to figure in that story as the source of fresh life and spirit.

Just as Klingsohr draws on works of Oriental, Hellenistic, and Nordic provenance to add a mythological dimension to his account, so too he assimilates biblical imagery, alchemical motifs, and scientific themes to introduce a cosmic element into the traditional form of the fairy tale. Klingsohr's tale opens with darkness: the "long night" has just begun. A frozen wintry landscape, dotted with brittle metallic trees and crystal flowers, unfolds before the reader's eyes to suggest sterility and rigidity—the absence of life and the triumph of "petrifying and petrified" reason. Like the poet's song in the story told by the merchants who befriend Heinrich von Ofterdingen, Klingsohr's *Märchen* heralds the regeneration of nature and the advent of an eternal golden age. But while the song of the poet in the merchants' tale only briefly sketches the sequence of events that will lead to redemption of the world, Klingsohr constructs so elaborate a scenario to describe this rejuvenation that it leaves virtually nothing to the reader's imagination.

The process of renewal begins when Fabel, the spirit of poetry, solves the riddle of the sphinx; it culminates in a "long kiss" that seals the "eternal union" between Eros and Freya. Once Fabel has demonstrated her wisdom by answering the questions posed by the sphinx, she can begin the task of breaking the evil spell woven over nature by reason. In order to accomplish this goal, she enlists the aid of three allies: Zinc, Gold, and Tourmaline.[33] Their first journey

[33] The following analysis of galvanic operations in Klingsohr's *Märchen* draws on Bruce Haywood, *Novalis: The Veil of Imagery*, Harvard Germanic Series, no. 1 (Cambridge, Mass.: Harvard University Press, 1956), pp. 113-133; Walter D. Wetzels, "Klingsohrs Märchen als Science Fiction," *Monatshefte*, 65 (1973), 167-175; and Johannes Hegener,

takes them to the giant Atlas, who has been mysteriously paralyzed by a stroke. Together they perform a most unusual operation to revive the immobilized Titan:

> Gold placed a coin in his mouth, and the flower gardener [Zinc] slid a basin under his loins. Fabel touched his eyes and emptied a vessel over his brow. As soon as the water ran over his eyes into his mouth and down into the basin, a flash of life quivered in all his muscles.[34]

The galvanic battery manufactured by Fabel produces a current of electrical energy that induces muscular contractions similar to those observed by Galvani and jolts Atlas back to life. Fabel, incidentally, selects her helpmates quite prudently. Zinc and gold, lying at opposite ends of the electrochemical series, are capable of producing a far more powerful electrical potential than most other combinations of metals.

Fabel and her attendants perform a similar service for the Father. Gold melts a coin to fill the vessel in which the Father is lying; Zinc places around Ginnistan's neck a chain that touches the stream of gold; and Ginnistan, by placing her hand on the Father's heart, closes the electrical circuit to resurrect him: "The Father arose; his eyes flashed" (I, 311).

After Fabel, Eros, Sophie, Ginnistan, and the Father participate in a communal rite by drinking a magical elixir in which the ashes of the Mother are dissolved, they pour the dregs into the earth.[35] A sudden transformation takes

---

Die Poetisierung der Wissenschaften bei Novalis, Abhandlungen zur Kunst-, Musik- und Literaturwissenschaft, no. 170 (Bonn: Bouvier, 1975), pp. 138-175.

[34] "Gold legte ihm eine Münze in den Mund, und der Blumengärtner schob eine Schüssel unter seine Lenden. Fabel berührte ihm die Augen, und goss das Gefäss auf seiner Stirn aus. Sowie das Wasser über das Auge in den Mund und herunter über ihn in die Schüssel floss, zuckte ein Blitz des Lebens ihm in allen Muskeln." (I, 310)

[35] As Wetzels points out, tourmaline, a metal that attracts dust and

place: "A mighty spring covered the earth. . . . Everything seemed animated. Everything spoke and sang. . . . Animals approached the newly awakened people with friendly nods. Plants regaled them with fruits and fragrances" (I, 312-313).

The permanence of this new order is guaranteed by a kiss sanctifying the compact between love and peace. Fabel leads Eros to the slumbering Freya who, at the beginning of the *Märchen*, had been charged with electrostatic energy by her ladies-in-waiting. An electrical spark leaps from Freya to the sword carried by Eros, and, charged with the energy thus derived, Eros flings away his sword to plant a kiss on Freya's lips.

Scientists and poets, according to Novalis, have always spoken the same language, and it is in Klingsohr's *Märchen* that Novalis literally depicts the spirit of poetry (Fabel) joining hands with science to usher in a new golden age. Echoing, but also adding a subtle twist to Goethe's dictum that science originally developed out of poetry and that the two will meet again on a higher plane, Novalis suggests that the union of these two arts will take place through the joint effort of poetic and scientific wisdom.[36]

The awakening of nature, the advent of an "eternal festival of spring," can be traced in large part to the galvanic and electrostatic feats performed by Fabel and her escorts. It is not surprising that Novalis described the revivification of nature as the work of powers that in his age were identified with vital forces. But at the end of Klingsohr's tale, nature is not only alive, it is also characterized as "animated" (*beseelt*). In view of Novalis's conviction that galvanism constitutes the "higher consciousness" of Nature and perhaps of "Nature's soul," it is entirely logical to find

---

ashes when heated, is the appropriate agent for collecting the ashes of the Mother. See "Klingsohrs Märchen als Science Fiction," pp. 171-172.

[36] Goethe, "Zur Morphologie," *Werke* (Sophienausgabe), 2d ser., VI (Weimar: Hermann Böhlau, 1891), 139-140.

that the galvanic current generated by Fabel injects both new life and fresh spirit into nature.

Novalis's concept of a future golden age rests on the triadic development of history and human consciousness—a pattern of thought that informs the writings of German poets and philosophers from Lessing through Goethe and Schiller to Kleist.[37] The path of this development can be visualized as an ascending spiral that takes as its point of departure a primal harmony between man and nature, proceeds through a period of differentiation and individuation brought on by the growth of reflection, and finally ends with restoration of the original harmony on a higher level. For many of the Romantics, self-consciousness represented both the cause of the discord that emerges in the second stage and the solution to it. Schelling, for example, believed that reflection had created a rift between nature and the mind of man, but he also sought, through philosophical reflection, to reestablish the identity of nature and spirit. In Hegel's view, the means of restoring the lost unity lay in thought and thought alone: "The hand that inflicts the wound is also the hand that heals it."[38] The third and final stage of this development turns back upon itself, for it implies reunification, though by incorporating that which has intervened between the first and third stage, it reaches a plateau higher than that of the first stage.

The primal division caused by reflection has many dimensions—aesthetic, moral, religious, and cognitive—but only the last need concern us here. Intuitive understanding of

[37] For a discussion of this triadic pattern in German literature, see Julius Petersen, *Die Sehnsucht nach dem Dritten Reich in deutscher Sage und Dichtung* (Stuttgart: Metzler, 1934). A more recent analysis focusing on the "circuitous journey" appears in a study of German and English Romanticism by M. H. Abrams, *Natural Supernaturalism: Tradition and Revolution in Romantic Literature* (New York: Norton, 1971).

[38] Hegel, *Enzyklopädie der philosophischen Wissenschaften*, in *Werke*, ed. Eva Moldenhauer and Karl Markus Michel, VIII (Frankfurt a. M.: Suhrkamp, 1970), 88.

nature, according to the cognitive pattern, is forfeited with man's growing awareness of his opposition to and conflict with nature. The ultimate redemption, however, will not only allow man to recover the original, undivided condition he once abandoned, but will also endow him with the ability to reflect on this condition, that is, to appreciate it in its full glory.

In Klingsohr's *Märchen*, reflection and the intuitive faculty for divining the mysteries of nature both appear in poetically veiled form. Novalis's notebooks show that he repeatedly defined thought as a galvanic process.[39] Not surprisingly, then, the by-product of the second galvanic resurrection in the *Märchen* is a magical mirror reflecting nature's wonders in their true form and preserving their primordial image. Sophie counsels Ginnistan and the Father to contemplate the images mirrored in this looking glass, a symbol of reflection in its purest form, whenever they require sustenance and guidance.

As noted previously, the galvanic and electrostatic operations engineered by Fabel, Zinc, and Gold also serve to infuse fresh feeling into nature and to establish a new order in which man participates in the life of nature. Novalis underscored the animating influence of galvanism when he described the phenomenon as an "inner light" and identified it with the "soul of the universe." In the same year that Novalis jotted down these thoughts in his notebooks, he wrote in "The Novices of Sais" that feeling (which he designated there as an "inner light") would ultimately bring back "the past age, the age we yearn for" (I, 96). For Novalis, the galvanic process thus figures as a poetic symbol for the synthesis of reflection and feeling. In his philosophical studies, he called this combination "intellectual intuition" and declared that it furnished the key to life (II, 561).

[39] "Unser Denken ist schlechterdings nur eine Galvanisation" (III, 263); "Dass Denken (*auch*) Galvanismus sey lässt sich äusserst wahrscheinlich machen" (III, 557).

IV

When Novalis characterized Ritter's galvanic experiments as a search for the "soul of nature," he astutely recognized connections between the vitalist theories of Romantic physics and the metaphysical doctrines of what Schelling called "higher physics." Although Schelling's *Weltseele*, as the Romantic philosopher himself conceded, owes its existence to the *nous* of Greek philosophers, it also bears some resemblance to the subtle fluids that furnished the Romantics with light, heat, electricity, and magnetism. Schelling's second major work, *On the World-Soul: A Hypothesis of Higher Physics to Explain the Collective Organism* (*Von der Weltseele: Eine Hypothese der höheren Physik zur Erklärung des allgemeinen Organismus*), unequivocally identifies the principle of life in nature with an ethereal fluid. How, asks Schelling, is it possible to explain why animals take fright when the atmosphere is charged with electricity, or why experiments with animal electricity meet with greater success during thunderstorms, without assuming the existence of an invisible fluid that permeates both the organic world and inorganic matter and fuses them into one living whole? Schelling's response to this rhetorical question is characteristically straightforward: one cannot hope to explain these phenomena without positing the existence of such a universal fluid. And this fluid, he adds, is the "very same substance that ancient philosophy hailed as the *Soul of Nature* and that some physicists of antiquity viewed as identical with the formative and creative ether."[40]

As Rudolf Haym suggests, Schelling cherished the belief that future generations would one day look upon his own age as a pioneering epoch in the history of the natural sciences, and he therefore sought to develop a comprehensive

[40] *Werke*, II, 569. Passages from Schelling's works are cited according to the text of the standard edition in twelve volumes: *Schellings Werke*, ed. Manfred Schröter (Munich: Beck und Oldenbourg, 1927).

philosophical system that would take into account the extraordinary scientific achievements of his time.[41] A philosopher who devotes the major part of his *magnum opus* to light, gravity, electricity, and irritability clearly possesses a deep-rooted belief in the complementary relationship between philosophy and science. But while the aims of Romantic philosophy and science are congruent, their methods remain radically different. Schelling, as the subtitle of his treatise on the *Weltseele* indicates, simply posited that nature was a gigantic living organism and did not feel obliged to support this statement with anything more than random observations. A Romantic physicist like Ritter, on the other hand, could not resort solely to the metaphysical dignity of the a priori. Ritter himself did not adhere strictly to orthodox scientific methodology, but he at least attempted to substantiate the hypothesis that nature is an organic whole by performing experiments and marshaling a wealth of empirical evidence to support his thesis.

Contrary to Schelling's hopes, scientists of the next generation displayed considerable contempt for his philosophy and looked askance at his liberal use of the a priori and nonexperimental approach to science. The noted chemist Justus von Liebig denounced Schelling's *Naturphilosophie* as the Black Death of the nineteenth century.[42] For the German Romantics, however, this "disease" seemed to provide a new vitality. Novalis hailed Schelling as the "*philosopher of the new chemistry*" (III, 266). In a brilliant pun that both characterizes Schelling's intelligence and identifies one of the substances that figured prominently in his philosophical system, Novalis christened him "the absolute Oxygénist" ("der abs[olute] Oxygénist"; III, 266).[43] Because Schelling's

[41] Rudolf Haym, *Die romantische Schule: Ein Beitrag zur Geschichte des deutschen Geistes*, 5th ed. (Berlin: Weidmann, 1928), p. 638.

[42] Cited in H. G. Schenk, *The Mind of the European Romantics* (London: Constable, 1966), p. 180.

[43] The isolation of oxygen in 1771 by Priestly and Scheele led to widespread speculation about the role of oxygen as the principle of

ideas provided a sophisticated justification for their own conception of nature and furnished a system that lay claim to total explanation, the Romantics embraced his philosophy as an expression of their most deeply held convictions. As the architect of a vast system that integrated the fragmentary knowledge accumulated through scientific experiments, Schelling took the first step toward promoting the philosophical cooperation of science and poetry called for by the Romantics. Friedrich Schlegel, for example, decreed that all art must become science and all science art; he recommended the study of poetry to those who wished to penetrate the mysteries of physics.[44] Schelling, by translating the language of science into the idiom of philosophy, poeticized the sciences and thus rendered them intelligible to the Romantics. The cornerstones of Schelling's philosophy—the concept of nature as an organic whole, the identity between nature and the human mind, the notion of a tripartite rhythm in the history of human consciousness, and the principle of polarity—came to serve as the very foundations of Romantic poetry.

Schelling's influence on contemporary psychological theories was of a far more subtle, but no less significant, nature. The principles set forth in his early philosophical inquiries shaped the major premises on which Romantic psychology rested. In those works, Schelling sought to demonstrate that nature is a visible manifestation of spirit and that spirit is

---

life. Like electricity it came to be depicted as a vital force in the universe. Note Novalis's observation: "Alle Naturkräfte sind nur eine Kraft. Das Leben der ganzen Natur ist ein Oxyd[ations] Process" (III, 659). On the significance of oxygen for the Romantics, see H.A.M. Snelders, "Romanticism and Naturphilosophie and the Inorganic Natural Sciences, 1797-1840: An Introductory Survey," *Studies in Romanticism*, 9 (1970), 193-215.

[44] *Kritische Friedrich-Schlegel-Ausgabe*, ed. Ernst Behler, Jean-Jacques Anstett, and Hans Eichner, II (Munich: Ferdinand Schöningh, 1967), 161, 266.

an invisible form of nature.[45] He posited an infinitely productive force in nature which, if there is to be any system in nature at all, must be checked by a second limiting force. The conflict between these two opposing forces led Schelling to conclude that there exists in nature an essence (the *Weltseele*) that organizes the world into a system.

For Schelling, higher forms of life develop through an intricate series of conflicts between opposing forces; the principle of polarity regulates and maintains the heartbeat of his cosmic organism. *Naturphilosophie*, he declared, aims primarily to achieve an understanding of polarity, for the principle of evolution through opposition represents one of nature's universal laws. Schelling's obsession with the problem of attracting and repelling forces led one contemporary, Jean Paul, to dismiss his philosophical system as little more than a belabored magnetic metaphor.[46]

Once Schelling had enthroned polarity as a universal law regulating development in nature, he adduced evidence from contemporary scientific investigations to corroborate this postulate. The relationship between light and gravity (in Schelling's view the primal polarity), between positive and negative electricity, the north and south poles of magnets, acids and bases, and between irritability and sensibility all confirmed for him the sovereignty of polar forces. Waving the "magic wand of analogy," Schelling could associate the masculine principle with the infinitely expansive force of light and the feminine with the limiting influence of gravity. Even the rhythmical alternation between sleeping and waking presented further evidence of a constant struggle between opposing forces.[47]

Intrigued by Schelling's view that waking hours foster

[45] "Die Natur soll der sichtbare Geist, der Geist die unsichtbare Natur seyn" (Schelling, *Werke*, I, 706).

[46] Jean Paul, *Flegeljahre*, in *Sämtliche Werke*, ed. Preussische Akademie der Wissenschaften, section 1, X (Weimar: Hermann Böhlaus Nachfolger, 1934), 16.

[47] Schelling, *Werke*, I, 44.

ceaseless activity and a drive toward individuation, whereas sleep returns man to the wellspring of his being, Romantic physicians and physiologists constructed neurological theories that promised to account for the biological cycle he had described. A cerebral system of nerves, they contended, governs all conscious, voluntary behavior; its polar opposite, the ganglionic system (sometimes known as the "sympathetic" system), controls involuntary activity. During sleep, the ganglionic system inhibits operation of the cerebral nerves; in waking hours, the cerebral system checks the activity of ganglionic nerves.

By 1814, the year in which Gotthilf Heinrich Schubert, a Romantic physician and philosopher of sorts, published *The Symbolism of Dreams* (*Die Symbolik des Traumes*), the concept of neurological polarity had gained wide acceptance in German medical and philosophical circles. Schubert's own remarks on the subject are highly derivative, but for precisely this reason they provide an ideal summation of psychological theories prevalent at the time. Schubert maintained that a bundle of nerves located in the solar plexus regulates the functions of the ganglionic system, just as the brain orchestrates the activities carried out by the cerebral nerves. The solar plexus, identified by Schubert as the organ of intuitive knowledge, figures as a link between the individual nervous system and an ethereal spirit or subtle fluid that organizes the universe into a living whole. That anatomical organ invests man with a sixth sense analogous to the faculty of instinct in animals and endows him with the ability to transcend spatial and temporal limitations.[48] Schelling had also expressed faith in the existence of such a special organ when he described a sixth sense "which penetrates the barriers of time, foresees the future, and accounts for instinct in animals."[49] And the travelers of Novalis's "Novices of Sais" have a similar organ in mind when they

[48] Gotthilf Heinrich Schubert, *Die Symbolik des Traumes* (1814; reprint ed. Heidelberg: Lambert Schneider, 1968), pp. 132-133.

[49] Schelling, *Werke*, I, 438.

discuss a form of extrasensory perception that can be evoked through a kind of autohypnotic process. If a person directs his "undivided attention" at an object, they note, then a "new mode of perception" emerges, and thoughts arise that appear to be "nothing more than the strange contractions and figurations of an elastic fluid" (I, 96-97). This new mode of perception, mediated by the ethereal fluids in which eighteenth-century scientists bathed the universe, allows man to establish communication with the entire world.

For Schubert, the ability to transcend the isolation of the individual nervous system emerges in mental states characterized by an absence of cerebral activity. Poetic inspiration, dreams, magnetic trances, cataleptic seizures, and the lucid intervals of madmen, by breaking down the barriers between mind and matter, enable man to enter into a wholly harmonious relationship with nature and indeed to become a part of it. These mental states would therefore seem to represent a regression to an earlier and more primitive form of existence in which being takes precedence over consciousness. But because they offer a moment of clairvoyant vision that implies at once the negation of sight and the intensification of insight, they also possess a cognitive value.

Romantic scientists, philosophers, and psychologists offered competing, yet ultimately consistent, explanations for such mental states. It mattered little whether the immense network of communication allowing instantaneous contact with the universe was powered by electricity, by a world-soul, or by animal magnetism. (The discovery of galvanism and the popularity of Schelling's *Naturphilosophie* had, in fact, done much to legitimize the claims of animal magnetism and to strengthen its appeal.)[50] What Romantic thinkers considered essential was the unity of creation and the special gift of some men to apprehend that unity.

[50] Justinus Kerner, *Franz Anton Mesmer aus Schwaben: Entdecker des thierischen Magnetismus* (Frankfurt a.M.: Literarische Anstalt, 1856), pp. 105-108.

V

Until the French Revolution, few men outside of France had mastered the art of magnetizing. In the course of the nineteenth century, however, Mesmer's legacy changed hands frequently, and with each exchange it took on new meanings. During the first two decades of the century, mesmerism fell on evil days in France. East of the Rhine, it fared considerably better. German physicians had imported animal magnetism from their neighbors as early as 1785 in order to heal the sick; poets then fastened on the trance as a symbol of creative consciousness; and finally spiritualists used mesmerism to establish communication with another world.

In Germany, mesmerism first earned notoriety when Friedrich Wilhelm II turned to magnetism and electricity as a source of health. When he took ill in 1795, doctors rushed to his bedside with magnets, *baquets,* and electrical machines. Two "electrical baths" a day, with strong doses of magnetic fluid administered between each session in the tub, eventually brought him to his deathbed. The example of Friedrich Wilhelm did not, however, discourage others from trying similar cures. Friedrich Wolfart, who occupied one of two chairs for animal magnetism at the University of Berlin, attracted such luminaries as Schleiermacher, Savigny, Solger, and Wilhelm von Humboldt to his mesmerist clinic. Fichte kept a diary on animal magnetism in which he recorded observations made at Wolfart's clinic and entered notes on Mesmer's publications. Schiller briefly flirted with the idea of using magnetism to relieve his sufferings, but eventually considered it inappropriate for his particular illness. Jean Paul, a compulsive autodidact, read widely on the topic and learned enough about mesmerism to cure headaches and toothaches. Achim von Arnim published widely on electricity and magnetism, though at an early age he gave up his scientific aspirations. Whenever he was on the verge of a new discovery, he complained, Schelling or Ritter would publish an article on the subject. Nonetheless, a number of "magnetic experiments" later found their way into his literary work.[51]

Not all Germans, however, remained practical minded about the virtues of animal magnetism. Though a late convert, Friedrich Schlegel showed no lack of imaginative zeal in exploring the avenues opened by mesmerist therapy. From 1819 until his death he sought to communicate with Christine von Stransky, his companion in mystical ventures, by placing himself in rapport with her at appointed hours and by sending her magnetized tufts of cotton and locks of hair.[52]

Of the many Germans who took up the art of magnetizing, Justinus Kerner was perhaps the only one to appreciate fully Mesmer's pioneering role. In his pious biography of the man who "discovered" animal magnetism, he stressed Mesmer's reliance on feeling and intuition—only eight books, he noted with satisfaction, were found in Mesmer's

[51] On Friedrich Wilhelm, see Walter Artelt, *Der Mesmerismus in Berlin*, Abhandlungen der geistes- und sozialwissenschaftlichen Klasse, no. 6 (Wiesbaden: Akademie der Wissenschaften und der Literatur in Mainz, 1965), pp. 20-21. For further details on the mesmerist movement in Germany, see Walter Artelt, "Der Mesmerismus im deutschen Geistesleben," *Gesnerus*, 8 (1951), 4-14. Fichte's "Tagebuch über den animalischen Magnetismus" appears in his *Nachgelassene Werke*, ed. J. H. Fichte, III (Bonn: Adolph Marcus, 1835), 295-344. Schiller's encounter with mesmerism is described by David B. Richards, "Mesmerism in *Die Jungfrau von Orleans*," *PMLA*, 91 (1976), 856-870. On Jean Paul and mesmerism, see A. T. MacKay, "The Religious Significance of Animal Magnetism in the Later Works of Jean Paul," *German Life and Letters*, 23 (1970), 216-225. Arnim's allusions to mesmerism appear in *Gräfin Dolores*, in *Sämtliche Romane und Erzählungen*, ed. Walther Migge, 3 vols. (Munich: Hanser, 1962), I, 100, 254.

[52] See Jean-Jacques Anstett, *La Pensée religieuse de Friedrich Schlegel* (Paris: Société d'Edition *Les Belles-Lettres*, 1941), pp. 320-332; Hans Eichner, *Friedrich Schlegel* (New York: Twayne, 1970), pp. 128-129; and *Friedrich Schlegels Briefe an Frau Christine von Stransky, geborene Freiin von Schleich*, 2 vols. (Vienna: Verlag des literarischen Vereins, 1907).

estate.[53] Kerner's own experiments with animal magnetism led him into regions of the mind hitherto unexplored. In 1826 he began to treat Friederike Hauffe, a woman who proved to be Europe's most versatile medium. In his five-hundred-page case study of the "Seeress of Prevorst," Kerner documented the astonishing "facts" about the spiritual world disclosed during the three years she remained in his care. When mesmerized, Frau Hauffe could cure the sick, predict the course of future events, summon spirits, and speak a tongue that she described as the original language of mankind.[54]

Mesmerism did not, however, serve only the special needs of the medical world and the occult community. For German poets the trance took on the character of a mental state charged with revelation. Though deprived of sight, mesmerist mediums seemed to experience a moment of enlightenment; they were endowed with a higher vision—with insight in its literal and figurative meaning. The venerable theme of blindness and insight (as expressed in the works of Sophocles, Shakespeare, and Goethe) and the time-honored motif of darkness and illumination in mystical thought supported the sacred character of such visions.[55]

A capital example to illustrate the heightened awareness, if not the infallible vision, of mediums comes from a

[53] Justinus Kerner, *Franz Anton Mesmer aus Schwaben*, p. xi.

[54] Justinus Kerner, *Die Seherin von Prevorst, Eröffnungen über das innere Leben des Menschen und über das Hereinragen einer Geisterwelt in die unsere* (Stuttgart: Cotta, 1829).

[55] The Romantic shift in emphasis from the eye and external senses to an inner light represents for Werner Vordtriede a retreat from Enlightenment ideas to a secularized form of mystical thought. See *Novalis und die französischen Symbolisten: Zur Entstehungsgeschichte des dichterischen Symbols* (Stuttgart: Kohlhammer, 1963), pp. 148-149. On analogies between the Romantic conception of poetic inspiration and mystical moments of revelation, see Albert Béguin, *L'Ame romantique et le rêve: Essai sur le romantisme allemand et la poésie française* (Paris: José Corti, 1939).

most unlikely source: Goethe's *Elective Affinities (Die Wahlverwandtschaften).*[56] A demonstration of the so-called pendulum experiments, in vogue at the time when Goethe wrote the novel, first introduces the mesmerist theme. It shows Ottilie, one in a star-crossed quartet, ideally suited to play the role of medium for such experiments: when she takes the pendulum in hand and holds it over various metals, it first describes a circular path, then follows an elliptical orbit, and finally swings back and forth in a straight line. Near the end of the novel, shortly after the death of Charlotte's child, Ottilie falls into a "trancelike slumber" that replicates an earlier experience. Upon awakening, she describes the first occurrence of that state to Charlotte:

> Shortly after my mother's death, while still a small child, I had moved my stool up close to you: you were, as now, sitting on the sofa; my head was resting on your knee, I wasn't asleep, but I wasn't awake; I was slumbering. I understood everything that was happening around me, especially all that was said; and yet I could not move, or speak, or even if I had wanted to, give any sign of consciousness.[57]

While in that trance, she came to understand her personal situation and silently formulated rules to guide her conduct.

Ottilie's second, more recent trance also prompts her to draw up a new code of behavior. She tells Charlotte:

[56] Otto Brahm was the first to suggest connections among the various allusions to somnambulism and divination in *Die Wahlverwandtschaften.* See "Eine Episode in Goethes *Wahlverwandtschaften,*" *Zeitschrift für deutsches Altertum und deutsche Literatur,* 26 (1882), 194-197.

[57] "Kurz nach meiner Mutter Tode, als ein kleines Kind, hatte ich meinen Schemel an dich gerückt; du sassest auf dem Sofa wie jetzt; mein Haupt lag auf deinen Knieen, ich schlief nicht, ich wachte nicht; ich schlummerte. Ich vernahm alles, was um mich vorging, besonders alle Reden sehr deutlich; und doch konnte ich mich nicht regen, mich nicht äussern und, wenn ich auch gewollt hätte, nicht andeuten, dass ich meiner selbst mich bewusst fühlte." Goethe, *Werke* (Hamburger Ausgabe), VI (Hamburg: Wegner, 1951), 462.

> Resting on your lap, half benumbed, I hear once again, as if from an alien world, your gentle voice at my ear; I learn what my situation is; I shudder at myself; but as once before, so now, in my deathlike sleep, I have mapped out a new path for myself.[58]

In her nearly catatonic condition, Ottilie gains insight into herself and uses this knowledge to forge a new destiny.

Although Goethe does not grant Ottilie the unerring prophetic vision bestowed on some other literary dreamers, he nonetheless shares with Romantic writers the view that subtle fluids are in part responsible for second sight. "We do not know what stirs in the atmosphere surrounding us, or what connections exist between our own minds and that atmosphere," he reported in conversation. "But it is clear that, under certain circumstances, the antennae of the soul can reach beyond corporeal limits so that premonitions or even a glimpse of the near future are vouchsafed to it."[59]

Yet the visions of some somnambulists contrast sharply with reality. Kreuzgang, the poet manqué who makes the rounds in *The Night Watches of Bonaventura (Die Nachtwachen des Bonaventura)*, draws attention to the fatal discrepancy between the world of sleepwalkers and that of men awake. If prematurely aroused, the sleepwalker, who may be either physically or mentally removed from other men ("on a roof or in an inspired state"), runs the risk of breaking his neck.[60] In German Romantic literature, disparities between somnambulist visions and the prevailing reality are especially marked, and these disparities inevitably lead to a

[58] "Auf deinem Schosse ruhend, halb erstarrt, wie aus einer fremden Welt vernehm ich abermals deine leise Stimme über meinem Ohr; ich vernehme, wie es mit mir selbst aussieht; ich schaudere über mich selbst; aber wie damals habe ich auch diesmal in meinem halben Totenschlaf mir meine neue Bahn vorgezeichnet." Ibid., pp. 462-463.

[59] Johann Peter Eckermann, *Gespräche mit Goethe in den letzten Jahren seines Lebens*, ed. Heinrich Düntzer, 3 vols. (Leipzig: Brockhaus, 1899), III, 136. The conversation is dated 7 October 1827.

[60] *Die Nachtwachen des Bonaventura* (Heidelberg: Lambert Schneider, 1955), p. 27.

conflict between an individual's sense of his own fate and the claims of a social or political order.

Characters in the dramas of Heinrich von Kleist, for example, unfailingly elect to follow the destiny foreshadowed in their dreams or trances, though by so doing, they place themselves in opposition to conventional codes of behavior. Disregarding the obstacles placed in their paths, they move toward the realization of their dreams with the same blind tenacity that characterizes a sleepwalker's march toward his goal. But for Kleist, as we shall see, "sleep-waking" rather than somnambulism exemplifies the true moment of cognition, the fusion of visionary experience with creative consciousness.

In the tales of E.T.A. Hoffmann, the dream and the trance give characters access to the world of the marvelous and the fantastic. But in order to sustain the poetic experience of these mental states, the characters must sever their ties with society. True liberation from the conflicts between the sphere of poetry and the realm of everyday existence comes only in a visionary moment preceding death. Kleist chose the symbol of "sleep-waking" to express the possibility of transcendence; for Hoffmann, as for Novalis, the perception of the self in a mirror figures as the metaphoric vehicle for describing the union of intuitive knowledge with self-conscious reflection. The word "mirror," as Pierre Mabille reminds us, derives from the Latin word meaning "to wonder at" or "to marvel," and recognition of this etymology does much to explain why the images reflected in a mirror stand on the threshold of the marvelous.[61] As a symbol of both pure reflection and sight subverted, the mirror is the perfect complement to the mesmerist trance, a symbol of pure intuition and sight occluded.

For the German Romantics, the trance thus represented only one half of the equation for poetic inspiration. Like the great mystics of past ages, they urged the necessity of

[61] Pierre Mabille, *Le Miroir du merveilleux* (Paris: Sagittaire, 1940), p. 15.

Mesmer. The inscription honors the Viennese physician as a heroic benefactor of mankind. Having disposed of the evils set free by Pandora, he stands without rivals in the art of healing. (Bibliothèque Nationale)

An eighteenth-century engraving of Mesmer's salon. The patients seated around the *baquet* use rods and ropes to draw the magnetic fluid to their eyes, hands, and feet, while two violinists provide soothing music. In the left foreground, Mesmer ministers to a patient in the throes of a crisis. Note that a smaller *baquet*, in the room to the left, is being put to use by less affluent patients. (Bibliothèque Nationale)

A mesmerist session in full swing. Astrological beams and the traditional *baquet* provide the patients with a copious supply of the magnetic fluid. The mesmerist (who can be identified in this and other contemporary cartoons by the ass's head) is much in demand for his magnetic virtues. The patients in the center and in the left foreground keep the fluid in circulation by forming magnetic chains and making contact with the "poles" of other bodies. (Bibliothèque Nationale)

A literalist's view of animal magnetism. (Bibliothèque Nationale)

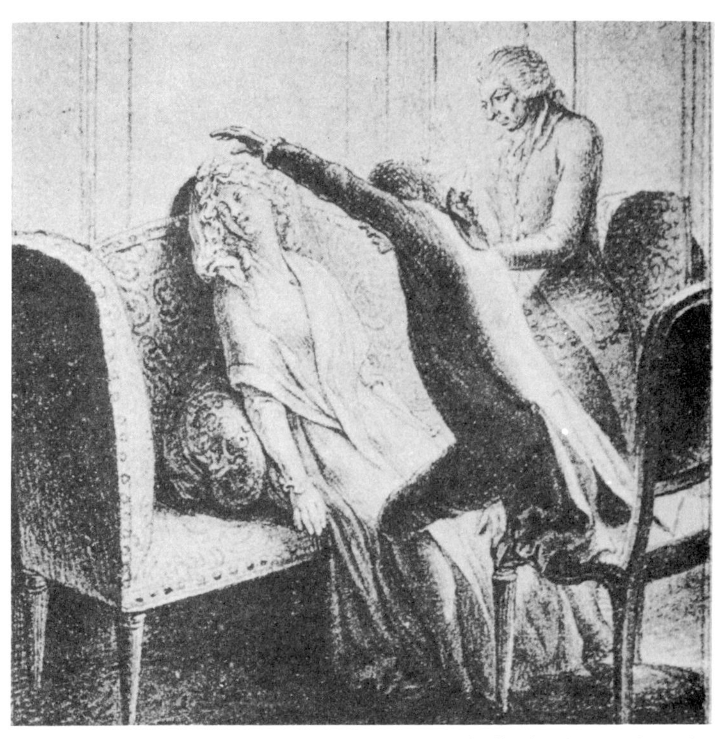

An eighteenth-century etching by Daniel Chodowiecki showing the mesmerist at work. (Archiv für Kunst und Geschichte, Berlin)

A satirical view of mesmerist phenomena. Mesmer announces that there is only one disease and that he has the remedy for it at his fingertips. He tries out his cure on a young lady, appoints a valet to assist him, establishes the Society of Harmony, and installs a *baquet* in his apartment. The artist caps this sequence of events with a sketch showing the tombstones of Mesmer's victims. (Houghton Library, Harvard University)

Samuel Collings's "Magnetic Dispensary" (1790) shows patients drawing magnetic effluvia from the *baquet*. One patient is ready to be escorted to the "crisis room"; others appear merely amused or bored by the proceedings. Note the electrical machine in the background. (Yale Medical Library)

The "magnetized elm" of Buzancy. Puységur leads his patient Victor Race to a tree that has been invested with healing powers. Mesmerist cures were no doubt a welcome relief from the household chores that had to be discharged on Puységur's estate. (Bibliothèque Nationale)

Au génie de Franklin. Fragonard shows Benjamin Franklin snatching the thunder from the skies to strike down tyrants. (Bibliothèque Nationale)

Charcot lecturing at the Salpêtrière to physicians and writers. Although Charcot denied the importance of suggestion, he inadvertently utilized that very technique in his demonstrations. The verbal explanations, the painting on the wall, and the outstretched hands of the attendant have all provided the patient with cues for her behavior. (Bibliothèque Nationale)

pushing beyond the trance state to reach an ever purer clarity of mind in which, as Novalis put it, intoxication and self-consciousness are daringly mingled (I, 197). Yet they did not ignore the steps leading to that clarity, and mesmerist theories seemed to answer some of the questions about the exalted states of consciousness that precede the creative process.

Mesmerist ideas returned to their point of origin in France only after the German Romantics had ceased to draw inspiration from them. Beginning in 1820 and continuing for several decades, Balzac and other French writers related animal magnetism to their own specific preoccupations and to those of their contemporaries; theories of energy and will, the problem of psychological domination, and the mysteries of a spiritual world became linked with mesmerist ideas. But for the French, the mesmerist, rather than the medium, moved into the limelight. One of the many evil geniuses haunting the pages of French Romantic novels, that sinister figure commanded the attention and controlled the destinies of those around him. By mid-century, when mesmerists began to weave their spells on the other side of the Atlantic, they reached an audience that had been schooled to their tricks. The showmen who wandered from town to town with their trance maidens figured as highly suspect characters. Yet because the activities of such men perfectly matched a central concern of American writers—the violation of innocence—mesmerism left its unique impression on the literature of the 1840s and 1850s. In the course of the nineteenth century, mesmerism thus became enmeshed with a wide variety of themes ranging downward from the sublime to the sordid. The chronological survey of mesmerist literature that follows will, by necessity, chart that decline.

CHAPTER 3

Thunder, Lightning, and Electricity: Moments of Recognition in Heinrich von Kleist's Dramas

"Fear no more the lightning flash,
Nor the all-dreaded thunder-stone."
—Shakespeare, *Cymbeline*

The interludes of idyllic peace that momentarily arrest the narrative flow of Kleist's short stories or retard the dramatic action of his plays are not without sinister overtones. Most frequently these interludes take the form of love trysts or engagement scenes. Almost inevitably they herald a crisis of catastrophic dimensions. In Kleist's "Betrothal in Santo Domingo" ("Die Verlobung in St. Domingo"), Toni and Gustav share such a moment of intimacy, though for Toni that moment is clouded by her failure to tell Gustav of the evil intentions she once harbored toward him. Toni later confesses her sins, prays for the strength to reveal them to Gustav, and enters his bedroom firmly resolved to alert him to the danger threatening his life. But when she hears him whisper her name in his sleep and perceives that his thoughts dwell upon the events of the previous evening, her courage falters: "She could not bring herself to pull him down from the heaven of sweet illusions into the depths of a base and wretched reality." ("Sie konnte sich nicht entschliessen, ihn aus den Himmeln lieblicher Einbildung in die Tiefe einer gemeinen und elenden Wirklichkeit herabzureissen.")[1] Congo Hoango has returned to the planta-

[1]Heinrich von Kleist, *Sämtliche Werke und Briefe*, ed. Helmut Sembdner, 3rd ed. (Munich: Hanser, 1964), II, 184. Subsequent references in the text will be to this edition; passages from the dramas are cited by act, scene, and line number.

tion ahead of schedule, and when Toni hears his voice in the courtyard, she becomes literally "paralyzed with fear, as if a lightning bolt had struck her" (II, 185). The sudden intrusion of grim reality strikes Toni with the devastating violence of an elemental force.

Metaphorical claps of thunder or bolts of lightning repeatedly immobilize Kleist's characters at the moment they confront events that fail to conform with their expectations or facts that contradict their perceptions.[2] The Marquise von O . . . , for example, troubled by recurring physical pains that bear a disturbing resemblance to sensations she experienced during pregnancy, summons her physician. "Thunderstruck" by the doctor's announcement that she is indeed pregnant and by his refusal to entertain the possibility of error in this diagnosis, she struggles to her feet intending to denounce his impertinent behavior to her father. But the physician's stern bearing, we learn, "immobilized every limb" (II, 120).

Lightning strikes with a similar degree of intensity in "The Foundling" ("Der Findling"). Elvire, concerned about her husband's sudden indisposition, rushes to the pantry to fetch a household remedy, but is struck down by an "invisible lightning bolt" (II, 204) when she sees a figure (her foster son Nicolo) dressed in the costume of the man who once saved her life. The cause of her sudden collapse remains shrouded in mystery, for the sight of what seems to

[2] Friedrich Koch views this situation—the conflict between reality and consciousness and the so-called destruction of consciousness that attends confrontation with reality—as the central theme of Kleist's works. See his *Heinrich von Kleist: Bewusstsein und Wirklichkeit* (Stuttgart: Metzler, 1958), pp. 35-45. The titles and controlling ideas of major critical studies on Kleist, though couching the conflict between opposing forces in different terms, reflect the centrality of this problem in Kleist scholarship. See especially, Gerhard Fricke, *Gefühl und Schicksal bei Heinrich v. Kleist: Studien über den inneren Vorgang im Leben und Schaffen des Dichters* (Berlin: Junker und Dünnhaupt, 1929); Walter Müller-Seidel, *Versehen und Erkennen: Eine Studie über Heinrich von Kleist* (Cologne: Böhlau, 1961); and Hermann Reske, *Traum und Wirklichkeit im Werk Heinrich von Kleists* (Stuttgart: Kohlhammer, 1969).

be the man she worships not only deprives her of the ability to maintain her balance, but also conveniently impairs the faculty of speech. She is neither able nor does she desire to disclose why she was struck dumb.

Toni, the marquise, and Elvire all share a predilection for "sweet illusions"; they wish to disturb neither their own tranquillity nor that of others. Toni hopes to preserve Gustav's love in its pristine state as long as possible; the marquise cherishes a belief in her own moral purity; Elvire deifies a disembodied Colino who cannot possibly pose a threat to her fidelity. But it is precisely in the "heaven of sweet illusions" that all three women prove most vulnerable to cruel strokes of lightning and fateful blasts of thunder.

Thunder and lightning are, for obvious reasons, privileged metaphoric vehicles for expressing a sudden shock and for describing the intrusion of a malevolent force. Disaster strikes like lightning; thunderbolts descend upon a doomed head; and bolts from the blue can deliver a stunning blow. If Kleist had only occasionally indulged in meteorological metaphors to intensify the strokes of fate sustained by his characters, we might easily dismiss these figures of speech as uninspired products of a normally fertile imagination. But these meteorological metaphors are so persistently woven into the dramatic action of Kleist's plots —and at such strategic positions—that they come to take on a special meaning.

It is only in Kleist's later works that both electricity and animal magnetism begin to play a significant role. When he was writing *Penthesilea,* Kleist's metaphorical language was still predominantly electrical. Visionary experience and moments of recognition are repeatedly attended by crashes of thunder and bolts of lightning. Once Kleist acquainted himself with the miracles of animal magnetism, he continued to take advantage of electrical metaphors, but rendered his characters less prone to fainting spells and hallucinations than to somnambulism and trances.

This gradual shift in interest from electricity to animal

magnetism coincided with a change in Kleist's intellectual outlook. The steady erosion of his faith in man's ability to acquire knowledge and truth triggered a decision to turn his attention from empirical sciences to existential questions. The quasi-scientific explanations he advanced in his early letters and essays to elucidate the complexities of the human mind progressively gave way to psychological, at times parapsychological, speculations. Unlike the vast majority of authors who concerned themselves with mesmerist ideas, Kleist did not immediately identify electricity with magnetism. Instead he first studied correlations between electrical reactions and mental processes, then explored the dimensions of animal magnetism.

The evolution of thoughts, as Kleist himself would insist, requires the critic's attention as much as the final idea. A study of Kleist's electrical theories can not only clarify our understanding of certain metaphors in his work, but also illuminate the avenues of thought that led him to animal magnetism.

I

Kleist's letters to his fiancée Wilhelmine von Zenge reveal a nearly obsessive interest in acquiring insight into human nature. He proceeded by drawing analogies between the laws governing physical nature and those operating in human behavior. From Berlin he wrote to Wilhelmine about the great pleasure he derived from putting questions to nature and applying the answers to man. "Every day, as a means of recreation, I devote an hour or so to this activity," he reported, "and it is never without joy that I think back on the moment (in Würzburg) when I first hit upon the idea of taking lessons in this way from the great Mistress Nature" (II, 604). Kleist was undoubtedly alluding to the November afternoon on which he had passed under the stone arch of the Würzburg city gate and had suddenly been struck by the thought that this arch could remain standing only because *"all the stones bid fair to collapse at the same time"* (*"alle Steine auf einmal einstürzen wollen"*; II, 593). By analogy he reasoned that, if ever deprived of all external support, he too could stand his ground. His courage was greatly sustained by this lesson which, as he put it, nature had taught him.

Over a period of several months Kleist engaged in a spirited "image hunt" (*Bilderjagd*) and entertained Wilhelmine with its spoils. He also compiled a notebook in which he diligently recorded correlations that he had discerned between physical and psychological phenomena. Urging his fiancée to follow his example, he instructed her to search for the wider significance of observations emerging from close scrutiny of nature by constantly asking the questions: "What does that mean, if it is applied to *man*? or: what kind of analogy emerges by way of comparison with a *human situation*?" (II, 596).[3] With the hope of sharpening Wilhelmine's analytic faculties, Kleist supplied her with a series of riddles on the order of: "If storms blow out weak flames, but make strong ones even stronger, in what way are they like misfortune?" (II, 613), and "Storms uproot trees, but not violets; the most gentle evening breeze makes violets flutter, but not trees. —What excellent comparison comes to mind?" (II, 594). Kleist hoped that Wilhelmine would amass a large capital from the "moral revenues" that her answers were to provide; he himself was later to invest the assets accumulated from this form of entertainment in poetic images.

In the characteristically condescending manner he adopted when writing to his fiancée, Kleist suggested that she cultivate the ability to draw comparisons by first posing

[3] Hans Joachim Kreutzer maintains that the images in Kleist's letters derive solely from "observation" and "interpretation" of nature. See *Die dichterische Entwicklung Heinrich von Kleists: Untersuchungen zu seinen Briefen und zu Chronologie und Aufbau seiner Werke*, Philologische Studien und Quellen, no. 41 (Berlin: Erich Schmidt, 1968), p. 125.

relatively simple questions and drawing up lists of answers. "What is terrifying?" he suggests as one possible query and furnishes the response: "an approaching storm." "What is alarming?" similarly yields the answer: "a clap of thunder and a bolt of lightning" (II, 606).

The pointed use of specific atmospheric conditions—the lightning and thunder that attend a storm—to define a menacing situation can also be traced throughout Kleist's correspondence. Lightning especially figures often as the medium of fate. In a letter to his tutor Christian Ernst Martini, Kleist declared his intention to resign his military post and henceforth to devote his energies to philosophy and mathematics. With his destiny firmly secured, he no longer felt vulnerable to a sudden blow of fate (*Blitz des Schicksals*, II, 485).

Two anecdotes published more than a decade later, in 1810, characterize lightning as a form of divine retribution. The first of these, published under the title "Event of the Day" ("Tagesbegebenheit") in the *Berliner Abendblätter*, reports the fate of a laborer named Brietz who, during a storm, arrogantly refuses an army officer shelter. Moments later, lightning strikes the tree beneath which he stands, felling the uncharitable laborer. In "The Stylus of God" ("Der Griffel Gottes"), a Polish noblewoman who has led a less than exemplary life leaves her fortune to a convent and receives in return not only absolution for her sins, but also a magnificent tombstone inscribed with an epitaph commemorating her generosity. The following day, lightning strikes the stone and eradicates her epitaph—with the exception of a group of letters which, when read in sequence, yield a new inscription: "She is condemned!"

In his dramas and prose works, Kleist often rendered a blow of fate as a stroke of lightning. In *Prince Friedrich of Homburg* (*Prinz Friedrich von Homburg*), for example, Natalie, receiving word of the elector's alleged death on the battlefield, asks Homburg: "After this thunderstroke that rives the ground / Beneath me, what—ah, what—am I to do?" ("Ja, was soll ich, nach diesem Wetterschlag, / Der unter mir den Grund zerreisst, beginnen?" II.vi.589-90) And the narrator of *Saint Cecilia; or The Power of Music* (*Die heilige Cäcilie oder Die Gewalt der Musik*) reports that God has struck down "as if by invisible strokes of lightning" (II, 225) the four iconoclasts who intended to destroy a convent. Although the Christian God does not always inflict punishment in the form of a flash of lightning, his Greek, Roman, and Germanic counterparts have traditionally wielded the thunderbolt to express irritation or to vent their wrath. Descriptions of Jupiter and Wotan in *Amphitryon* and *The Battle of Arminius* (*Die Hermannsschlacht*) show Kleist's awareness that these gods can enlist the service of elemental forces. In *Amphitryon*, Jupiter identifies himself as the "god of thunder" (II.v.1336), and Sosias refers to him as the "god of lightning" (II.vi.1590). The leader of the Cheruscans in *Die Hermannsschlacht* realizes that if his own plans run counter to those of a divine will, a stroke of lightning will fell his messenger.

Thunder and lightning clearly appealed to Kleist's imagination. The moments of recognition that so many of his characters experience and the blows of fate that buffet their senses found for several reasons poetic expression in claps of thunder and flashes of lightning. With their capacity to overwhelm man—to blind, deafen, and paralyze him—thunder and lightning represent appropriate metaphoric vehicles for conveying the mental shock that jars Kleist's characters when they face an event that contradicts their basic assumptions or most deeply held convictions. As the weapons of the gods for visiting punishment on man, these natural forces take on the quality of symbols for divine intervention and are thus endowed with an added dimension of stark fatality.

Kleist perceived a correlation not only between the overbearing strength of natural forces and the staggering powers of destiny, but also more generally between the activity of nature and the behavior of human beings. This latter observation led him to describe the interaction of natural forces in terms of human conflict. A thunderstorm he witnessed in Würzburg, for example, inspired the following description:

> A few days ago we witnessed this *spectacle* [*Schauspiel*] —O it was a splendid *scene*! A nocturnal thunderstorm was stationed in the west and raged like a *tyrant*, and in the east, the sun rose calmly and quietly, like a *hero*. And the thunderstorm hissed and shot bolts of lightning at it and cursed it loudly with its voice of thunder —but the divine star was silent, and rose, and looked down majestically to the restless mist at its feet. . . . — And the thunderstorm hurled one last terrifying bolt. . . . —But the sun did not falter in its course and advanced undaunted to ascend heaven's throne.[4] (my emphasis)

The italicized words of the passage reveal that Kleist perceived this spectacle as a cosmic drama, with the sun and thunderstorm pitted against each other as protagonist and antagonist. (A decade later he was to introduce a strikingly similar account of a thunderstorm into the narrative framework of *Die heilige Cäcilie* and to characterize it there also as a *Schauspiel* [I, 225].)[5] In his other works, especially in

[4] "Wir hatten hier vor einigen Tagen dies Schauspiel—o es war eine prächtige Szene! Im Westen stand das nächtliche Gewitter und wütete, wie ein Tyrann, und von Osten her stieg die Sonne herauf, ruhig und schweigend, wie ein Held. Und seine Blitze warf ihm das Ungewitter zischend zu und schalt ihn laut mit der Stimme des Donners—er aber schwieg der göttliche Stern, und stieg herauf, und blickte mit Hoheit herab auf den unruhigen Nebel unter seinen Füssen. . . . —Und einen letzten fürchterlichen Donnerschlag schleuderte ihm das Ungewitter entgegen. . . . —Aber die Sonne wankte nicht in ihrer Bahn, und nahte sich unerschrocken, und bestieg den Thron des Himmels." (II, 581)

[5] See also Kleist's description of Würzburg as a gigantic amphitheater in which the sun, figuring as an oversized chandelier in a somewhat strained metaphor, sets "wie ein Held" (II, 579-580).

Penthesilea, Kleist capitalized on his study of clashing forces in nature and, reversing the procedure used in the passage cited above, invested the human protagonists of his drama with traits characteristic of nature.

Before examining Kleist's inversion of the pathetic fallacy and the function of this poetic technique in his dramas, it will be helpful to explore his views on the electrical discharge that accompanies all thunderstorms. In his essay "On the Gradual Formation of Thoughts during Speech" ("Über die allmähliche Verfertigung der Gedanken beim Reden") and in a satirical companion piece entitled "The Very Latest Educational Scheme" ("Allerneuester Erziehungsplan"), Kleist discusses electrical reactions in detail.[6] The aim of the first essay is to illustrate that problems unresolved by silent meditation will often yield to solution in conversation with a passive but attentive partner. A sympathetic glance or an animated facial expression, Kleist argues, can assist in setting the thought process in motion and will often lift a person to the height of eloquence.

But the first example Kleist cites in his essay—an episode involving the thunderbolt (*Donnerkeil*) with which Mirabeau dispatched an envoy sent by Louis XVI to dissolve the Estates General—makes a quite different point. A hostile opponent can, in fact, figure as a powerful source of inspiration. Mirabeau, in Kleist's view, had no preconceived notion of how he would respond to the envoy's announcement and to his query whether the deputies had understood the king's

[6] The two essays have, to my knowledge, received relatively little critical attention. Books on Kleist generally mention "Über die allmähliche Verfertigung der Gedanken beim Reden" only in passing. Exceptions are the chapters devoted to it in studies by Heinz Ide, *Der junge Kleist* (Würzburg: Holzner, 1961), pp. 16-22; by Hans Heinz Holz, *Macht und Ohnmacht der Sprache: Untersuchungen zum Sprachverständnis und Stil Heinrich von Kleists* (Frankfurt a.M.: Athenäum, 1962), pp. 26-33; and by Horst Turk, *Dramensprache als gesprochene Sprache: Untersuchungen zu Kleists "Penthesilea,"* Abhandlungen zur Kunst-, Musik- und Literaturwissenschaft, no. 31 (Bonn: Bouvier, 1965), pp. 35-47.

orders. He began by addressing himself solely to the rhetorical question posed by the envoy. While thus stalling for time, he found his cue and fired off a volley of rhetoric culminating in the declaration that the deputies would leave their seats only under threat of the bayonet. The thunderstruck envoy must have been in a state of "mental bankruptcy" after this verbal assault, Kleist asserts, and to support this conviction he adduces an electrical analogy. When an uncharged body (the envoy) comes in the vicinity of a positively charged body (Mirabeau), it becomes negatively charged; Mirabeau's energetic response thus drained the passions of his opponent. To continue the analogy, Kleist points out that further contact with the negatively charged body intensifies the positive charge of the other body; hence Mirabeau drew added strength from his adversary's utter defeat. Having vented his anger on the envoy, Mirabeau then reverted to a "neutral" state—just as a Leyden jar loses its electrical energy once it has been discharged. Kleist's interpretation of the events that led up to an "upheaval in the order of things" and his comparison of electrical reactions with psychological responses conclude with an intriguing assertion. "We have here," he declares, "an unusual concordance between the phenomena of the physical and moral world which, if one were to explore it further, would hold true for the minor details as well." ("Dies ist eine merkwürdige Übereinstimmung zwischen den Erscheinungen der physischen und moralischen Welt, welche sich, wenn man sie verfolgen wollte, auch noch in den Nebenumständen bewähren würde." II, 321)

As if to warn his readers and future critics not to take this statement too seriously, Kleist published a short essay on "The Very Latest Educational Scheme," which illustrates the hazards attending unqualified acceptance of such an idea. C. J. Levanus, the benighted author of that essay, proposes to establish an institution where principles derived from the physical sciences will be applied to the moral education of children. Citing the same kinds of electrical reactions described in "On the Gradual Formation of Thoughts during Speech," he points out that the laws governing such reactions also hold for the sphere of human feelings, emotions, opinions, and desires. "The universal law of contradictions," a law that obeys the fiendish logic of Poe's imp of the perverse, dictates that a person in an emotionally neutral state will cease to remain so the moment he comes in contact with a person who expresses a strong sentiment or conviction: "In fact his disposition shifts . . . entirely over to the opposite pole; he takes on a positive charge, when the other has a negative charge, and a negative charge, when the other has a positive charge" (II, 330). Applying this insight to pedagogic strategies, Levanus suggests breaking with traditional methods of education: he exhorts parents to dismiss the models of virtue now employed to educate their children and to replace them with reprobates, gluttons, misers, cowards, and bigots.

In much the same way that Kleist mercilessly made game of Penthesilea's passions and the Marquise von O . . . 's "swoon" in his distichs, so too he used the essay form to parody views that in fact he took quite seriously. A passage from his "Essay on the Sure Way of Finding Happiness" ("Aufsatz, den sichern Weg des Glücks zu finden") suggests that a less mature Kleist recognized, but still recoiled from, the possibility that his thoughts on the correspondences between physical laws and moral principles would be held up to ridicule. "Don't laugh, my friend," he cautioned Rühle von Lilienstern, "the law governing the moral world rules in the physical world as well" (II, 308). No work of Kleist's better illustrates the universality of the law of contradictions that reigns in both worlds than *Penthesilea,* a work whose titular heroine is ruled by a fatal spirit of contrariness.

II

Although the first encounter between Penthesilea and Achilles takes place before the play begins, the reader receives reports about this meeting from two sources.[7] In the first scene of the drama, Odysseus gives a detailed account of Penthesilea's capricious behavior at that meeting and of Achilles' strange effect on her. When Penthesilea first comes face to face with the Greek army, she surveys its ranks with a blank expression; but as soon as her eye lights upon the son of Peleus, a feverish glow colors her countenance. Dismounting her horse "with a shock and quiver," Penthesilea demands to know what the Greeks desire. Odysseus replies that he and his men would welcome an alliance with her warriors against the Trojans. But as he notes with some astonishment, the queen of the Amazons remains deaf to his overtures. Betraying the focal point of her attention, she turns to one of her attendants to declare: "O such a man as this, my Prothoe, / Otrere, my dear mother, never saw!" (i.89-90). When Penthesilea finally responds to Odysseus' offer, she rejects the proposed alliance, storms off in a rage, and prepares to attack both the Greek and the Trojan armies.

Penthesilea's own recollection of this episode sheds some light on her inscrutable behavior. During an intimate exchange with Achilles, she reveals how stunned she was at the sight of him:

> It could not have been otherwise if he
> Himself had come with his white chariot team,
> Driving in thunder from Olympus' heights,
> Ares, the god of war, to greet his bride!
> Dazzled I stood, when you escaped from me,
> By such an apparition—as at night

[7] Mary Garland views the presentation of two different interpretations for the same event in Kleist's dramas as a "constant reminder that there are two sides to the appearance of things and the situation before us." See *Kleist's "Prinz Friedrich von Homburg": An Interpretation through Word Pattern*, Anglica Germanica: British Studies in Germanic Languages and Literatures, no. 11 (The Hague and Paris: Mouton, 1968), p. 56. The two reports, it should be added, often draw attention to the discrepancy between a person's memory of an event and an observer's perception of it.

When lightning strikes before a wanderer,
The gates of Elysium with din
Fly open for a spirit, and are closed.[8]

Penthesilea does not invoke images attended by thunder and lightning arbitrarily. Though only the gods or the heavens can actually generate thunder and lightning, Achilles seems to brandish forces of equal power. Momentarily deafened and blinded by the clap of thunder and the lightning bolt that he dispatches, Penthesilea is rendered insensible to her surroundings in much the way that Toni, the marquise, and Elvire are temporarily immobilized.

By her own admission, Penthesilea has long harbored a covert and, according to the laws of the Amazon state, illicit love for Achilles. "My constant thought in every waking hour, / My every dream was you!" (xv.2187-88), she confesses to the Greek hero. Thus the lightning that flashes when she sees Achilles for the first time does not disclose anything new or foreign, but rather something familiar that has hitherto been concealed. If we recall the various occasions on which thunder and lightning appear in Kleist's stories, then it becomes clear that the revelation of a forbidden wish, a secret desire, or repressed knowledge elicits a reaction from the heavens, if only in a metaphorical sense. Yet thunder and lightning, even though used in mere figures of speech, can stun Kleist's characters with a strength equal to that of their literal counterparts.

Penthesilea, however, recovers speedily from her dazed state and returns to the battlefield to pursue her martial

[8] "So müsst es mir gewesen sein, wenn er
Unmittelbar, mit seinen weissen Rossen,
Von dem Olymp herabgedonnert wäre,
Mars selbst, der Kriegsgott, seine Braut zu grüssen!
Geblendet stand ich, als du jetzt entwichen,
Von der Erscheinung da—wie wenn zur Nachtzeit
Der Blitz vor einen Wandrer fällt, die Pforten
Elysiums, des glanzerfüllten, rasselnd,
Vor einem Geist sich öffnen und verschliessen."
(xv.2208-16)

aims with renewed vigor. During combat, her passions reach such a pitch that she appears as fierce and refractory as the intractable forces of nature. The thunderbolt sent by Achilles has much the same effect on Penthesilea as the invisible bolt of lightning that strikes the four iconoclasts of *Die heilige Cäcilie*. Deprived of their senses (*sinnberaubt*), the four brothers of that story engage in perpetual prayer. Penthesilea, repeatedly described as a woman deprived of her senses ("die Sinnberaubte"), relentlessly tracks the object of her passions in an equally monomaniacal, but more violent, fashion. The first five scenes of the drama, dominated by images of the hunt, portray Penthesilea alternately as a wild beast pursuing her quarry and as an untamed natural force riding roughshod over obstacles in her path. Driving the Trojans forward "like a stormy wind," she appears intent on blowing them off the face of the earth. She sweeps the enemy from her path "like a raging torrent in a forest," blasts hostile forces "with a crash of thunder," and launches an assault that scorches "like a lightning bolt."

Achilles reacts to this explosive discharge of energy in the same way that Penthesilea responded to the sight of the Greek hero. After his narrow escape from Penthesilea, he returns to camp; barely taking cognizance of his wounds, he refuses medical attention. Just as Odysseus' bid for an alliance with the Amazons fell on deaf ears, so the commands that he issues Achilles make no impression. When Odysseus asks the wounded warrior whether he has understood his instructions, Achilles answers: "Have said to me? / No, nothing. Why, what do you want?" (iv.566-67). But Achilles soon rouses himself from his torpor and boldly prepares to take on the Amazons single-handedly.

Penthesilea and Achilles thus pass through a sequence of pointedly similar psychological situations. Both are struck by forces resembling lightning bolts and are momentarily dazed by the blow. Deprived of their normal mental faculties, they linger in a realm entirely removed from the sphere of conscious experience. But in each case the stroke of lightning only temporarily arrests the flow of consciousness; moments later Penthesilea and Achilles appear galvanized into action by the electrifying force of the thunderbolts that struck them. Charged with psychic energy rivaling the power of electrical energy, the queen of the Amazons and the Greek hero fall upon each other with the force of "two thunderbolts."

After this second clash of arms, the relationship between Achilles and Penthesilea closely resembles that between Mirabeau and the king's deputy in Kleist's essay on the formation of thoughts. Achilles, repeatedly denounced for his presumptuous manner and audacity, triumphantly marches into the Amazons' camp, never once wavering in the pursuit of his goal. He remains insensible to the ominous threats delivered by the female warriors. Penthesilea, defeated in battle, is led back to camp by her attendants and remains in a state similar to the "mental bankruptcy" induced in the envoy by Mirabeau's bold remarks. "She is out of her senses!" Prothoe cries out. "Her fall / Has robbed her of her wits." ("Sie ist von Sinnen! . . . Der Sturz / Hat völlig ums Bewusstsein sie gebracht." ix.1193-95) Penthesilea's attempts to marshal a psychological defense against her humiliating defeat miscarry when she discovers the wreaths of roses gathered for the erotic festival that was to crown her victory. Her poignant declaration, "I will get hold of myself," gives way to the plaintive question, "How, tell me, how can I get hold of myself?" Having run the gamut of emotions, she finally escapes from the painful reality of defeat by taking refuge in unconsciousness.[9]

When Penthesilea recovers from her swoon, she continues to shut out knowledge of her defeat—now by taking shelter

[9] Dorrit Cohn suggests that Penthesilea's loss of consciousness has wider implications. The fainting spell bears a "dual significance": it promises to efface all memory of the "forbidden and desired act of love that will predictably ensue," and it is "the only behavior on Penthesilea's part that can bring this act about" ("Kleist's 'Marquise von O . . .' : The Problem of Knowledge," *Monatshefte*, 67 [1975], 129-144).

in the "heaven of sweet illusions." So freely does her imagination soar that Prothoe is tempted to arrest its flight by disclosing the truth. But Penthesilea's own words make clear that the illusion is not complete.[10] "Let this poor heart / Two moments in this stream of keen delight / Plunge like a dirty child" (xiv.1674-76), she implores Prothoe. When Penthesilea notices that the other Amazon warriors are not in the camp, she is puzzled, but blithely accepts Prothoe's explanation that her warriors are pursuing the Greeks. In short, she deliberately deludes herself because she senses that acceptance of defeat—according to the laws of the Amazon state—obviates the possibility of an erotic encounter with Achilles. Even when the truth is finally revealed, Penthesilea is prepared to strike a compromise, to settle for a verbal admission of defeat from her opponent in battle. Achilles, however, stands his ground and insists that only he, as victor, is entitled to make demands.

Later, when Achilles returns to camp, he resolves to let Penthesilea win him by force of arms and sends a messenger to inform the queen of his intention. Penthesilea, learning only that Achilles wishes to challenge her in battle, fails to divine his motives. Overwhelmed by the realization that she has mistakenly believed in her own supremacy, she could not be more vulnerable to error than at the moment when Achilles' messenger arrives. "Have my hands wreathed an image carved in stone?" (xx.2391) is the rhetorical question that marks the transition from lingering doubt to settled belief in Achilles' duplicity. Dismissing Prothoe's plea to reject the challenge, Penthesilea responds to the message in a manner consonant with the "spirit of opposition" that rules her emotions. Flying into a rage, she declares her intention to defy Achilles. The clap of thunder capping her announcement lends added emphasis to the decision.

[10] John Gearey makes this point: see *Heinrich von Kleist: A Study in Tragedy and Anxiety*, University of Pennsylvania Studies in Germanic Languages and Literatures (Philadelphia: University of Pennsylvania Press, 1968), pp. 132-134.

Although the high priestess warns Penthesilea that this ominous sign portends the gods' displeasure, Penthesilea interprets the rumblings in the heavens as an answer to her appeal for support from Mars: "I call him / With all his thunderbolts down to me" (xx.2405-2406). And as the thunder peals a second time, Penthesilea again invokes the aid of Mars:

> Ah! —down to me, your chariot of bronze:
> That I may set foot within it, seize
> The reins and harness, hurtle through the fields,
> And from the storm clouds like the thunderbolt
> Fall down upon this Greek and cleave his skull![11]

Amidst violent thunder and lightning, she takes to the field with her train of wild beasts.

Penthesilea's recognition that Achilles has defeated her is accompanied by the same atmospheric conditions that prevail during other moments of revelation in Kleist's works. But on this occasion, when thunder and lightning are literally a part of the climate, Penthesilea fails to fully comprehend her situation. She remains immune to the thunderbolts that normally figure as symbols of enlightenment or divine intervention by usurping their power and transforming herself into a human agent of fate.

So blinded by the passion of revenge that she cannot notice Achilles' conciliatory intentions, Penthesilea falls upon him with uncontrolled fury. Now it is Achilles who is plunged into a state of "mental bankruptcy" to remain transfixed by the violence of Penthesilea's wrath. Once she has torn the helpless Achilles limb from limb with her pack of dogs, Penthesilea stands silently before the corpse, her

[11]"Oh! —deinen erznen Wagen mir herab:
Dass ich den Fuss in seine Muschel setze,
Die Zügel greife, durch die Felder rolle,
Und wie ein Donnerkeil aus Wetterwolken,
Auf dieses Griechen Scheitel niederfalle!"
(xx.2434-38)

emotions discharged, staring vacantly into space. In a nearly catatonic state she returns to camp and gazes steadily at the high priestess of her tribe. Again she cannot recall the events that occurred before her battle with Achilles, but now she shows considerably less resistance to recovering her memory. A group of Amazon warriors who hope to remove Achilles' corpse from her view are detained by the question: "What are you carrying? I demand to know. Stop!" ("Was tragt ihr dort? Ich will es wissen. Steht!" xxiv.2881) "I demand to see him!" ("Ich will ihn sehn!" xxiv.2895), she insists, despite Prothoe's urgent plea to check her curiosity. And when Penthesilea finally discovers the mutilated body of Achilles, she declares: "But this I demand to know, / Who my rival was in such godless love!" ("Das aber will ich wissen, / Wer mir so gottlos neben hat gebuhlt!" xxiv.2914-15)

When Penthesilea hears the truth at last, she nonetheless makes one final attempt to deny it:

> No, hear me, you will not make me believe it.
> And were it written in the night with lightning,
> And did I hear it in the thunder's voice
> Still I would cry to both of them: you lie![12]

But in fact, thunder and lightning are not required to transmit knowledge of her act; Penthesilea's own relentless questioning has already yielded it. The attainment of that goal endows her with the power to take her own life. Knowledge destroys Penthesilea in much the same way that—in a strikingly different poetic climate—it deals a fatal blow to the titular hero of Tieck's *The Fair-Haired Eckbert* (*Der blonde Eckbert*).

Of Kleist's seven completed dramas, *Penthesilea* is per-

[12]"Nein, hört, davon nicht überzeugt ihr mich.
Und stünds mit Blitzen in die Nacht geschrieben,
Und rief es mir des Donners Stimme zu,
So rief ich doch noch beiden zu: ihr lügt!"
(xxiv.2963-66)

haps the richest in poetic images. It is thus not without reason that *Penthesilea* has inspired a large number of studies focusing on Kleist's use of metaphorical language.[13] Images of the hunt, as noted earlier, figure prominently in the first five scenes of the drama to underscore the unflagging energy of the heroine in pursuing her quarry. In order to point up both the martial impulses and the carnal desires of Penthesilea, Kleist deliberately charged the language and imagery of the drama with ambiguous meaning. The arrows that traverse the battlefield are invested with the power of Cupid's weapons. The verb "smite" (*treffen*), repeatedly woven into the texture of the drama, supports both a physical and a psychological interpretation. And the animal imagery further sustains this blending of instinctual aggression and uninhibited eroticism. Linked with the language of the hunt is a group of kinetic and spatial images that maintains a dramatic tension between heights and depths and between the pinnacles and abysses that betoken victory and defeat. The second scene of the drama, which describes Penthesilea's attempt to capture Achilles in a terrain dominated by rugged cliffs, mountain peaks, and yawning chasms, provides the largest number of such images.

Another series of images echoes the passages in Kleist's letters that depict a conflict between the sun and a gathering storm. Both the Greeks and the Amazons identify the object of Penthesilea's pursuit with the sun—a heavenly body that remains hopelessly out of human reach. When Achilles appears with his carriage on the horizon, a Greek warrior proclaims: "Just so the sun / In glory rises on a fair spring day!" (iii.368-69). On the battlefield, the gloomy landscape serves as a backdrop to enhance the dazzling effect of Achilles' figure, which is illuminated by a single ray of sunshine

[13] Paula Ritzler, "Zur Bedeutung des bildlichen Ausdrucks im Werke Heinrich von Kleists," *Trivium*, 2 (1944), 178-194. I cannot, however, agree with Ritzler's statement that the hypertrophy of metaphors in this drama demonstrates that "Kleists Drängen nach dem Du den Höhepunkt erreicht hat."

emerging from thick storm clouds. In her madness, Penthesilea's attention is riveted on the sun. She announces to her incredulous attendants that she intends to seize Helios by his flaming hair in order to draw him down to her. Finally, the thunderstorm, emblematic of strife in nature, functions as the dominant image of the drama. *Penthesilea* closes with one of Kleist's favorite images, the sturdy oak that crashes to the ground because it cannot weather a storm's full blast.[14]

In their interpretations of *Penthesilea*, literary critics have not failed to discuss the significance of these and other images.[15] Yet the motifs of thunder and lightning, which appear throughout the text so frequently that they acquire the resonance of symbols, have received surprisingly little attention.

In *Penthesilea*, peals of thunder and flashes of lightning bring a sudden spiritual illumination that is followed by the eclipse of consciousness. Once Penthesilea is exposed to these forces, she is ruled by reason no longer, but rather driven by passions. Each encounter with Achilles further intensifies the degree of her mental derangement: after the first meeting she is "blinded"; the second renders her "de-

[14] For a brief discussion of this image, see Donald H. Crosby, "Heinrich von Kleist's 'Oak-Image,'" *German Quarterly*, 38 (1965), 14-19. I have also profited from Martin Stern's suggestive essay on the same topic: "Die Eiche als Sinnbild bei Heinrich von Kleist," *Jahrbuch der deutschen Schillergesellschaft*, 8 (1964), 199-225.

[15] See especially Joachim Henry Senger, *Der bildliche Ausdruck in den Werken Heinrich von Kleists*, Teutonia: Arbeiten zur germanischen Philologie, no. 8 (Leipzig: Eduard Avenarius, 1909); Fritz Kanter, *Der bildliche Ausdruck in Kleists "Penthesilea,"* Diss. Jena, 1913 (Leipzig: Robert Noske, 1913); Helene Hermann, "Studien zu Heinrich von Kleist," *Zeitschrift für Ästhetik und allgemeine Kunstwissenschaft*, 18 (1924), 273-304; Hans Albrecht, "Die Bilder in den Dramen Heinrich von Kleists: Ihr Wesen und ihre Bedeutung," Diss. Freiburg, 1955; Marie-Luise Keller, "Die Bildlichkeit in der Tragödie Heinrich von Kleists: Bilder als Phänomene des Tragischen," Diss. Tübingen, 1959; and Denys Dyer, "The Imagery in Kleist's *Penthesilea*," *Publications of the English Goethe Society*, 31 (1961), 1-23.

prived of her senses"; during the third she is described as "out of her senses"; and finally she is "beside herself." Once dispossessed of her normal human faculties, Penthesilea obeys the same laws that prevail in the sphere of nature. She and Achilles hurl themselves at each other like "two stars," fly at each other like "two thunderbolts," and rage like "storms of thunder."

In both thunder and lightning, Kleist found vehicles for describing a sudden shift in the human mind from normal consciousness to a radically altered state of mind. Lightning held a special appeal for him because it represents a discharge of atmospheric electricity, and it was in electrical reactions that Kleist found striking parallels with human behavior.

Finally, the thunderstorm suggests itself as the central controlling image of *Penthesilea,* for it constitutes the generating matrix of other motifs and images within the drama. The nouns "water," "fire," "thunder," and "lightning" (with their verbal counterparts "flow," "burn," "blast," and "smite") are all drawn together in Prothoe's vision of the raging storm that fells Penthesilea.[16]

III

If we bear in mind Kleist's use of meteorological metaphors in *Penthesilea,* the surname of the male protagonist in *Käthchen of Heilbronn* (*Das Käthchen von Heilbronn*) seems almost painfully contrived. Graf Wetter vom Strahl does in fact prove eminently worthy of his patronymic which, when stripped of its nobiliary particle, means flash of lightning.[17] In the first scene of the drama, Theobald

[16] Although Stern believes that the image of the oak laid low by a storm is somewhat infelicitous because it suggests that Penthesilea succumbs to "äussere Gewalt" ("Die Eiche als Sinnbild," p. 204), analysis of other metaphors and images within the text points to the possibility that Penthesilea represents in a sense both oak and storm.

[17] Note in this context Walter Müller-Seidel's remarks: "Was sich im Inneren dieser Figur [Käthchens] abspielt, erinnert in Wendungen wie

Friedeborn describes Wetter vom Strahl's visit to his workshop. He recounts in vivid detail the jolt that Käthchen received when she came face to face with the count:[18]

> Mind you, if the Lord himself had appeared on earth before me, I would have reacted as she did. The moment she sees the knight, she drops dishes and glasses and food; and pale as a corpse, . . . she throws herself at his feet, just as if lightning had struck her down![19]

Suddenly flushing with color, Käthchen appears spellbound by the count and rivets her gaze upon him. Käthchen and Penthesilea, whom Kleist himself viewed as "one and the same, but considered in situations utterly different" (II, 818), suffer the same emotional agitation when they see the men who embody their destinies. Theobald's description of the impression that the count makes on Käthchen echoes Penthesilea's report of Achilles' impact on her. Both men seem to possess superhuman attributes. Their electrifying qualities endow them with the power to upset the emotional equilibrium of Kleist's heroines.

Kleist's gift for translating metaphor into symbolic action operates not only in the sphere of electrical reactions, but also in the domain of magnetic fields. The affinity between Käthchen and Wetter vom Strahl is rendered as a powerful

---

'Blitz' oder 'Strahl' an den Einbruch elementarer Gewalten, wie es überdies im Namen des Grafen Wetter vom Strahl zum Ausdruck kommt" (*Versehen und Erkennen*, p. 80).

[18] See also Graf Otto's question: "Warum, als Friedrich Graf vom Strahl erschien, / . . . bist du zu Füssen, / Wie man vor Gott tut, nieder ihm gestürzt?" (I.ii.423-25), and Wenzel's description of Käthchen when she meets vom Strahl at the *Vehmgericht*: "Im Staub liegt sie vor ihm— . . . / Wie wir vor dem Erlöser hingestreckt!" (I.ii.442-43).

[19] "Nun seht, wenn mir Gott der Herr aus Wolken erschiene, so würd ich mich ohngefähr so fassen, wie sie. Geschirr und Becher und Imbiss, da sie den Ritter erblickt, lässt sie fallen; und leichenbleich . . . stürzt sie vor ihm nieder, als ob sie ein Blitz nieder geschmettert hätte!" (I.i.158-64)

magnetic pull that inexorably draws Käthchen to the count. Like Penthesilea, she seems bereft of reason after her encounter with the physical embodiment of a visionary ideal and does not hesitate to leap from a window thirty feet above the ground in order to keep the count in sight. Guided by the gleam of his countenance ("Strahl seines Angesichts"), she pursues him relentlessly, paying no heed to the obstacles in her path.

The uncanny attraction between Käthchen and the count, like the mysterious New Year's Eve dream and the intervention of heavenly powers at critical moments, contributes a supernatural ingredient to Kleist's drama.[20] Since the genesis of *Das Käthchen von Heilbronn* falls within the period of Kleist's association with the Romantic physician and *Naturphilosoph* Gotthilf Heinrich Schubert, literary critics have sought to elucidate some of the more puzzling scenes in the drama by establishing thematic connections between Kleist's writings and Schubert's theories.[21]

During the winter months of 1807 and 1808, Schubert, Kleist, Adam Müller, and others organized a social circle which met frequently to discuss contemporary literary, philosophical, and scientific issues. In his autobiography, Schubert reports that his friends regarded him as an authority on animal magnetism—and not without reason. He had pored over the recent literature on the topic, discussed it in detail with his professional colleagues, and even tried a few experiments of his own. Although normally reserved in manner and not particularly adept at glib conversation, Schubert became positively loquacious when the subject of

[20] Robert E. Helbling, the most recent critic to discuss the fantastic aspects of the drama, suggests that some of its excesses stem from a deliberate attempt at parody on Kleist's part. See *The Major Works of Heinrich von Kleist* (New York: New Directions, 1975), pp. 175-176.

[21] See especially Max Morris, *Heinrich von Kleists Reise nach Würzburg* (Berlin: Conrad Skopnik, 1899), pp. 34-43, and Spiridion Wukadinović, *Kleist-Studien* (Stuttgart: J. G. Cotta'sche Buchhandlung Nachfolger, 1904), pp. 135-172.

animal magnetism was broached. "I spoke so spontaneously and with such competence about it that it was a pleasure for me and, if I may venture to say so, for the others as well," he reported in his memoirs. "For Kleist especially, the information I offered was so fascinating that he could not hear enough about it and drew as much out of me as possible."[22]

Schubert later delivered a course of lectures on *Naturphilosophie* in Dresden. Critics have generally cited passages from these fourteen lectures, published in 1808 under the title *Views on the Nocturnal Aspect of Natural Science* (*Ansichten von der Nachtseite der Naturwissenschaft*) as evidence that it was Schubert who introduced Kleist to animal magnetism, somnambulism, and related mental phenomena. But rather than explore the problem of how heavily Kleist was indebted to Schubert for ideas relating to the shadowy side of the human psyche, we might turn to a more fruitful question and ask why animal magnetism so intrigued him.[23] The discussion of Kleist's letters and of *Penthesilea* suggests that correlations between psychological and physical processes were a source of unending speculation for him. Animal magnetism, by its very name, promised to demonstrate that the laws of the physical sciences could explain certain patterns of human behavior. Moreover, animal magnetism was, according to Schubert, the legitimate

[22] Gotthilf Heinrich Schubert, *Der Erwerb aus einem vergangenen und die Erwartungen von einem zukünftigen Leben: Eine Selbstbiographie*, 2 vols. (Erlangen: Palm und Enke, 1856), II, 228.

[23] Because I work under the assumption that Kleist learned about animal magnetism from Schubert, it will be necessary to answer briefly Ursula Thomas's argument that Schubert acquired his knowledge of animal magnetism from his acquaintances in Dresden ("Heinrich von Kleist and Gotthilf Heinrich Schubert," *Monatshefte*, 51 [1959], 249-261). Such a view would first of all contradict the autobiographical remarks (cited in my text) of a physician who was famed for his honesty and self-effacing modesty. In addition, it would seem odd that a man who had written a dissertation on galvanism and who idolized Röschlaub and Reil (both of whom had written extensively on animal magnetism) would know less about the "Nachtseite der Naturwissenschaft" than either Adam Müller or Kleist.

successor to animal electricity.[24] In view of Kleist's interest in electricity, it is not surprising that he listened with such rapt attention to Schubert's accounts. Finally, as the analysis of *Penthesilea* has shown, Kleist had already concerned himself with dreams, trances, and madness. The study of animal magnetism held out the hope of providing further insights into such mental states. Closer examination of Kleist's *Käthchen von Heilbronn* will reveal to what purpose Kleist drew on his discussions with Schubert on mesmerism.

A mental rapport between Count Wetter vom Strahl and Käthchen is first established on a New Year's Eve, almost two years before their fateful meeting in Theobald Friedeborn's workshop. On that night, the count lay in a state of suspended animation. His physician had nearly relinquished all hope of bringing him back to life:

> The doctor really believed that his spirit [*Geist*] had departed; called him anxiously by name; tried to arouse him with aromatics; poked at him with needles and pins; plucked out a hair so that blood came; in vain: he didn't twitch a muscle and seemed to be dead.[25]

The physician's diagnosis is not entirely erroneous—the count did in fact give up the ghost, or, more accurately, his spirit abandoned its corporeal abode for another dwelling place. After interrogating Käthchen, Wetter vom Strahl himself recognizes that, during his illness, his spirit was freed to consummate an ethereal union with Käthchen:

> Stand by me now, ye gods: I have a double!
> A spirit 'tis and walks about at night!
> . . . .
> What seemed a dream, 'tis naked truth:
> In my castle at Strahl, deathly ill with fever,

[24] Gotthilf Heinrich Schubert, *Ansichten von der Nachtseite der Naturwissenschaft* (1808; reprint ed. Darmstadt: Wissenschaftliche Buchgesellschaft, 1967), pp. 329-330.

[25] "Der Arzt meinte in der Tat, sein Geist habe ihn verlassen; rief ihm ängstlich seinen Namen ins Ohr; reizt' ihn, um ihn zu erwecken, mit

I languished away and yet, led forth
By a cherub from heaven, my spirit
Visited her in the chamber at Heilbronn![26]

Although these events place inordinate demands on the imagination of a twentieth-century audience, in Kleist's day they may have appeared somewhat less exotic. Johann Christian Reil, one of Schubert's mentors, reported in a study of mental illness that the souls of somnambulists can at any time undertake a spiritual migration.[27] Furthermore, Schubert himself pointed out that persons invested with magnetic powers forge strong bonds with their mediums no matter how vast the physical distance separating them. In addition, he noted that swoons, cataleptic fits, and magnetic trances—all of which are closely allied with death—have a "salutary" effect. Patients who awaken from such exalted states feel refreshed and, in general, are freed from their previous ailments.[28] Wetter vom Strahl draws strength from his own visionary experience and, as Schubert could have predicted, miraculously recovers from his illness.

Although the bond of sympathy joining Käthchen to Wetter vom Strahl seems to be of divine origin, only Käthchen unquestioningly accepts it as such. For her, the

---

Gerüchen; reizt' ihn mit Stiften und Nadeln, riss ihm ein Haar aus, dass sich das Blut zeigte; vergebens: er bewegte kein Glied und lag, wie tot." (II.ix.1193-98)

[26]"Nun steht mir bei, ihr Götter: ich bin doppelt!
Ein Geist bin ich und wandele zur Nacht!
. . . .
Was mir ein Traum schien, nackte Wahrheit ists:
Im Schloss zu Strahl, todkrank am Nervenfieber,
Lag ich danieder, und hinweggeführt,
Von einem Cherubim, besuchte sie
Mein Geist in ihrer Klause zu Heilbronn!"
(IV.ii.2144-45;2147-51)

[27] J. C. Reil, *Rhapsodieen über die Anwendung der psychischen Curmethode auf Geisteszerrüttungen* (1803; reprint ed. Amsterdam: E. J. Bonset, 1968), p. 66.

[28] Schubert, *Ansichten*, p. 357.

count is like a god who has descended from the heavens. She herself, "a child in whom God delights," has been elevated to celestial status by both her father and the villagers: "Whenever she crossed the street in her simple finery . . . , a murmur was heard at every window: That's Käthchen of Heilbronn. Käthchen of Heilbronn, my lords, as if the firmament above Swabia had begotten her and the city beneath it, impregnated by a kiss, had given birth to her" (I.i.73-80). But after her "fall," when she yields to the compelling attraction for vom Strahl, she appears to have debased herself and, in the count's words, behaves like a common strumpet. Theobald, who views vom Strahl as "Satan incarnate," is convinced that diabolical forces have been wielded to "seduce" his daughter. The count, on the other hand, describes Käthchen's nearly pathological submissiveness as a derangement "stirred up by the devil."

In *Das Käthchen von Heilbronn*, Kleist draws on the same two traditions that he blended in "Die Marquise von O . . ." to heighten the ambiguities surrounding the erotic act in that story.[29] By describing the count as a god, as Käthchen's "sovereign lord," and by disclosing that his spirit visited Käthchen in Heilbronn, Kleist sets up associations with the myth of classical provenance in which a god impregnates a woman of celebrated beauty and with the Christian variant of that myth in which the Holy Ghost visits a woman of humble origins. At the same time, Theobald's insistence that vom Strahl is Satan incarnate suggests links with legends that depict devils and other fiendish creatures taking on human form in order to ravish sleeping women. Although the meeting between Käthchen and the count represents no more than a cohabitation of souls, the erotic resonances are unmistakable.

For Käthchen, the memory of the New Year's Eve events remains cut off from normal consciousness. When the count

[29] The remainder of this paragraph follows Dorrit Cohn's analysis of these traditions. See "Kleist's 'Marquise von O . . .' : The Problem of Knowledge," p. 138.

interrogates her to determine the origin of her infatuation, she answers:

> My sovereign lord! You're asking me too much.
> If I were kneeling, as I kneel before you now,
> At the feet of my own consciousness:
> Enthrone it in a golden tribunal,
> And let all the terrors of the conscience
> Tower in blazing armor at its side;
> My every thought would still reply
> To what you ask: I do not know.[30]

During a different kind of dialogue—a probe rather than a cross-examination—Käthchen finally recovers the memory of her first meeting with the count.[31] In the trance, a state in which mediums are privy to knowledge of what they experienced in similar mental states, Käthchen unravels the mystery of her existence. The count, having resolved to try an "experiment" on Käthchen, induces the trance by putting his arms around her, thus establishing a magnetic rapport.[32] Only after he releases her from his embrace does she

[30]"Mein hoher Herr! Da fragst du mich zuviel.
Und läg ich so, wie ich vor dir jetzt liege,
Vor meinem eigenen Bewusstsein da:
Auf einem goldnen Richtstuhl lass es thronen,
Und alle Schrecken des Gewissens ihm,
In Flammenrüstungen, zur Seite stehn;
So spräche jeglicher Gedanke noch,
Auf das, was du gefragt: ich weiss es nicht." (I.ii.460-67)

[31] Herbert Singer distinguishes two types of *Verhöre* in Kleist's works. The *Examen* constitutes a cross-examination that only confirms the truth of what is already self-evident. A second type of interrogation, for which he is unable to suggest a suitable term, provides knowledge of a hidden truth. See "Kleists 'Verhöre,'" *Studi in onore di Lorenzo Bianchi*, ed. Horst Rüdiger (Bologna: Zanichelli, 1960), pp. 423-442.

[32] Hermann J. Weigand makes this point: "Zu Kleists 'Käthchen von Heilbronn,'" in *Studia philologica et litteraria in honorem L. Spitzer*, ed. A. G. Hatcher and K. L. Selig (Bern: Francke, 1958), pp. 413-430, reprinted in *Heinrich von Kleist: Aufsätze und Essays*, ed. Walter Müller-Seidel (Darmstadt: Wissenschaftliche Buchgesellschaft, 1967), pp. 326-350.

awaken. But while under his spell, Käthchen obediently answers his every question and reveals that her own experience on the New Year's Eve accords with his dream on that night. Käthchen, however, needs no confirmation of this congruity. She has allowed herself to be guided by unconscious instincts from the moment she set eyes on vom Strahl. On a conscious level she still cannot identify the source of her attachment to the count, but she nonetheless unquestioningly obeys the dictates of her subliminal memories. As the passive partner of a magnetic rapport, she has, one may add, little choice in the matter.[33]

Vom Strahl's monologue at the beginning of the second act reveals that he is moved by the same overpowering attraction that draws Käthchen to him. But unlike Käthchen, he refuses to entertain the possibility of succumbing to his subconscious feelings: the class barriers that separate him from her seem insurmountable, and love alone cannot overcome such an obstacle. Although the count seems to retain a clear memory of the events linked with the New Year's Eve dream, he persistently denies any knowledge of Käthchen's role in that dream.[34] Käthchen, however, insists that he is perfectly capable of fathoming her behavior. When the count asks why she dogs his footsteps so tenaciously, she replies: "Why are you asking? You surely know!" ("Was fragt Ihr doch? Ihr wissts ja!" I.i.293) or "Ah, stern master! You surely know!" ("Ei gestrenger Herr! Ihr wissts ja!" IV.ii. 2041) But he nonetheless continues to disavow knowledge:

[33] In his *Ansichten,* Schubert attaches special significance to the "unschuldige Zuneigung . . . , welche die Somnambülen an den Magnetiseur und an Alles was sein ist, fesselt" (p. 345).

[34] The count remembers the message of the dream, but he has "forgotten" a number of important details that would have invalidated Kunigunde's claims from the start. These details curiously made a far more vivid impression on those who simply heard about the dream. Brigitte, for example, can describe the birthmark by which the count was to identify his bride, and she also recalls that the count was addressed in his dream as "mein hoher Herr."

when Käthchen later rehearses the events of the New Year's Eve, he responds by punctuating her narrative with the disclaimer, "I know nothing about that." ("Davon weiss ich nichts." IV.ii.2105) Moments later, however, he himself begins to describe the details of that evening.

Kleist carefully marked the transition between the count's mystification and his enlightenment with a stage direction that reads: "He stands lost in dreams." The significance of the stage direction can be clarified by means of a passage from Kleist's essay "On the Gradual Formation of Thoughts during Speech." The essay concludes with a description of oral examinations in which students are barraged with such questions as "What is the state?" and "What is property?" Kleist points out that under normal circumstances the students might well answer such questions competently, but when the questions are posed outside any frame of reference —without preliminary remarks that can generate a kind of "mental excitation"—the students inevitably make a poor showing. "*We* don't know," Kleist reasons, "it is first and foremost a certain *state* of mind that knows." ("Denn nicht *wir* wissen, es ist allererst ein gewisser *Zustand* unsrer, welcher weiss." II, 323) A person's ability to summon up knowledge is thus contingent on the psychic situation that has been developed through the attitude of the examiners and the tone of the examination.

For both Käthchen and Graf Wetter vom Strahl, the "state of mind that knows" is the dream state. Käthchen "knows" what happened on that special New Year's Eve after she is mesmerized; the count "remembers" what occurred when he is lost in thought. A hypnotic or semihypnotic state—as Freud noted nearly a century later—by replicating the condition in which the forgotten event was experienced, recovers knowledge of it. But the prerequisite for such a rapport is the desire to know, and vom Strahl cannot learn what accounts for Käthchen's attachment until he makes up his mind that he wants to know. The count's mood before Käthchen survives her ordeal by fire contrasts sharply with his disposition after that event. In the third act, he sits thoughtfully in a room of the castle strumming chords on a lute; when Käthchen tries to deliver a letter, the count reacts in a violent fashion. Three times he announces: "I don't want to know anything of her." ("Ich will nichts von ihr wissen.") But after Käthchen has proven her near divine powers, he gently approaches her while she is sleeping and declares: "I *can't* look upon this misery any longer. . . . I have to know why I am condemned to have her follow me around like a strumpet; to know why she keeps tagging after me like a dog, through fire and water" (IV.ii.2029-34). Wetter vom Strahl thus attains the "state of mind that knows" through the will to knowledge. But only after receiving a sign from heaven does he abandon his brutal cross-examination and allow Käthchen to provide him with the cues that will summon forth self-knowledge and knowledge of the "other."

IV

Like Penthesilea and Käthchen, the hero of Kleist's last drama is impelled into action by the discovery of a congruence between subconscious desires and reality. In the first scene of the drama, we see Homburg ("half waking, half sleeping" as the stage directions describe him) intently fashioning a wreath of laurels. Escorted by Hohenzollern, the elector and his entourage intrude upon his fantasy world. Somewhat irritated by the symbolic overtones of Homburg's actions, the elector decides to try an experiment. He takes the wreath, entwines his own chain around it, and hands it to Natalie for a mock crowning ceremony. But the elector brings the pantomime to an abrupt halt when he discovers that Homburg is perfectly amenable to assuming a heroic role in his *mise en scène*. The episode culminates with the elector's angry reproof of Homburg:

To nothingness return, Lord Prince of Homburg,
To nothingness, to nothingness! Tomorrow
We'll meet, so please you, on the battlefield.
In dreams such things as these are never won![35]

Although the events of Homburg's dream have failed to win him the rewards to which the elector refers in his reprimand, they have secured for him at least one object. That object, the glove that Homburg snatches from Natalie in his eagerness to seize the wreath, soon takes on far-reaching significance, for it provides Homburg with tangible evidence for the reality of his "dream." When Homburg later learns that it belongs to Natalie, the stage directions describe him as if "struck by lightning."

One need hardly belabor the point that this first scene is crucial to an understanding of the drama. Building an arch over the dramatic action, it sets the stage for and prefigures the action of the final scene. Its importance is further underscored by the fact that two characters, Homburg and Hohenzollern, hark back to its main events and summarize them from their own points of view. When Homburg later picks up Natalie's glove (which he initially considered so insignificant that he casually tossed it away), he becomes pensive and recalls his strange dream:

It seemed as if a kingly palace opened
Suddenly, all in gold and silver gleaming,
And down its marble balustrade to me
Descended all the conclave of persons
Whom in my heart I hold most dear.[36]

[35]"Ins Nichts mit dir zurück, Herr Prinz von Homburg,
Ins Nichts, ins Nichts! In dem Gefild der Schlacht,
Sehn wir, wenns dir gefällig ist, uns wieder!
Im Traum erringt man solche Dinge nicht!" (I.i.74-77)

[36]"Mir war, als ob, von Gold und Silber strahlend
Ein Königsschloss sich plötzlich öffnete,
Und hoch von seiner Marmorramp' herab,
Der ganze Reigen zu mir niederstiege,
Der Menschen, die mein Busen liebt." (I.iv.141-45)

The elector, with the "brow of Zeus," handed a wreath to a woman—but just when Homburg was about to receive this token of love and esteem from her, the figures of his dream suddenly vanished:

> Beneath my tread the ramp itself stretches up
> In endless vistas to the gate of heaven.
> I sweep my empty arms to left and right
> In anguish to encompass one dear person.
> In vain! The palace door abruptly opens,
> A bolt of lightning from within consumes them.
> The door itself closes shut before my eyes.[37]

The series of images, "brow of Zeus," "gate of heaven," and "bolt of lightning," suggests that Homburg has transformed a royal pageant into a divine spectacle. It also explains why Hohenzollern later reports to the elector that Homburg interpreted his dream as a sign from the heavens.

In the last act of the drama, Hohenzollern describes the dream sequence and subsequent events to the elector. His narrative dwells in detail on the moment at which Homburg learned that the glove salvaged from his nocturnal engagement belongs to Natalie. The prince, he alleges, tried to keep his composure, but—as the stage directions of that scene also reveal—he was overwhelmed by his discovery and reacted in a fashion that will come as no great surprise to readers familiar with *Penthesilea* and *Das Käthchen von Heilbronn*:

> He was a stone. His pencil in his hand,
> He stood there, to be sure, and seemed alive,
> But all his senses were extinguished in him

[37]"Die Rampe dehnt sich, da ich sie betrete,
Endlos, bis an das Tor des Himmels aus,
Ich greife rechts, ich greife links umher,
Der Teuren einen ängstlich zu erhaschen.
Umsonst! Des Schlosses Tor geht plötzlich auf;
Ein Blitz der aus dem Innern zuckt, verschlingt sie,
Das Tor fügt rasselnd wieder sich zusammen." (I.iv.181-87)

As though by strokes of magic. And not until
Next morning, when the cannon of the battle
Thundered, did he return to life. . . .[38]

Lightning flashed out at the moment when Penthesilea saw Achilles and Käthchen encountered Wetter vom Strahl. In *Prinz Friedrich von Homburg* the ostensible merging of dream and reality summons up "strokes of magic" that mysteriously paralyze the prince. The bolt from the blue that strikes Penthesilea, Käthchen, and Homburg robs them of their rational faculties. Penthesilea, we recall, is described as "deprived of her senses"; Käthchen acts "like a lost one, deprived of her five senses"; and Homburg is characterized as a "bewildered dreamer," "confused," and "rash." Although it is tempting here to draw an analogy between these sense-less figures of the dramas and the inanimate puppets of Kleist's *Marionettentheater*, the behavior of the dramatic characters will not support this hypothesis.[39] It is true that Penthesilea, Käthchen, and Homburg propel themselves toward their goal in a manner that admits neither reflection nor its physical concomitant, affectation (*Ziererei*), but it remains difficult to equate their lack of dexterity with the gracefulness (*Grazie*) of Kleist's marionettes. While pursuing Achilles, Penthesilea nearly plunges to her death;

[38] "Ein Stein ist er, den Bleistift in der Hand,
Steht er zwar da und scheint ein Lebender;
Doch die Empfindung, wie durch Zauberschläge,
In ihm verlöscht; und erst am andern Morgen,
Da das Geschütz schon in den Reihen donnert,
Kehrt er ins Dasein wieder. . . ." (V.v.1693-98)

[39] In a pioneering study of Kleist's essay on the "Marionettentheater," Paul Böckmann argues that "die dichterischen Gestalten haben den Vorteil, dass sie antigrav sind und die Bewegungen rein zur Auswirkung bringen können; ferner, dass sie sich nicht zieren, d.h., dass sie [den] Einbruch . . . elementaren Geschehens nicht durch die Reflexion aufzuheben suchen oder zerstören." See "Kleists Aufsatz 'Über das Marionettentheater,'" in *Kleists Aufsatz über das Marionettentheater: Studien und Interpretationen*, ed. Helmut Sembdner and Walter Müller-Seidel (Berlin: Erich Schmidt, 1967), pp. 32-53.

Käthchen hurls herself from a window ledge; on the way to meet his troops, Homburg falls from his horse. In each case the "fall" is symbolic not of the biblical fall, but rather of the hazards attending unconstrained spontaneity owing, as it were, to the "precarious organization of the world" ("gebrechliche Einrichtung der Welt").

Homburg's impulsive behavior leads him into conflict with laws governing the state in much the same way that Penthesilea's uninhibited passion for Achilles places her in opposition to the Amazon code and that Käthchen's attachment to Wetter vom Strahl runs counter to social custom. Only in *Prinz Friedrich von Homburg*, however, has this conflict between the law and the individual been thought to take on a dynamic quality. The uncompromising claims of Kleist's heroines and the equally inflexible nature of the laws whose validity they challenge is seen to give way to a dialectical relationship between the rights of the individual and the standards prevailing within a community of men.[40] Homburg, once the "bewildered dreamer," learns to master his own passions and thereby divests himself of those characteristics that occasioned a contradiction between his desires and the authority of the law. While composing a response to the elector's letter, he composes himself and agrees to accept the penalty for his presumptuous manner and arrogant behavior.[41] But the purity of Homburg's motives

[40] This interpretation of the drama has attained perhaps the widest currency. For discussions of critical responses to the drama, see Richard Samuel's introduction to *Heinrich von Kleist: Prinz Friedrich von Homburg. Ein Schauspiel* (London: G. G. Harrap, 1957); V. C. Hubbs, "Heinrich von Kleist and the Symbol of the Wise Man," *Symposium*, 16 (1962), 165-179; and J. M. Ellis, *Kleist's "Prinz Friedrich von Homburg": A Critical Study*, University of California Publications in Modern Philology, no. 97 (Berkeley: University of California Press, 1970), pp. 3-10.

[41] Sigurd Burckhardt calls attention to Kleist's play on the words *Fassung* and *sich fassen* ("*Egmont* and *Prinz Friedrich von Homburg*: Expostulation and Reply," in *The Drama of Language: Essays on*

remains questionable. His initial reaction to the elector's letter betrays a tinge of envy: "How honest, how befitting. / Ah, that is how a noble heart must speak!" (IV.iv.1343-44). And after formulating his answer, he triumphantly declares:

> I will not stand unworthily before
> A man who faces me so worthily.
> Guilt weighs, profound guilt weighs, upon my heart,
> As I well realize. If he can only
> Forgive my having balked at his decision,
> Then I want to hear nothing of his mercy.[42]

Homburg has, however, challenged a master in the game of one-upmanship, for the elector crosses the prince's will once again. The last two scenes of the drama echo events of the first scene and, as many critics argue, translate the prince's dream into reality.[43] While it is true that the final

---

Goethe and Kleist, by Sigurd Burckhardt, ed. Bernhard Blume and Roy Harvey Pearce [Baltimore and London: The Johns Hopkins Press, 1970], pp. 94-100).

[42] "Ich will ihm, der so würdig vor mir steht,
Nicht, ein Unwürdger, gegenüber stehn!
Schuld ruht, bedeutende, mir auf der Brust,
Wie ich es wohl erkenne; kann er mir
Vergeben nur, wenn ich mit ihm drum streite,
So mag ich nichts von seiner Gnade wissen." (IV.iv.1380-85)

Lawrence Ryan advances persuasive arguments to call in question the view that Homburg's acceptance of the death penalty signals a newly awakened sense of duty: "Ein Gesetz zu 'verherrlichen' steht . . . kaum in der Macht desjenigen, der einer durch dieses Gesetz verfügten Strafe verfällt. . . . Ähnliches gilt auch für die ekstatische Begrüssung der Unsterblichkeit . . . und die Vorwegnahme des triumphalen Aufstiegs in 'stille Ätherräume,' die sich sonst im Munde desjenigen, der sein Leben schuldhaft verwirkt haben will, etwas sonderbar ausnehmen müssten" ("Die Marionette und das 'unendliche Bewusstsein' bei Heinrich von Kleist," in *Kleists Aufsatz über das Marionettentheater*, pp. 171-195).

[43] For a discussion of these critics' views, see Roy Pascal, "'Ein Traum, was sonst?' Zur Interpretation des 'Prinz Friedrich von Hom-

scenes recapitulate and vary the action of the first scene, they do not simply corroborate the prophetic quality of Homburg's dream, but rather show us a second dream and a second rude awakening. In the penultimate scene of the drama, the prince is no longer a somnambulist in the literal sense of the word, but he is still very much a dreamer. Deprived of sight by his blindfold, though not of consciousness, he is endowed with the same visionary insight he experienced during the somnambulist episode that opened the play. The ethereal soliloquy he delivers is dominated by images of light that signal a moment of awakening and illumination. Having lost sight, he gains new insight:

> Now I possess you, Immortality!
> You penetrate the blindfold of my eyes
> With flashing splendor of a thousand suns![44]

But reality—once again in the form of the elector—intrudes upon his dream and, although it now promises to fulfill an earlier dream, it ultimately cannot satisfy his deepest desires. The thunder rolling at the end of the drama would seem to signalize the perfect blending of dream and reality, if we did not know that this thunder comes from the roar of cannon set off to give the finishing touch to yet another scenario staged by the elector.

V

In each of the dramas discussed above, a fateful stroke of lightning flashes at the moment when the content of a dream

---

burg,'" in *Formenwandel: Festschrift zum 65. Geburtstag von Paul Böckmann*, ed. Walter Müller-Seidel and Wolfgang Preisendanz (Hamburg: Hoffmann und Campe, 1964), pp. 351-362. For an exhaustive analysis of parallels between the two scenes (many of which have been overlooked by other critics), see J. M. Ellis, *Kleist's "Prinz Friedrich von Homburg,"* pp. 7-9, 58-64.

[44] "Nun, o Unsterblichkeit, bist du ganz mein!
Du strahlst mir, durch die Binde meiner Augen,
Mit Glanz der tausendfachen Sonne zu!" (V.x.1830-32)

takes on palpable form. The appearance of Achilles, for example, brings a shock of recognition that jolts Penthesilea and temporarily immobilizes her. Käthchen and Homburg do not require a prophecy concerning their destinies from an outside source; the somnambulist trance allows them to divine their fate. Once confronted with it, however, they also are stunned by a lightning bolt that deprives them of their senses. Deeply stirred by the incarnation of a forbidden ideal that represents their most profound desires, all three characters cast off their inhibitions and remain guided solely by the human embodiment of that visionary ideal.

The lightning that attends all three moments of recognition is interpreted by each character as a sign from the heavens sanctioning an illicit desire. Penthesilea compares the appearance of Achilles to the descent of Mars and to a vision of the gates of Elysium; Käthchen lies prostrate before vom Strahl as if he were God the Father; and the royal family that appears in Homburg's "dream" vanishes behind the gate of heaven. While all three characters consider themselves the beneficiaries of divine condescension, other figures in the drama view them as instruments of diabolical possession, or as madmen (the modern version of men possessed). Penthesilea, Käthchen, and Homburg are, however, neither the vessels of divine grace nor of satanic forces, but rather the victims of their own subliminal desires. The persons or events that bring lightning down from the heavens have all figured significantly in their unconscious lives—though they have, by necessity, been banned from waking existence. The only possible way to legitimize the attainment of their subliminal desires is to invest the human embodiment of these desires with divine qualities.

None of Kleist's characters manages to fulfill a wish through this act of self-deception. They all impetuously grasp at (*greifen nach*) the object of their desires, but succeed only in making themselves incomprehensible (*unbegreiflich*) to others. To a great extent, the confusion they experience stems from a refusal to distinguish between the world of their dreams, the heaven of "sweet illusions," and that of physical reality. A resolution to the tensions within the plots of *Penthesilea, Das Käthchen von Heilbronn,* and *Prinz Friedrich von Homburg* comes only with knowledge of what has taken place in both arenas of experience. It is ultimately the act of speaking that, when preceded by the desire to know, yields knowledge. As Kleist puts it (in a deliberately tortured syntactical form):

> . . . because I have a dim notion that stands in some remote connection with what I am searching for, my mind develops while I am speaking—so long as I make a bold beginning—this confused notion (owing to the necessity of finding an end for a beginning) to full clarity, in such a manner that knowledge, to my astonishment, is there with the end of the sentence.[45]

When Kleist's characters stop saying "I don't want to know," or "It doesn't matter," and suddenly insist on knowing, they are never far from fully understanding their situation. In the language of Freud, they have abolished their inner resistances and are at last prepared to accept the truth.

If we turn from the world of Kleist to that of E.T.A. Hoffmann, we encounter characters somewhat less passionate and headstrong. Penthesilea, Käthchen, and Homburg abandon all inhibitions to seize hold of the ideal previewed in their dreams. But the figures who inhabit the fictional world of E.T.A. Hoffmann show far more caution and restraint. They hesitate to accept the reality of their visions and dreams—and yet that hesitation proves as hazardous as the resolute determination of Kleist's characters.

[45] ". . . weil ich doch irgend eine dunkle Vorstellung habe, die mit dem, was ich suche, von fern her in einiger Verbindung steht, so prägt, wenn ich nur dreist damit den Anfang mache, das Gemüt, während die Rede fortschreitet, in der Notwendigkeit, dem Anfang nun auch ein Ende zu finden, jene verworrene Vorstellung zur völligen Deutlichkeit aus, dergestalt, dass die Erkenntnis, zu meinem Erstaunen, mit der Periode fertig ist." (II, 319-320)

CHAPTER 4

Blindness and Insight: Visionary Experience in the Tales of E.T.A. Hoffmann

". . . that serene and blessed mood,
In which the affections gently lead us on,
Until, the breath of this corporeal frame,
And even the motion of our human blood
Almost suspended, we are laid asleep
In body, and become a living soul:
While with an eye made quiet by the power
Of harmony, and the deep power of joy,
We see into the life of things."
—Wordsworth, *Tintern Abbey*

Heinrich Heine once advised literary critics to abandon their efforts at interpreting E.T.A. Hoffmann's works; the task of dissecting these tales, he felt, should be delegated exclusively to physicians. In his view, Hoffmann, like Novalis, had made the unfortunate error of confounding poetry with disease.[1] Heine surely never expected physicians to take

[1] Heinrich Heine, *Sämtliche Werke*, ed. Ernst Elster (Leipzig: Bibliographisches Institut, n.d.), V, 302. Heine also parodied Romantic views on electricity. In *Die Bäder von Lucca*, he set forth an amusing theory of electrical love that echoes passages cited in this chapter from Hoffmann's works: "Einige Naturphilosophen haben behauptet, [die Liebe] sei eine Art Elektrizität. Das ist möglich; denn im Momente des Verliebens ist uns zu Mute, als habe ein elektrischer Strahl aus dem Auge der Geliebten plötzlich in unser Herz eingeschlagen. Ach! diese Blitze sind die verderblichsten, und wer gegen diese einen Ableiter erfindet, den will ich höher achten als Franklin. Gäbe es doch kleine Blitzableiter, die man auf dem Herzen tragen könnte, und woran eine Wetterstange wäre, die das schreckliche Feuer anderswohin zu leiten vermöchte!" (III, 319).

this statement to heart, nor did he propose that critics turn to medical treatises for their studies of Hoffmann's tales. Yet literary scholars of our own age have not hesitated to document Hoffmann's acquaintance with contemporary medical literature and to draw upon such sources in order to shed light on "The Magnetizer" ("Der Magnetiseur"), "The Uncanny Guest" ("Der unheimliche Gast"), "The Pledge" ("Das Gelübde"), and other stories in which mesmerist trances and related mental states play a significant role in the development of plot.[2]

Hoffmann's principal sources of information about the medical and philosophical foundations of mesmerism included David Ferdinand Koreff, Adalbert Friedrich Marcus, and Gotthilf Heinrich Schubert—all three of whom managed to preserve untarnished reputations as physicians in spite of their endorsement of mesmerist doctrines. Koreff, who served as the model for Vinzenz of the *Serapionsbund,* supplied Hoffmann with firsthand information about his own patients and those of Mesmer's dwindling band of disciples in France. Marcus gave Hoffmann a guided tour of the sanitorium in which he performed mesmerist cures. After that visit, Hoffmann noted in his diary: "Saw for the first time a somnambulist at the hospital—doubts!"[3] Finally, Schubert introduced Hoffmann to the "dark side of natural science" and shaped his views on the broader implications of mesmeric control and hypnotic trances. It was Schubert, for example, who suggested to Hoffmann the connections

[2] See especially Paul Sucher, *Les Sources du merveilleux chez E.T.A. Hoffmann* (Paris: Félix Alcan, 1912); Hans Dahmen, *E. T. A. Hoffmanns Weltanschauung* (Marburg: N. G. Elwert, 1929); Karl Ochsner, *E.T.A. Hoffmann als Dichter des Unbewussten: Ein Beitrag zur Geistesgeschichte der Romantik,* Wege zur Dichtung, no. 23 (Frauenfeld and Leipzig: Huber, 1936); and Hans-Georg Werner, *E.T.A. Hoffmann: Darstellung und Deutung der Wirklichkeit im dichterischen Werke,* Beiträge zur deutschen Klassik, no. 13 (Weimar: Arion, 1962), pp. 84-109.

[3] E.T.A. Hoffmann, *Tagebücher,* ed. Friedrich Schnapp (Munich: Winkler, 1971), p. 186.

linking magnetic trances with poetic inspiration, the lucid intervals of madmen, and visionary moments preceding death.[4]

Because Hoffmann frequently indulges in lengthy digressions on mesmerism and takes pains to document his direct borrowings from psychological sources, it is easy to miss the way in which mesmerism also colors his imagery and style. In *The Golden Pot (Der goldne Topf)*, for example, Hoffmann uses the language of mesmerism to describe the electrifying events that take place in the first two chapters, or "vigils," of his tale. He also explores those states of consciousness that Schubert associated with the mesmerist trance. The elusive quality of *Der goldne Topf* and of other tales stems in part from certain words, motifs, and metaphors that Hoffmann employs to depict the mental state of his heroes. To a great extent this vocabulary derives from nineteenth-century psychology, and for that reason a study of Hoffmann's allusions to mesmerism can enlarge our understanding of his works.

I

Hoffmann's obsession with eyes and with optical instruments accounts in some measure for his fascination with mesmerism.[5] The burning gaze of fiendish creatures and the

[4] On Koreff and his friendship with Hoffmann, see Friedrich von Oppeln-Bronikowski, *David Ferdinand Koreff: Serapionsbruder, Magnetiseur, Geheimrat und Dichter. Der Lebensroman eines Vergessenen* (Berlin and Leipzig: Gebrüder Paetel, 1928). A discussion of Marcus's views on animal magnetism appears in his biography by Speyer and Marc: *Dr. A. F. Marcus nach seinem Leben und Wirken geschildert* (Bamberg and Leipzig: C. F. Kunz, 1817), p. 153. For a discussion of Schubert's influence on Hoffmann, see Hans Dahmen, "E.Th.A. Hoffmann and G. H. Schubert," *Literaturwissenschaftliches Jahrbuch der Görres-Gesellschaft*, 1 (1926), 62-111.

[5] For a suggestive essay on the significance of eyes in Hoffmann's works, see Helga Slessarev, "Bedeutungsanreicherung des Wortes: Auge. Betrachtungen zum Werke E.T.A. Hoffmanns," *Monatschefte*, 63 (1971), 358-371.

benighted orbs of madmen haunt the minds of his heroes; the charming blue eyes of bourgeois maidens weave magical spells over musicians, poets, and painters; the sublime gaze of celestial eyes lifts his artists into a kingdom of poetic imagination. Optical aids endow his characters with superhuman powers of vision and allow them to penetrate the surface of appearances to a higher reality. The mysterious mirror that reflects images normally hidden from view in "The Deserted House" ("Das öde Haus"), the strange spectacles hawked by Celionati in *Princess Brambilla (Prinzessin Brambilla)*, and the magic lens that allows Peregrinus Tyss of *Master Flea (Meister Floh)* to divine the thoughts of others are all instruments of second sight. The optical aids bestowed on figures in Hoffmann's tales rarely sharpen or intensify the powers of the human eye. They appear instead to block normal visual perception and to open the gateway to another world—one bearing little resemblance to empirical reality.

In Hoffmann's stories, blinding rays of light and bolts of fire frequently herald the transition from ordinary vision to creative insight. The vision of Anselmus in Atlantis, for example, is granted to the narrator of *Der goldne Topf* only after he has been deprived of sight, first by a fine mist, then by dazzling rays of light:

> The azure dissolves from the walls and floats to and fro like a fragrant vapor. . . . blinding rays shoot through the fragrance. . . . brighter and brighter shoots beam upon beam until, in boundless expanse, a grove opens before my eyes, and there I see Anselmus in the splendid brilliance of the sun.[6]

[6] "Das Azur löst sich von den Wänden und wallt wie duftiger Nebel auf und nieder. . . . blendende Strahlen schiessen durch den Duft. . . . immer blendender häuft sich Strahl auf Strahl, bis in hellem Sonnenglanze sich der unabsehbare Hain aufschliesst, in dem ich den Anselmus erblicke." E.T.A. Hoffmann, *Fantasie- und Nachtstücke*, ed. Walter Müller-Seidel and Wolfgang Kron (Darmstadt: Wissenschaftliche Buchgesellschaft, 1968), p. 253. Subsequent references to Hoffmann's works

The introductory paragraphs of "The Contest of the Singers" ("Der Kampf der Sänger") outline a similar situation. In that story, the unnamed reader of Wagenseil's study of the mastersingers closes the volume to gaze into the crackling flames on the hearth before him. Veils placed over his eyes by invisible hands blur his vision; everything around him seems engulfed in an "ever-thickening mist." A voice announces that these veils signal the advent of a dream which will open an "inner eye" to disclose glorious images of a higher reality. An obligatory dash marking a sudden change in perception precedes the moment of illumination: "—A blinding light flashed forth like a firebolt; the veiled man opened his eyes to find his sight no longer hampered either by veils or clouds of mist" (II, 275).[7]

The story of the mastersingers is one in a collection of tales narrated by Theodor, Lothar, Cyprian, Ottmar, Sylvester, and Vinzenz, members of a fictional literary club known as the *Serapionsbund.* Although the tale becomes the target of a devastating attack at a meeting of the Serapion Brethren, the poetic vision that introduces it is singled out by Ottmar as worthy of praise. The depiction of such a vision, he maintains, is entirely consonant with the "Serapiontic Principle" (*serapiontisches Prinzip*), a rule that guides the league's literary efforts. When Lothar first formulated that principle, he had instructed his colleagues that

---

will be to this edition of the collected works. Since the publisher did not assign numbers to the volumes, I have arranged them in the following order. Volume I refers to the *Fantasie- und Nachtstücke*; volume II to *Die Serapions-Brüder,* ed. Walter Müller-Seidel and Wulf Segebrecht, 1967; volume III to *Die Elixiere des Teufels / Lebens-Ansichten des Katers Murr,* ed. Walter Müller-Seidel and Wolfgang Kron, 1969; volume IV to the *Späte Werke,* ed. Walter Müller-Seidel and Wulf Segebrecht, 1967; and volume V to *Schriften zur Musik / Nachlese,* ed. Friedrich Schnapp, 1968.

7 For a discussion of the veil motif and its connection with cognition in German literature of the late eighteenth century, see Alexander Gode-von Aesch, *Natural Science in German Romanticism* (New York: Columbia University Press, 1941), pp. 97-116.

there exists "an inner world and the spiritual power to see it in true clarity, in the ultimate splendor of its full animation." But he also reminded his friends that "the world in which we live functions as the lever setting that power in motion" (II, 54).

The external world thus assumes a crucial role in the creative act. Impulses from that sphere give rise to the poetic process by animating an internal sensorium that summons up a spectacle so vivid as to rival reality. Only those individuals blessed with a poetic spirit are privy to such exalted visions, and they rank as true artists. But these artists must also learn how to bring their visions down to earth, to reconstruct them using the words, notes, or colors of this world. Unless they can develop a serene command over the images emerging from a spiritual domain and at the same time stake out clear boundaries between the poetic realm and the ordinary world, they will find it impossible to translate their visionary experiences into an idiom comprehensible to others. *Besonnenheit* (composure) is the term that Hoffmann's characters habitually use to identify the mental disposition that lends itself to the creative act.[8] Without this gift, the painter's canvas remains empty, the writer's manuscript consists of blank pages, the composer's score contains not a single note, and the artist in general is branded a madman by society.[9]

While the genesis of the work of art normally proceeds in three stages—provocation, inspiration, and composition—Hoffmann rarely devotes much attention to the last stage.

[8] Kreisler speaks of "die hohe Besonnenheit, welche vom wahren Genie unzertrennlich ist" (I, 44). Ottmar declares that the creative process demands "die grösste Besonnenheit" (II, 995).

[9] On this point, see Peter von Matt, *Die Augen der Automaten: E.T.A. Hoffmanns Imaginationslehre als Prinzip seiner Erzählkunst* (Tübingen: Max Niemeyer, 1971), pp. 31-37, and Diane Stone Peters, "The Dream as Bridge in the Works of E.T.A. Hoffmann," *Oxford German Studies*, 8 (1973), 60-85.

Generally he directs his energy at depicting the first two stages and the transition between them. Since this transition is so often attended by sparks and flashes of light, it is not surprising that Hoffmann breaks off the narrative thread of one story to outline a scientific theory for explaining radical shifts in perception. One eminent professor of physics, he notes, contends that

> the world spirit, known to be a capable experimenter, has built somewhere a highly efficient electrical machine; from it mysterious wires run all over the earth, and we would be wise to avoid them by sneaking around them. But at one time or another we are sure to step on one of them: a shock will then jolt our innermost being, and everything will suddenly take on a new shape.[10]

The passage suggests one possible explanation for the sudden changes in perception that allow Hoffmann's characters to catch a glimpse of a higher reality. But the electrical machine with its intricate mechanism and strategically placed wires is a superfluous source of energy in Hoffmann's works: his female characters are endowed with an electrical current sufficient to charge the atmosphere of the tales and to spark the imagination of poets. Johannes Kreisler even maintains that Princess Hedwiga must be a kind of "Leyden jar" (III, 416) or "gymnotus electricus" (III, 442), for she repeatedly delivers electrical shocks to others by the mere touch of a hand. The electrifying charm of Donna Anna, Albertine, and Dörtje Elwerdink—to cite only a few examples—generates an inner light that illuminates the minds

[10] "Der Weltgeist habe als ein wackrer Experimentalist irgendwo eine tüchtige Elektrisiermaschine gebaut, und von ihr aus liefen gar geheimnisvolle Drähte durchs Leben, die umschlichen und umgingen wir nun bestmöglichst, aber in irgendeinem Moment müssten wir darauftreten, und Blitz und Schlag führen durch unser Inneres, in dem sich nun plötzlich alles anders gestalte." (II,150)

of Hoffmann's artists and allows them to perceive a second world of their own creation.[11]

Another "lever that triggers inner visions" controls a different, though related, kind of energy. During the course of a heated debate on animal magnetism, Ottmar urges his poetic brethren in the *Serapionsbund* not to disparage mesmerist powers, for they too can serve as an "excellent lever . . . for setting mysterious, unknown powers into motion" (II, 274). He reminds his companions that even Lothar, the most incorrigible skeptic among them, does not hesitate to introduce magnetic miracles into his stories. The figure Marie in his "Nutcracker and the King of Mice" ("Nussknacker und Mäusekönig"), he claims, bears the characteristic signs of a somnambulist. From Schubert, Hoffmann had learned that during the magnetic trance a ganglionic (or sympathetic) system of nerves usurps the powers of the cerebral system. The operation of the ganglionic system not only inhibits external sensory perception, but also activates a unique organ that is attuned to a spiritual world.[12]

For Hoffmann, the mesmerist trance is an analogue of the dream, and it too serves as a vehicle for introducing the marvelous and the supernatural into his fictional world. During the trance, the same process that Lothar describes as genuinely "Serapiontic" occurs. External senses slumber. An inner eye awakens to contemplate a magical kingdom in which the spatial and temporal laws governing empirical reality no longer hold. Just as the dreamer of "Der Kampf der Sänger" enters a timeless realm inhabited both by the

[11] Bolts of lightning are dispatched by Donna Anna's eyes in "Don Juan" (I, 71); when Albertine embraces Edmund in "Die Brautwahl," the narrator observes that "ein ganzes Feuerwerk von elektrischen Schlägen . . . begann zu rauschen und zu knistern" (II, 569); and Dörtje Elwerdink sends an "elektrischer Strahl" from her fingertips to Georg Pepusch's heart in *Meister Floh* (IV, 713).

[12] Gotthilf Heinrich Schubert, *Die Symbolik des Traumes* (1814; reprint ed. Heidelberg: Lambert Schneider, 1968), pp. 132-133.

poets of another era and by the man who, after their deaths, recorded their feats, so the mesmerist medium dwells in an eternal realm of the spirit that exists independently of the everyday world.

Some characters in Hoffmann's works combine electrical and magnetic attributes. If we recall that Galvani conducted his experiments on animal electricity at the same time that Mesmer was using animal magnetism to cure his patients in France, then it should not seem unusual that a character in *Kater Murr* speaks of an "electrical fluid" (III, 424) in connection with mesmerism. The narrator of the *Fantastic Sketches in the Style of Callot* (*Fantasiestücke in Callots Manier*) meets a lady who possesses powers at once electrifying and mesmerizing. At a performance of Mozart's *Don Giovanni*, he divines the presence of this woman, who fixes on him the "penetrating gaze of her soulful eyes." Her deep blue eyes emit sparks and flashes of light that touch off his imagination and transport him into a mental state that he himself calls "a kind of somnambulism." The woman returns to the stage to sing the role of Donna Anna, and the narrator—now in an entirely different frame of mind—listens to Mozart's masterpiece. "It was as if the long promised fulfillment of my most beautiful, unearthly dreams were actually taking on life; as if the most esoteric thoughts of an enraptured soul were fixed in tones and mysteriously arrayed to reveal the most marvelous knowledge" (I, 72), he writes to his friend Theodor. Later that evening he senses the presence of the enigmatic Donna Anna once again. "A warm electrical breath of air" discloses her proximity. When the narrator hears her voice, he addresses a distant spiritual realm that he now hopes to enter:

> Let me penetrate the circle of your enchanting visions! May the dream, which you have chosen to serve as both a frightening and friendly messenger to earthbound creatures—may that dream, when sleep holds the body

captive in leaden bonds, carry my spirit to ethereal fields.[13]

The narrator of *Der goldne Topf* echoes the words of this passage when he declares that the world of dreams is "full of glorious wonders that can suddenly evoke the highest rapture and the deepest horror" (I, 197-198). Since mesmerists control the content of their mediums' dreams and can summon up images that touch any point on the spectrum ranging from rapture (*Wonne*) to horror (*Entsetzen*), animal magnetism is potentially a "dangerous instrument." For this reason, one of the *Serapionsbrüder* refuses to allow any magnetizer to tamper with his own ganglia. In the hands of an evil agent, mesmerism can call forth "all the horrors of an alien spiritual world" (II, 264). In Hoffmann's works, those who unwittingly wield mesmerist and electrical powers generally exercise a salutary influence over their mediums; those who deliberately seek to cast a spell on others and to use them as mediums of knowledge exert a power that is fatal to their subjects. Before investigating the gifts of Hoffmann's electrical muses, let us first turn our attention to the mesmerist figures in his works.

II

A penetrating gaze and basilisk-like eyes are the most salient characteristics of the magnetic personalities in Hoffmann's tales. The narrator of "Don Juan" ascribes the magical powers of the rattlesnake to the hero of Mozart's opera. In "Das öde Haus," Theodor becomes entranced by a woman who possesses the "penetrating gaze of a rattlesnake" (I, 480). And in "Der Magnetiseur," Maria summons up a lurid image of her physician's eyes: "Bright, glossy basilisks wrig-

[13] "Lass mich eintreten in den Kreis deiner holdseligen Erscheinungen! Mag der Traum, den du, bald zum Grausen erregenden, bald zum freundlichen Boten an den irdischen Menschen erkoren—mag er meinen Geist, wenn der Schlaf den Körper in bleiernen Banden festhält, den ätherischen Gefilden zuführen." (I, 78)

gled with revolting dexterity from his fiery red eyes" (I, 168). In his monumental study of the evil eye, Siegfried Seligmann points out that in many cultures the gaze of snakes and basilisks is thought to exercise a pernicious, and often fatal, hypnotic influence.[14] Hoffmann appears to have taken advantage of this superstition by regularly endowing the evil mesmerizers in his tales with eyes resembling those of reptiles, or indeed containing such cold-blooded creatures. Whenever Hoffmann wishes to suggest that one individual wields hypnotic control over another, he is also at pains to stress the "piercing eyes" or "burning gaze" of that person. In "Der Magnetiseur" especially, fiery eyes and a spellbinding gaze are directly connected with magnetic prowess.

"Der Magnetiseur" contains three separate episodes demonstrating the remarkable hold that mesmerists can acquire over their mediums. In "Dreams Are Froth" ("Träume sind Schäume"), the first installment in a collection of documents gathered by the "traveling enthusiast" of the *Fantasiestücke*, an aged baron, patriarch of the family gathered around the hearth in the opening scene, recalls a terrifying encounter with a Danish major. The major, a teacher at the boarding school attended by the baron, literally mesmerizes his pupils. Despite a violent temper and gruff manner, he manages to bewitch them by means of a deep, resonant voice, the searing gaze of his eyes, and the "irresistible

[14] Siegfried Seligmann, *Der böse Blick und Verwandtes: Ein Beitrag zur Geschichte des Aberglaubens aller Zeiten und Völker* (Berlin: Hermann Barsdorf, 1910), I, 126-133. That Hoffmann was familiar with the legendary powers of basilisks becomes clear from the following passage in *Kater Murr*: "Es ist etwas Entsetzliches in diesem Prinzen; als er mich anblickte, ich kann dir's nicht beschreiben, was in meinem Innern vorging. —Ein Blitzstrahl fuhr tötend aus diesen dunklen unheimlichen Augen, von dem getroffen ich Ärmste vernichtet werden konnte. . . . Man spricht von Basilisken, deren Blick, ein giftiger Feuerstrahl, augenblicklich tötet, wenn man es wagt, sie anzuschauen. Der Prinz mag solchem bedrohlichen Untier gleichen" (III, 462). See also "Die Abenteuer der Silvester-Nacht" (I, 258).

power" of his hand. Strange rumors circulate in both the school and the village that the major can cure illnesses by a mere touch of the hand or gaze of his eyes. The major is especially well disposed to the young baron and cultivates his friendship. "It was as if I were forced by a higher power to remain loyal to the man," the baron reports, "as if the withdrawal of my affection would also be the moment of my ruin" (I, 145).

Eerie events attend the major's death. Shortly before his corpse is discovered, the baron has a painfully vivid nightmare in which the major draws a knife and threatens to perform a gruesome operation on his pupil's brain. The baron remains haunted by the dream and is further tormented by an obsessive fear that the major will one day rise from the dead to hunt him down. The adolescent trauma clearly shapes his expressed conviction that dreams are agonizing experiences. His son Ottmar, however, takes a quite different view. Dreams, he believes, lift men into a kingdom where they can really see, not just intuit, the life of an "alien spiritual world" (I, 142). He in turn tells a story designed to persuade his family that dreams, as well as trances induced by magnetic influence, exert only a beneficial influence on man. Theobald, the hero of his account, is a disciple of the Marquis de Puységur and uses hypnotic powers to cure his fiancée Auguste of a passionate attachment to an Italian officer. After several mesmerist sessions with Auguste, Theobald is able to control her thoughts, to deflect them from the fiery Italian to himself, and finally to cure her of the mad infatuation to which she had succumbed.

Vulnerability to magnetic influence appears to be passed on from generation to generation. The baron's relationship to the major is mirrored in his daughter's rapport with Alban, the titular villain of the story. Alban's eyes bear an arresting similarity to those of the major, and he makes a most forceful impression on Maria by means of the "penetrating gaze" that he fixes upon her. She submits to his bidding in all matters and faithfully adheres to the mesmerist regimen prescribed for her. In a letter to her friend Adelgunde, Maria asserts that in her dreams she has developed an "entirely new faculty" that allows her to identify colors, distinguish between various types of metal, and read the printed page with her eyes shut. Although she occasionally suspects that Alban is exercising a malevolent influence over her, she dismisses such fears as the product of an overwrought imagination. "What if he is secretly using fiendish means to enslave me?" (I, 167), she asks, only to add immediately that she cannot entertain such a possibility.

The master-slave relationship nonetheless emerges as the most obvious common denominator for the three mesmerist alliances depicted in "Der Magnetiseur." Whenever the baron, Auguste, or Maria slumber, they are completely at the mercy of a powerful psychic force emanating from the eyes of mesmerist agents. In "Der unheimliche Gast," another story describing the strength of mesmerist bonds, this psychic force is so powerful that it takes on a tangible character by weaving a web of fire around its victim. The theme of psychological domination gives way to that of physical confinement. Angelika, the heroine of the story, dreams that she feels drawn to a mysterious elder tree. In its branches, she discerns a pair of human eyes gazing intently at her:

> The eyes [stood] right in front of me, and a snow-white hand, which was describing circles around me, became visible. The circles became narrower and narrower and continued to spin threads of fire around me until I finally could not stir or budge in the dense web. I felt then as if the frightful gaze of the horrifying eyes were controlling my innermost being and taking complete possession of me.[15]

[15] "Die Augen [standen] dicht vor mir, und eine schneeweisse Hand wurde sichtbar, die Kreise um mich her beschrieb. Und immer enger und enger wurden die Kreise und umspannen mich mit Feuerfaden,

Only later does Angelika learn that Graf S——i, a disciple of the Marquis de Puységur, has been using magnetic powers to control her thoughts.

The description of the mesmerist operation performed under the elder tree exhibits striking parallels in language and imagery to other passages in Hoffmann's works that depict mental anguish in terms of physical constraints. The sequence of events leading to Anselmus's imprisonment in a crystal jar, for example, recapitulates the pattern of Angelika's account. Cataracts of fire bursting forth from the maws of gigantic snakes shower down upon the hero of *Der goldne Topf*: "It was as if the *currents of fire* were congealing about his body and turning into a solid ice-cold mass. . . . When he came to, he could not *stir or budge*" (I, 239; my emphasis).[16] Although the sources for the threads of fire woven around Angelika and the currents of fire aimed at Anselmus are different, the effect of both substances is the same.

The similarity between these two episodes is further underscored by the fact that the shattering of crystal (*Kristall*) figures as a symbol of liberation in both stories. In *Der goldne Topf, Kristall* assumes the shape of a prison for the body. When Anselmus breaks through that prison, he is freed to bask in the glowing warmth of Atlantis. In "Der unheimliche Gast," *Kristall* is internalized as a symbol of

---

dass ich zuletzt in dem dichten Gespinst mich nicht regen und bewegen konnte. Und dabei war es, als erfasse nun der furchtbare Blick der entsetzlichen Augen mein innerstes Wesen und bemächtige sich meines ganzen Seins." (II, 619)

[16] Angelika's description of her response to the dream also closely resembles Anselmus's reaction to the gigantic serpent that assaults him at the entrance to Lindhorst's home. "Der Schrei, den ich ausstossen wollte," Angelika reports, "konnte sich nicht der mit namenloser Angst belasteten Brust entwinden, er wurde zum dumpfen Seufzer" (II, 619). Anselmus too tries in vain to voice his fears: " 'Töte mich, töte mich,' wollte er schreien in der entsetzlichen Angst, aber sein Geschrei war nur ein dumpfes Röcheln" (I, 191).

the heroine's mental captivity. On the day designated for her marriage to Graf S——i, Angelika falls into a deep magnetic trance and awakens to learn of his death. "At the very moment he died," she reports, "it seemed as if a crystal were shattering within me" (II, 631). The death of her oppressor signals the end of her painful thralldom and her exposure to the terrors of an alien spiritual world.

Maria, the victim of Alban's magnetic influence, experiences the same sense of constraint imposed on Angelika by Graf S——i. She does not dare to step out of the circle into which Alban has banished her. Her thoughts, in addition, are haunted both by the evil eyes that cast a spell on Angelika and by the serpents that assaulted Anselmus:

> I saw Alban surrounded by unusual instruments and by loathsome plants and animals and stones and gleaming metals in his room; I saw how his arms and hands described strange circles with convulsive movements. . . . Bright, glossy basilisks wriggled with revolting dexterity from his fiery red eyes.[17]

Maria also develops a curious aversion for lilies. Whenever the perfume of these flowers fills the air, she falls into a faint and later explains her swoon as a reaction to the "bright and glossy hissing basilisks" that lurk in the calyxes of such flowers.

Lilies, however, as readers familiar with Hoffmann's *Der goldne Topf* will recall, are not always *fleurs du mal,* nor are serpents always pernicious creatures. The cold gleam of the basilisks in Maria's daydreams and the chilling effect of the snakes in Lindhorst's chambers contrast sharply with the radiant warmth emitted by Serpentina, the enchanting

[17] "Ich sah Alban in seinem Zimmer mit unbekannten Instrumenten und hässlichen Pflanzen und Tieren und Steinen und blinkenden Metallen umgeben, wie er in krampfhafter Bewegung seltsame Kreise mit den Armen und Händen beschrieb. . . . Aus seinen glutroten Augen schlängelten sich in ekelhafter Schnelle blanke, glatte Basiliske." (I, 168)

green snake of *Der goldne Topf*. Far from exercising a restraining influence on Anselmus's imagination, Serpentina's eyes open new vistas for the budding poet of that story.

III

The eyes of Serpentina flash out at Anselmus in the very first vigil of *Der goldne Topf*. Before examining their powers, let us briefly review the circumstances that prompt Anselmus to forego the Ascension Day festivities in Dresden. After inadvertently upsetting an applecart, Anselmus is obliged to compensate its irate proprietress for the damages. He feels compelled to escape from the crowd that has witnessed his humiliation and seeks out a deserted path that leads him to the banks of the Elbe. Brooding over his misfortune in the shade of an elder tree, he indulges in a lengthy reverie about the sublime delights of the local celebration.

Strange melodies and whispers issuing from the tree distract him from his thoughts and call attention to the acoustic wonders of the landscape in which he is situated. Anselmus strains to comprehend every word and phrase in the mellifluous blend of whispers, murmurs, and chimes that he hears. Convinced that the words he finally distinguishes must be the product of his imagination, he naturally seeks a rational explanation for the sudden intrusion of the supernatural. The voices he hears are no doubt merely the sound of the evening wind, and the emeralds sparkling in the foliage are likewise merely an optical illusion caused by the rays of the evening sun playing in the elder bush. The air of ambiguity surrounding all of Anselmus's perceptions is made eminently clear by the narrator's persistent use of such introductory locutions as "it was as if" or "it seemed as if" before each descriptive statement.[18] But when Anselmus

[18] According to Tzvetan Todorov, this stylistic device keeps the reader suspended between the world of the marvelous and that of every-

receives an electrical shock and sees Serpentina's eyes gazing at him he discards all rational explanations, and the narrator also abandons modalizing formulas and the subjunctive mood. Emeralds now fall from the tree's branches to surround Anselmus; the elder, the wind, and the rays of the sun all speak to him. As Anselmus becomes increasingly entranced by Serpentina's eyes, nature comes to life for him:

> More and more deeply absorbed in the gaze of those glorious eyes, his longing grew stronger, his desire more ardent. Suddenly everything around him stirred and moved as if awakened to joyous life. The flowers and blossoms released their fragrance around him—their perfume was like the glorious song of a thousand flute-like voices; and the echo of what they sang was carried away by golden evening clouds that sailed off into distant lands.[19]

The appearance of Serpentina's eyes neatly divides the passage accorded to Anselmus's visionary experience into two parts of equal length. In the first part Anselmus and the narrator both hesitate to admit that nature can establish direct communication with man. But once Anselmus beholds Serpentina's glorious blue eyes and is jolted by an electrical current, he and the narrator no longer doubt nature's ability to commune with man. The eyes and the bolt of lightning clearly occupy a pivotal position in this episode.

Because the hypnotic trance so closely replicates the men-

---

day reality. See *The Fantastic: A Structural Approach to a Literary Genre*, trans. Richard Howard (Ithaca, N.Y.: Cornell University Press, 1975).

[19] "Und immer inniger und inniger versunken in den Blick des herrlichen Augenpaars, wurde heisser die Sehnsucht, glühender das Verlangen. Da regte und bewegte sich alles, wie zum frohen Leben erwacht. Blumen und Blüten dufteten um ihn her, und ihr Duft war wie herrlicher Gesang von tausend Flötenstimmen und was sie gesungen, trugen im Widerhall die goldenen vorüberfliehenden Abendwolken in ferne Lande." (I, 183-184)

tal state conducive to poetic inspiration, Hoffmann introduced mesmerist motifs into his story to describe the shift in Anselmus's mind from normal perception to visionary insight. The serpentine movements in the elder tree, the melodic rustling of leaves, and the steady gaze of seductive eyes all seem to have a mesmerizing effect on Anselmus. The description of the landscape, suggestive of the classical *locus amoenus,* is also reminiscent of settings for mesmerist sessions in Kleist's *Käthchen von Heilbronn* and Hoffmann's "Der unheimliche Gast." Although Serpentina does not share Graf S——i's sinister qualities, she wields the same kind of hypnotic power over Anselmus that the count exercises over Angelika.

The serpentine mesmerist of *Der goldne Topf* seems, however, to possess electrical rather than magnetic properties. When Serpentina extends her head from the elder tree's branches toward Anselmus, he is jolted by an "electrical shock." Sitting next to Serpentina, Anselmus imbibes the "electrical heat" of her body. He marvels at the "thousand sparks" glittering on the slender bodies of Serpentina and her siblings.

The spark of love dispatched by Serpentina endows Anselmus with the power to understand the language of nature. The elder tree reminds the student: "You lay in my shadow; perfume surrounded you, but you did not understand me. Perfume is my language *when it is kindled by love*" (my emphasis). The wind and the sunbeams take up the same refrain: "The breeze is my language when it is kindled by love" and "Heat is my language when it is kindled by love" (I, 183).

Serpentina appears to have inherited her electrical attributes from Phosphorus, her maternal grandfather. The myth narrated by Lindhorst in the third vigil contains the history of Serpentina's ancestors, the youth Phosphorus and his consort, the fire lily.[20] When the lily first met Phos-

[20] For extensive analysis of that myth, see Robert Mühlher, "Liebestod und Spiegelmythe in E.T.A. Hoffmanns Märchen 'Der goldne

phorus, she became inflamed with love for him and implored him to remain with her. He, however, warned that

> the salutary longing now glowing within you will split into hundreds of rays that will torture and torment you; senses will be born of sense, and the ultimate bliss, kindled by the spark I shall cast into you, is also the hopeless pain through which you will perish, only to rise again in new form. —This spark is thought![21]

Sparks also fly when Anselmus meets Serpentina. The spark that this enchanting snake casts into Anselmus kindles love, and that love, as Anselmus himself reflects, is also thought (I, 218). Gazing at Serpentina, he feels a mixture of pain and bliss, the same combination of emotions ignited by the spark cast into the lily by Phosphorus. Whenever Anselmus's thoughts dwell on Serpentina, the narrator introduces a new variant of the oxymoron "blissful pain" to render the intensity of Anselmus's emotions.

Topf,'" *Zeitschrift für deutsche Philologie*, 67 (1942), 21-56; Aniela Jaffé, "Bilder und Symbole aus E.T.A. Hoffmanns Märchen 'Der goldne Topf,'" in C. G. Jung, *Gestaltungen des Unbewussten: Mit einem Beitrag von Aniela Jaffé* (Zurich: Rascher, 1950), pp. 237-616; Otto Friedrich Bollnow, "'Der goldene Topf' und die Naturphilosophie der Romantik: Bemerkungen zum Weltbild E.T.A. Hoffmanns," in *Unruhe und Geborgenheit im Weltbild neuerer Dichter* (Stuttgart: Kohlhammer, 1953), pp. 207-226; Kenneth Negus, "E.T.A. Hoffmann's *Der goldne Topf*: Its Romantic Myth," *Germanic Review*, 34 (1959), 262-275; and by the same author, *E.T.A. Hoffmann's Other World: The Romantic Author and His "New Mythology"* (Philadelphia: University of Pennsylvania Press, 1965); and Günter Wöllner, *E.T.A. Hoffmann und Franz Kafka: Von der "fortgeführten Metapher" zum "sinnlichen Paradox,"* Sprache und Dichtung, no. 20 (Bern and Stuttgart: Paul Haupt, 1971), pp. 69-73.

[21] "Die Sehnsucht, die jetzt dein ganzes Wesen wohltätig erwärmt, wird in hundert Strahlen zerspaltet, dich quälen und martern, denn der Sinn wird die Sinne gebären, und die höchste Wonne, die der Funke entzündet, den ich in dich hineinwerfe, ist der hoffnungslose Schmerz, in dem du untergehst, um aufs neue fremdartig emporzukeimen. —Dieser Funke ist der Gedanke!" (I, 192-193)

In a study of Hoffmann's stylistic peculiarities, Helmut Müller isolates and analyzes phrases repeatedly used to punctuate the transition from the world of everyday reality to the realm of poetic imagination.[22] The imagery of these recurring expressions, or *Konflikt-Formel* as Müller calls them, forms a coherent and consistent pattern in the tales and novels. Whenever sparks fly, eyes flash, or electricity pulses through the atmosphere, we know that the hero is about to enter a strange and marvelous fairy-tale world—in *Der goldne Topf* a magical kingdom harboring spellbinding serpents, loquacious plants, and temperamental salamanders. It is a realm that radiates heat, sheds light, and casts reflections. At the same time, images of coldness and rigidity often signal either a return to the prosaic life of bourgeois society or exposure to the demonic potential of a spiritual realm. The sensation of chilly water coursing through the veins generally precipitates the hero's rude awakening. He feels as if gripped by a frigid hand or doused with ice water and then freezes with terror. His limbs stiffen to become as lifeless and inflexible as those of a statue. Hoffmann's repeated use of such phrases as "struck by lightning" on the one hand, and "motionless as a statue" on the other, seems to border on the compulsive. Müller himself speaks of "pathological repetition," and other literary critics have taken a dim view of the "formulaic sentimental diction" and "linguistic clichés" scattered throughout Hoffmann's writings.[23]

22 Helmut Müller, *Untersuchungen zum Problem der Formelhaftigkeit bei E.T.A. Hoffmann*, Sprache und Dichtung, no. 11 (Bern: Paul Haupt, 1964).

23 René Wellek, "Why Read E.T.A. Hoffmann?" *Midway*, 8 (1967), 49-56, and Horst S. Daemmrich, *The Shattered Self: E.T.A. Hoffmann's Tragic Vision* (Detroit: Wayne State University Press, 1973), p. 74. I cannot agree with Wellek's observation that "Hoffmann is obviously laughing at himself" (p. 50) when he uses set phrases, nor with Daemmrich's view that such phrases point to a "devaluation of reality" and to "the characters' stereotyped conceptions of the world." For the judgments of other critics on this matter, see Müller, *Untersuchungen*, pp. 28-32.

Yet these expressions are not arbitrarily inserted into the text merely to evoke an emotional response to a character's dilemma, nor are they introduced for want of a better phrase. In many instances the imagery of such formulations aptly describes the mental state of a character and is inextricably bound up with contemporary psychological explanations for shifts in emotion. The electrical metaphors, for example, are deliberately invoked whenever an artist enters the realm of poetic imagination in order to suggest connections between his own perceptions and the visionary experience of mesmerist mediums.

It is curious that those critics who take Hoffmann to task for the repetitiveness of his language and imagery have paid little heed to the nearly monotonous logic of his plots. In his remarks on Hoffmann's lack of mental equilibrium, Eichendorff obliquely called attention to the predictability of those plots. "Like a passionate gambler," he noted, "Hoffmann always staked everything on a *single* card with an intensity and stubbornness increasing in proportion to his losses in body and soul."[24]

The archetypal pattern of stories centering on artists emerges perhaps most clearly in *Der goldne Topf*. The narrative begins with a description of the hero's problematic existence in bourgeois society. The plot is then set in motion by a visionary experience that introduces a new dimension into the story—a psychic space inhabited by figures whose counterparts often exist in the real world. The conflict between everyday reality and a poetic world of the mind produces a radical polarization of the self. Anselmus can live mentally in Atlantis, yet physically he remains moored in Dresden. From the moment that he experiences

[24] Joseph Freiherr von Eichendorff, *Geschichte der poetischen Literatur Deutschlands*, ed. Wilhelm Kosch (Kempten and Munich: Kösel'sche Buchhandlung, 1906), p. 499. Note also Freud's view that every writer has a "mannerism," a stereotyped set of motifs that points up the "limits" of his art (Ernest Jones, *The Life and Work of Sigmund Freud*, 3 vols. [New York: Basic Books, 1953], I, 75).

the mental bliss (*Wonne*) of Atlantis, he also senses the physical pain (*Schmerz*) of life in Dresden.[25] This pain is vastly intensified when Anselmus is imprisoned in a crystal jar situated on a shelf in Lindhorst's library. Confinement in that vessel inhibits motion and brings on complete physical paralysis. In order to understand the full implications of the medium in which Anselmus is suspended, it will be necessary to investigate the meaning of *Kristall* in several other stories by Hoffmann.

IV

In "The Mines of Falun" ("Die Bergwerke zu Falun"), Elis Fröbom's dream evokes an association between oceanic depths and *Kristall*:

> It seemed as if he were drifting on a beautiful ship in full sail on crystal clear seas, and above him arched a dark, cloudy sky. But when he looked down into the waves, he soon realized that what he had taken for the sea was a solid, transparent, sparkling mass. In its shimmer, the entire ship mysteriously dissolved so that he was left standing on a crystal surface and saw above him a dome of darkly gleaming metal.[26]

[25] Hoffmann's concept of *Schmerz* closely parallels Hegel's use of that term in the section of the *Phänomenologie* describing "unhappy consciousness": "Das Bewusstsein des Lebens, seines Daseins und Tuns ist nur der Schmerz über dieses Dasein und Tun, denn es hat darin nur das Bewusstsein seines Gegenteils, als des Wesens, und der eigenen Nichtigkeit" (*Phänomenologie des Geistes*, in *Werke*, ed. Eva Moldenhauer and Karl Markus Michel [Frankfurt a.M.: Suhrkamp, 1970], III, 164-165).

[26] "Es war ihm, als schwämme er in einem schönen Schiff mit vollen Segeln auf dem spiegelblanken Meer, und über ihm wölbe sich ein dunkler Wolkenhimmel. Doch wie er nun in die Wellen hinabschaute, erkannte er bald, dass das, was er für das Meer gehalten, eine feste durchsichtige funkelnde Masse war, in deren Schimmer das ganze Schiff auf wunderbare Weise zerfloss, so dass er auf dem Kristallboden stand, und über sich ein Gewölbe von schwarz flimmerndem Gestein erblickte." (II, 177-178)

Beneath this surface Elis sees myriads of virginal nymphs whose hearts sprout metallic plants and flowers. Just as Anselmus feels bliss mingled with pain and tries to jump ship when he sees the snakes gliding along in the waves, so Elis, seized by an "ineffable sense of pain and desire," desperately attempts to penetrate the crystal surface. He later descends into the depths of a mine in Falun to fetch a sparkling stone from the queen who rules over this underground paradise. Elis never returns from his excursion into a realm similar to the crystalline sphere of his dream, but is trapped in the mine and buried alive. In "Die Bergwerke zu Falun," the nether world of *Kristall* is associated with a fall from grace; it is a region that preserves the body alone, keeping it in an eternal state of suspended animation.[27]

Both the crystal jar and the alluring world of the mines represent constricting spaces that compel Anselmus and Elis to remain in agonizing limbo.[28] But Elis is never released from his underground trap: the subterranean pit finally becomes his grave. Because he failed to perceive the true nature of the lower world and confused it with a celestial paradise, he is punished with paralysis and petrifaction. Berthold, the eccentric painter of "The Jesuit Church in G." ("Die Jesuiterkirche in G."), recognizes the perils of confounding these two spheres. In striving to comprehend nature's marvels, he warns, the artist must constantly remain on guard, for "he stands at the edge of a precipice, on a narrow strip—beneath him a yawning abyss! A fiendish hoax lets the bold sailor who hovers over it see *below* what he intended to find above the stars!" (I, 419). Anselmus, on the other hand, only briefly confuses the bliss of Atlantis with the pleasures of Dresden, and he is ultimately liberated from

[27] Gaston Bachelard finds in the story a struggle between animal magnetism and mineral magnetism. See *La Terre et les rêveries de la volonté* (Paris: José Corti, 1948), p. 261.

[28] Lothar Pikulik makes this point. See "Anselmus in der Flasche: Kontrast und Illusion in E.T.A. Hoffmanns *Der goldne Topf*," *Euphorion*, 63 (1969), 341-370.

his glass prison to bask in the blazing splendor of Atlantis, a world that seems diametrically opposed to the frigid bleakness of *Kristall.*

In *Prinzessin Brambilla, Kristall* also figures as a medium of confinement. The moment of redemption for King Ophioch and Queen Liris in the myth narrated by Celionati does not occur until a "prism of shimmering crystal" melts to serve as the source for a bright, placid lake. As in the *Märchen* told by Klingsohr in Novalis's *Heinrich von Ofterdingen,* the thawing of ice signals the end of a long, cold season and the advent not merely of spring, but of a new era.

Ice and fire, emblematic of the terrors and delights of a "distant spiritual world," represent opposite ends of the spectrum in Hoffmann's aesthetics. Paralysis, intense cold, and rigidity are the hallmarks of a zone that imprisons both body and mind; luminosity and warmth pertain to the radiant brilliance of an ethereal dwelling place for the mind alone. The radical extremes of temperature in these two realms correspond to the difference between two artistic modes that one of the *Serapionsbrüder* defines:

> How does it happen that many a work of art, though not at all bad in terms of form and design, appears as insipid as a faded picture? It fails to lift our spirits, and the brilliance of its language only intensifies its chilling effect on us. It happens because the poet has not really seen what he tells us, and because the deed or event that presented itself to his mind's eye . . . has failed to inspire him and to kindle his imagination to such a degree that the flames within him can blaze forth as fiery words.[29]

[29] "Woher kommt es denn, dass so manches Dichterwerk das keineswegs schlecht zu nennen, wenn von Form und Ausarbeitung die Rede, doch so ganz wirkungslos bleibt wie ein verbleichtes Bild, dass wir nicht davon hingerissen werden, dass die Pracht der Worte nur dazu dient den inneren Frost, der uns durchgleitet, zu vermehren. Woher

Kristall, however, often appears to blend properties normally attributed to both fire and ice. In the crystal jar, Anselmus is physically paralyzed by the painful constraints of everyday life. At the same time he is literally blinded by a glaring light that colors the objects around him in all the hues of the rainbow. Imprisonment in crystal thus allows him to sense both the chilling gloom of one world and the blazing splendor of the other, but leaves him an alien in both.

Through his love for Serpentina and his steadfast faith in the world she inhabits, Anselmus breaks free from his corporeal prison and enters Atlantis. Readers of Hoffmann's works are accustomed to search for—and inevitably to find—an elaborate rational explanation for each supernatural event. But an alternative explanation for Anselmus's poetic life in Atlantis appears to be conspicuously absent from this story: the narrator only casually mentions that Anselmus has simply disappeared from Dresden.

In a provocative essay on *Der goldne Topf,* James M. McGlathery argues that Anselmus's death could account for his otherwise puzzling absence from Dresden.[30] As the first two vigils demonstrate, Serpentina's natural habitat is the river, and Anselmus nearly plunges into the water several times in order to prevent her departure. When Anselmus is ostensibly imprisoned in the glass jar, he is, according to the testimony of five other students, actually standing on a bridge gazing into the Elbe. Lindhorst finally liberates him from his prison, and the glass in which he is trapped shatters. Anselmus then "throws himself" into the arms of Serpentina. These facts suggest that Veronika's decision to

kommt es anders, als dass der Dichter nicht das wirklich schaute wovon er spricht, dass die Tat, die Begebenheit vor seinen geistigen Augen sich darstellend . . . , ihn nicht begeisterte, entzündete, so dass nur die inneren Flammen ausströmen durften in feurigen Worten." (II, 54)

[30] James M. McGlathery, "The Suicide Motif in E.T.A. Hoffmann's 'Der goldne Topf,'" *Monatshefte,* 58 (1966), 115-123.

cast the mementos of her brief flirtation with Anselmus into the Elbe does not entirely lack meaning. She delivers the mementos to Heerbrand and instructs him to throw them into the river from the bridge at the spot "where the cross stands." McGlathery marshals persuasive evidence for Anselmus's suicide, yet he fails to mention the most obvious and perhaps the most compelling indication that Anselmus finds death in Atlantis: Anselmus would have to plunge into the Elbe and swim through its waters in order to reach that submerged paradise.

For Anselmus, the moment of liberation, the sudden passage from blindness to insight, coincides with the appearance of a flash of lightning that strikes him to the quick and brings his martyrdom to an end by releasing a divided self. His body may remain trapped in the waters of the Elbe, but his soul soars into an empyrean realm of art. Dresden becomes the locus of paralysis, rigidity, and death, whereas the aesthetic world of Atlantis takes on all the warmth and vividness ordinarily associated with life.[31]

The climactic moment of recognition in the last vigil, when past revelations of the unconscious mind are suddenly experienced on a conscious level, crowns Anselmus's bliss. The soul celebrates its joyous union with nature in Atlantis. For the mundane counterpart of that moment we must return to the first vigil, in which Anselmus's thoughts still cling tenaciously to the bliss of a bourgeois paradise replete with raucous music, potent spirits, and smartly attired maidens. The fundamental tension between the inner vision of Atlantis and the conventional reality of Dresden resonates

[31] For the painter Reinhold in "Meister Martin der Küfner und seine Gesellen," a similar reversal occurs. Reinhold's infatuation with Rosa, Martin's charming daughter, sharply diminishes once he completes her portrait. While putting the finishing touches on the painting, he is suddenly seized by the odd sensation that his portrait embodies the Rosa he loves, and that Martin's flesh-and-blood daughter is a mere imitation of his portrait. He gives up his apprenticeship as a cooper and hastily departs for Italy, an aesthetic paradise that he calls the "Heimat aller Kunst."

throughout the entire work. When Anselmus lay beneath the elder tree, his attention was deflected, for the first time, from an earthly paradise to a magical realm of nature. During his trancelike state, he discovered a poetic world of the unconscious mind and sensed its harmonious fusion with external nature.

But revelations of dreams and of the unconscious, as Hoffmann stresses in "Ritter Gluck," remain distinct from true cognition. In an engaging study of the myth of Atlantis, Robert Mühlher calls attention to a passage from *Prinzessin Brambilla* that succinctly formulates the main pattern of development emerging in *Der goldne Topf* and demonstrates how Anselmus moves from reverie to cognition:[32]

> Thought destroys perception, and man, torn from his mother's breast, staggers around without a home in a confused daze and blind stupor until thought's own mirror image provides it with the knowledge that it *exists*.[33]

The surface of the golden flowerpot, polished by rays of diamonds, mirrors the magical landscape of Atlantis. Like the *Kristall* of the "stream of consciousness" in Atlantis, it brings to Anselmus reflection in both the literal and figurative sense of the word. For Mühlher the moment of cognition coincides with Anselmus's perception of the flowerpot's surface, which both preserves and casts back to Anselmus not only his own image but also that of the thought inspired in him through Serpentina. In Hoffmann's tale, the spark that kindles thought in Anselmus produces anguish and despair, but it is also through thought (in the form of Serpentina's love) and "reflection" that Anselmus attains the highest

[32] Mühlher, "Liebestod und Spiegelmythe," pp. 47-49.

[33] "Der Gedanke zerstört die Anschauung und losgerissen von der Mutter Brust wankt in irrem Wahn, in blinder Betäubtheit der Mensch heimatlos umher, bis des Gedankens eignes Spiegelbild dem Gedanken selbst die Erkenntnis schafft, dass er *ist*." (IV, 257)

level of consciousness, knowledge of the "sacred harmony" of all things.

Atlantis, the fairy-tale estate of poetic imagination, nonetheless remains a mere aesthetic construct. The situation of the narrator at the end of the twelfth vigil unfolds the true dilemma facing the artist. Constantly aware that the everyday world of Dresden and the higher reality of Atlantis are incompatible, he is doomed to remain suspended between these two regions and to suffer the pain generated by that condition. Occasional moments of poetic inspiration will ignite his imagination, allow him to see the wonders of Atlantis, and even furnish the words required to describe that vision. Hoffmann himself could never resolve the contradictions between these two worlds, and in his tales and novels aesthetic utopias are either described in detail as fantastic fairy-tale kingdoms or sketchily defined as "Italy" or "Florence"—countries and cities geographically remote from the setting of the story.

Fulfillment, as the conclusion of *Meister Floh* suggests, comes only at the moment of death.[34] Symptomatic of Hoffmann's genuine belief that visionary insight coincides with the transition from life to death is a passage from a letter to his friend Dr. Speyer. Upon receiving the disturbing news of Julia Marc's divorce and learning of the depressions that plagued her, Hoffmann asked Dr. Speyer to tell Julia "that the angel of sweetest mercy, of divinest grace in female form, and of childlike virtue, who radiated joy in my most dismal moments of hellish gloom, cannot leave me even when I take my last breath. Indeed, only then will the unfettered psyche, in its natural state, truly catch a glimpse of the

[34] Peregrinus Tyss learns in that tale that fulfillment bears within it the seeds of physical destruction. "Das Mysterium ist erschlossen," he declares after Georg Pepusch and Dörtje Elwerdink have mysteriously disappeared. "Der höchste Augenblick alles erfüllten Sehnens war auch der Augenblick [des] Todes" (IV, 813).

being that embodied its longing, its hope, and its consolation."[35]

V

Hoffmann was of two minds about mesmerism, and his ambivalent attitude toward it emerges most clearly in the discussions of the *Serapionsbrüder.* Cyprian lavishes praise on mesmerism as a tool for divining nature's secrets; Lothar denounces it as a "dangerous instrument." Hoffmann himself explored both views in his tales and novels.

The mental state of mediums, as noted earlier, offers striking analogies with that of poetic inspiration, and for this reason Hoffmann borrowed freely from the lexicon of mesmerism to describe the shift from normal consciousness to visionary experience in the minds of his artists. As Lothar never tires of declaring, only men with clairvoyant powers merit the title of poet. Those who are not "genuine seers" can create nothing but "deceptive puppets." Serapion, the patron saint of their literary club, he notes, was an "authentic poet," for he really saw what he proclaimed. And his instructions to the *Serapionsbrüder* read as follows: "Each of us must be sure that he has really seen what he plans to make known" (II, 55).

During both the mesmerist trance and the poetic mood, normal vision is obscured, and an inner eye opens to see "what slumbers peacefully in the depths of the soul" (II, 263). If the poet is lifted to such heights that he can actually perceive this psychic space, he will also secure genuine faith in its wonders. Then he must descend from his lofty perch to reconstruct this vision and thus inspire others through his art. The narrator of *Der goldne Topf,* for example, suggests that his own poetic composition, informed by the vision of Anselmus in Atlantis, may well cast into a reader's breast a

[35] *E.T.A. Hoffmanns Briefwechsel,* ed. Hans von Müller and Friedrich Schnapp (Munich: Winkler, 1968), II, 249.

spark that will kindle his longing for one of Serpentina's sisters and allow him to see the kingdom of Atlantis. The poet himself thus exercises over his audience the same electrifying power that the figures of his stories wield over each other.

Hoffmann reserves his greatest contempt for those who seek merely to dominate and exploit weaker personalities through mesmeric control. Both Alban and Graf S——i seek to appropriate the visionary powers of the women they mesmerize. Inspired by nothing more than carnal love and the desire to harness nature's power to their own ends, they induce in their mediums a mental state that yields neither love nor knowledge. The victims of their designs suffer the same fate to which Anselmus is subjected when his thoughts turn from Serpentina to her mundane counterpart Veronika. Maria is haunted by repugnant snakes; Angelika is plagued by a recurring precognitive dream in which she is trapped in a ring of flames.

In the visions of those stirred by genuine love, the consuming fires of earthly desires modulate into the radiant warmth of spiritual illumination. Kreisler, who divides all men into two categories—musicians and nonmusicians—describes this transformation in the following manner:

> Now and then it happens that invisible hands suddenly remove the veils covering the eyes of musicians, and they see on earth the angelic image that slumbered peacefully in their breasts as a sweet and impenetrable secret. And now all the rapture and ineffable bliss of a higher life that springs from our innermost being flares up in a divinely pure fire that radiates light and heat, yet never consumes with destructive flames. The mind sends out a thousand antennae of passionate desire to capture the one it has seen; and it has her, yet never has her, for longing lingers on eternally! —And *she, she* herself, the glorious being, the dream that has taken on

> life, is the one who shines forth from the artist's soul as music—portrait—poem![36]

Hoffmann persistently described the transition from ordinary consciousness to sublime revelations of the unconscious mind in terms of a mesmerist operation. The penetrating eyes of his female characters and the electrical sparks that attend their presence allow those who are blessed with a poetic spirit to embark on a journey into the uncharted territory of the unconscious mind and to return with music, portrait, or poem.

[36] "Es begibt sich wohl, dass besagten Musikanten unsichtbare Hände urplötzlich den Flor wegziehen, der ihre Augen verhüllte, und sie erschauen, auf Erden wandelnd, das Engelsbild, das, ein süsses unerforschtes Geheimnis, schweigend ruhte in ihrer Brust. Und nun lodert auf in reinem Himmelsfeuer, das nur leuchtet und wärmt, ohne mit verderblichen Flammen zu vernichten, alles Entzücken, alle namenlose Wonne des höheren aus dem Innersten emporkeimenden Lebens, und tausend Fühlhörner streckt der Geist aus in brünstigem Verlangen, und umnetzt die, die er geschaut, und hat sie, und hat sie nie, da die Sehnsucht ewig dürstend fortlebt! —Und *sie, sie* selbst ist es, die Herrliche, die, zum Leben gestaltete Ahnung, aus der Seele des Künstlers hervorleuchtet, als Gesang—Bild—Gedicht!" (III, 431)

CHAPTER 5

The Metaphysics of the Will: Voyeurs and Visionaries in Balzac's "Comédie humaine"

"There are hardly any exceptions to the rule that a person must pay dearly for the divine gift of creative fire. It is as though each of us were endowed at birth with a limited capital of energy."
—Jung, *Psychology and Literature*

Of the many superhuman powers ascribed to Honoré de Balzac, irresistible charm and a prodigious strength of will figure most prominently. These two attributes decisively shaped the enduring legend surrounding the author of the *Comédie humaine*. At an early age Balzac learned how to take advantage of his special psychological gifts both in the sphere of his personal life and in the domain of literary creativity. According to his contemporaries, the powerful spell he cast on others owed its origin to the penetrating gaze (the same kind of glance designated as "magnetic" in Balzac's novels) with which he fixed his interlocutors. Reminiscences of Balzac so persistently stress the hypnotic quality of his eyes that little doubt can remain about the prominence of this feature. Théophile Gautier repeatedly called attention to the "lightning-like glances, so brilliant, so charged with magnetism" that flashed from the eyes of his literary colleague; Edmond Werdet was especially struck by Balzac's "searching gaze" and "magnetic eyes"; Sainte-Beuve felt that Balzac's personality exerted a sexual attraction so compelling that—in one of his perennial quarrels with the novelist—he accused him of wielding magnetic powers to conquer women's hearts.[1]

Balzac's powers of vision have divided critics of his works into two rival camps: those who regard him as the patient and careful observer, and those who consider him, to borrow a term first applied to Balzac by Philarète Chasles, a *voyant*.[2] Baudelaire was among the first to sense that a false dichotomy had been established. In the *Comédie humaine* he found evidence that the talents of both a penetrating observer and a passionate visionary were at work. Balzac himself he characterized as a man whose insatiable appetite for detail was stimulated by the desire "to see everything, . . . to divine everything."[3]

Closely allied to the seductive power of Balzac's eye is the nearly legendary force of his will. The desire to influence other men, to dominate them, and to plant into their minds his own aspirations obsessed the writer throughout his life. Balzac had always prided himself on the strength of his willpower. In his youth he developed an intense interest in animal magnetism, which, he felt, would help him cultivate this faculty. "His enthusiasm was passionate, his faith ab-

[1] Théophile Gautier, "Honoré de Balzac," *Portraits contemporains: Littérateurs, peintres, sculpteurs, artistes dramatiques*, 3rd ed. (Paris: Charpentier, 1874), p. 88; Edmond Werdet, *Portrait intime de Balzac: Sa vie, son humeur et son caractère* (Paris: Dentu, 1859), p. 357; Charles-Augustin Sainte-Beuve, *Causeries du lundi*, 3rd ed. (Paris: Garnier, n.d.), II, 64.

[2] Philarète Chasles, *Journal des Débats Politiques et Littéraires*, 24 August 1850.

[3] Charles Baudelaire, "Théophile Gautier," in *L'Art romantique*, *Oeuvres complètes*, ed. Y.-G. Le Dantec (Paris: Garnier, 1954), p. 1,037. The views of critics who emphasize Balzac's visionary powers (*Balzac voyant*) or his uncompromising realism (*Balzac réaliste*) are documented by Marc Blanchard: *Témoignages et jugements sur Balzac: Essai bibliographique, Recueil de jugements* (Paris: Honoré Champion, 1931), pp. 218-239.

solute, and his confidence unswerving," his friend Jules de Pétigny reported. "He watched the demonstrations of magnetizers, studied their gestures, and devoured their works."[4] To Pétigny, Balzac declared his intention to unravel the mysteries of animal magnetism; he boldly proclaimed that one day he would force all men to comply with his desires and all women to fall in love with him. Apparently he had already acquired a certain degree of magnetic prowess, for he allegedly capped his statement by pointing to a servant girl and announcing: "The bewitching power of my gaze will compel her to walk across this room and to throw herself into my arms."[5]

Critics and novelists have, however, remained more impressed by a different aspect of Balzac's will. Félix Davin predicted that one day Balzac would be honored as much for his willpower as for his literary accomplishments, and Zola fulfilled this prophecy by declaring that the *Comédie humaine* stood as a monument to a heroic effort of the will. Henry James marveled at "the twenty monstrous years . . . , years of concentration and sacrifice the vision of which still makes us ache," that Balzac devoted to his work.[6] Although it was surely more than sheer willpower that roused him from his sleep at the stroke of midnight to don monastic garb and to work at a pace matched by few other writers, Balzac took great pride in what he called his Napoleonic tenacity of spirit.[7]

[4] For Pétigny's account of Balzac's mesmerist activities, see Charles de Lovenjoul, *Histoire des oeuvres de H. de Balzac* (Paris: Calmann Lévy, 1879), p. 378.

[5] Ibid.

[6] Félix Davin, "Introduction aux *Etudes philosophiques*," *Contes drolatiques* (*Oeuvres ébauchées, II – Préfaces*), ed. Roger Pierrot (Paris: Gallimard, 1965), p. 205; Emile Zola, *Les Romanciers naturalistes* (Paris: Charpentier, 1881), p. 7; Henry James, "Honoré de Balzac," in *The Art of Fiction and Other Essays*, ed. Morris Roberts (New York: Oxford University Press, 1948), p. 26.

[7] Balzac, *Lettres à l'étrangère*, 4 vols. (Paris: Calmann Lévy, 1930), I, 515.

I

For Balzac, the human will, which played so important a role in his personal life and which occupies so central a position in his philosophical thought, was a material substance that operated according to the same laws as Mesmer's magnetic fluid. By 1820, the year in which Balzac claimed to have mastered the art of mesmerizing, animal magnetism had once again captured the imagination of Parisian society.[8] From the Napoleonic era up through the early years of the Second Empire, mesmerism rode the crest of a wave of religious mysticism that swept Frenchmen off their feet and carried them into occult regions that Mesmer himself had never dared to enter.[9] Those who embraced the spiritualist form of mesmerism that first emerged in the early nineteenth century and acquired its widest following in the 1840s appeared less intent on ministering to the needs of the ailing than on attending to the concerns of the departed. They abandoned the magnetic *baquet* to link hands around levitating tables; they used mirrors to enthrall spirits roaming the earth instead of to strengthen the effects of ethereal fluids; and they hearkened to the strains of a spiritual world rather than to the profane chords of the glass harmonica or pianoforte. The mesmerist physician who had once displayed such marvelous therapeutic talents eventually yielded his prestige to the somnambulist medium who summoned the spirits of the deceased.

Many postrevolutionary mesmerists, however, interpreted Mesmer's doctrines in a more conservative manner than

[8] Balzac, "Avant-propos," *La Comédie humaine*, ed. Marcel Bouteron, 10 vols. (Paris: Gallimard, 1949-55), I, 12. Subsequent passages from the *Comédie humaine* will be cited from this edition. References in the text to Balzac's other works will be to the eleventh volume of the same edition: *Contes drolatiques* (*Oeuvres ébauchées, II – Préfaces*), ed. Roger Pierrot (Paris: Gallimard, 1965).

[9] See Auguste Viatte, *Les Sources occultes du romantisme: Illuminisme —Théosophie, 1770-1820*, 2 vols. (Paris: Honoré Champion, 1928), for a discussion of the various mystical movements that flourished in France.

their spiritualist and theosophic colleagues. The literary figures of nineteenth-century France who fell under the spell of mesmerism, for example, generally charted a course midway between the animal magnetism of the 1780s and the occult version of mesmerist teachings developed by Swedenborgians, Illuminists, and Rosicrucians. For those writers, the magnetizer's compelling gaze and the subtle fluids he used to work his miracles proved as engaging as the visions of clairvoyant mediums and the spirits with whom those seers communicated.

A German physician who had once occupied one of two chairs for animal magnetism at the University of Berlin helped to steer French writers in the proper direction and became perhaps the most celebrated mesmerist authority for France's literary world. David Ferdinand Koreff crossed the Rhine in 1823—shortly after he had fallen out of favor with his patron Prince von Hardenberg—with the hope of recovering in Paris the influential position he had lost in Berlin.[10] Although Koreff never attained the prestigious station he had once held in Prussian society, he nonetheless became something of a celebrity in the French capital. A sparkling wit and cosmopolitan manner, enhanced by his reputation as a leader of the mesmerist movement and his fame as a confidant of princes, poets, and politicians, provided Koreff access to literary circles that included such luminaries as Hugo, Alexandre Dumas, Musset, Mérimée, Chateaubriand, and Balzac. Soon after his arrival in the French capital, he added Stendhal, Benjamin Constant, and Heinrich Heine to the list of eminent men who sought his advice in medical matters.

Parisians were as fascinated by Koreff's literary connections as by his therapeutic skills. The German physician's uncanny resemblance to E.T.A. Hoffmann, whose works were enjoying wide acclaim among the French in the 1830s,

[10] For further information on Koreff's career, see Marietta Martin, *Le Docteur Koreff: Un Aventurier intellectuel sous la Restauration et la Monarchie de Juillet* (Paris: Edouard Champion, 1925).

especially delighted habitués of the leading salons. As a former member of a literary club founded by Hoffmann in Berlin, Koreff stood to profit enormously from the vogue for his recently deceased friend. Although it is difficult to measure his precise influence on the French literary world, Koreff's conquest of Parisian society provides some evidence for the continuing popularity of mesmerism in the capital.

The title of a burlesque comedy performed at the Théâtre des Variétés in 1816 suggests in fact that history was once again repeating itself. *Le Magnétisomanie*, like *Les Docteurs modernes* of 1784, drew crowds to the box office. Even such a work as Frédéric Soulié's *Le Magnétiseur,* which harked back to the ideals of prerevolutionary mesmerists, became an instant best seller. The only striking difference between the language of M. de Lussay, the sinister physician of Soulié's novel, and that of Mesmer's first Parisian disciples is the use of the present rather than the future tense:

> For you, the French Revolution signifies the restoration of the social order; I see in it nothing but anarchy and misfortune. For me, magnetism signifies the regeneration of mankind; you find in it nothing but charlatanry and chaos. I don't know the first thing about politics, but you know nothing about medicine.[11]

When Lussay asserts that the somnambulist trance promises to usher in a "moral and physical revolution," he merely rehearses the arguments advanced several decades earlier by leaders of the Society of Universal Harmony.

It is not always easy to determine whether the spirits haunting nineteenth-century French novels were inspired by animal magnetism, or even whether the electrical sparks and

[11] "Pour vous, la révolution française est le renouvellement de l'ordre social, et je n'y vois qu'anarchie et malheur. Pour moi, le magnétisme est la régénération de l'humanité et vous n'y trouvez que charlatanisme et désordre. Si je n'entends rien en politique; vous n'entendez rien en médecine." Frédéric Soulié, *Le Magnétiseur* (Brussels: Louis Hauman, 1835), p. 101.

waves of magnetic fluid that set their plots in motion represented direct borrowings from mesmerist sources. Yet a large number of writers explicitly acknowledged the debt they owed Mesmer for providing what appeared to be a scientific explanation for the supernatural events in their works.[12]

In 1847 Alexandre Dumas assured the readers of the *Journal du Magnétisme* that he genuinely believed in the preternatural powers he had bestowed on Joseph Balsamo (alias Cagliostro), the *diabolus ex machina* of the four novels that comprise his "Marie-Antoinette cycle."[13] The "streams of magnetic fluid" emanating from his "flaming orbs" and the bolts of lightning flashing from his "tempestuous gaze" allow Balsamo to overcome even the strongest resistance to his will. The youthful, innocent maidens whom he hypnotizes serve unwittingly to enlarge the scope of his knowledge and power. When they close their eyes to the light of the world, an inner eye opens to contemplate the splendors of a supernatural world that holds the solution to all the mysteries Balsamo could ever hope to divine. Without his mediums, Balsamo could never have discovered the elixir of life or developed the formula for manufacturing gold and diamonds. After performing one of the many successful mesmerist operations described in the novel, Balsamo triumphantly proclaims: "Science is thus not an empty word like virtue! Mesmer has defeated Brutus."[14]

In his "Préface philosophique" to *Les Misérables*, Victor Hugo roundly denounced the Academy of Sciences for having halted the progress of science by refusing to sanction the

[12] Robert Darnton, *Mesmerism and the End of the Enlightenment in France* (Cambridge, Mass.: Harvard University Press, 1968), p. 150. See his discussion of mesmerism in French literature, pp. 127-159, to which I am greatly indebted.

[13] Alexandre Dumas, "Etudes sur le somnambulisme," *Journal du Magnétisme*, 5 (1847), 146-155.

[14] Alexandre Dumas, *Mémoires d'un médecin: Joseph Balsamo*, 3 vols. (Paris: Calmann Lévy, 1888), I, 113.

imaginative research of Mesmer, Puységur, and their successor Deleuze. "Science," he charged, "has turned pale at the sight of . . . magnetic trances, artificial catalepsy, and clairvoyance."[15] It has locked the door to knowledge, he added, instead of serving as the key to it. Living in exile on the Channel Islands in the 1850s, Hugo had few distractions; he directed much of his energy toward the search for a path that would lead him into the regions so carefully sealed off by scientists. With the aid of his mystical mentor Delphine de Girardin, he obtained access to this world through spiritualism. Using tipping tables that rapped out letters of the alphabet, Hugo claimed to have established contact with inhabitants of a spiritual kingdom. He spoke with the shades of Socrates, the lion of Androcles, and Charlotte Corday; he learned how to communicate with frogs, the blade of the guillotine, and the Angel of Light; and he even conversed with the spirit of his deceased daughter Léopoldine.[16] Never troubled that Dante and Shakespeare spoke to him in French using his own literary style and meter, Hugo embraced the revelations of the séances held at his home. He came to view himself as a prophet charged with the mission of preaching universal fraternity and helping mankind clear the path leading to salvation.

In contrast, Balthazar Cherbonneau, the mesmerist physician of Gautier's "Avatar," is unable to use his powers to summon the spirits of the dead. But Cherbonneau has little difficulty breaking the bonds that confine the human soul to its earthly prison and in thus allowing the psyche to roam freely through space or to plant itself in another human frame. His version of mesmerism relies principally on electrical machines, wooden *baquets*, and the "magnetic bat-

[15] Victor Hugo, "Préface philosophique," *Oeuvres romanesques complètes*, ed. Francis Bouvet (Paris: Jean-Jacques Pauvert, 1962), p. 889.

[16] Gustave Simon, ed., *Chez Victor Hugo: Les Tables tournantes de Jersey* (Paris: Conard, 1928). See also Auguste Viatte, *Victor Hugo et les Illuminés de son temps* (Montreal: Editions de l'Arbre, 1942).

tery" of the human eye to transfer the soul of Octave de Saville, a lovesick young Parisian, to the body of Olaf Labinski, the husband of the woman he loves. Just as Cherbonneau's "piercing gaze" separates Octave's soul from its body, so the "intellectual electricity" that radiates from the eyes of Paul d'Aspremont (in Gautier's "Jettatura") draws the soul of his fiancée, Alicia, from its mortal dwelling place. An Italian nobleman conversant with the superstitions of his compatriots explains that d'Aspremont does not torture Alicia by design: "The evil eye is usually cast unintentionally; it operates without the knowledge of those who possess that fatal gift."[17]

While Gautier recognized that an abundant supply of "intellectual electricity" can endow men with a highly destructive power, he did not believe that a copious fund of that substance necessarily transforms a man into an evil genius. Balzac, he observed, had resolved to become a "great man," and he had become one by "projecting that fluid more powerful than electricity, which he . . . so profoundly analyzed in *Louis Lambert*."[18] In that novel, Balzac first developed his theory of the will as a vital force akin to light, electricity, and magnetism—a force that lifts man into spiritual regions, bestows on him the faculty of second sight, and at the same time allows him to control life on earth. The marvelous powers of Balzac's adolescent genius prefigure the less ethereal, but equally spectacular, traits of the "exceptional beings" who assume leading roles in the *Comédie humaine*.

II

The narrator of *Louis Lambert* reports that the subject of his biographical study first discovered the coruscating power

[17] Théophile Gautier, "Jettatura," in *Romans et contes* (Paris: Charpentier, 1923), p. 190.

[18] Théophile Gautier, *Portraits contemporains*, p. 71.

of his eye in the classroom.[19] Roused one day from his meditations by the voice of a schoolmaster berating him for indolence, Lambert flashes at his persecutor a look so full of contempt that it seems "charged with thought as a Leyden jar is charged with electricity" (X, 376). This "ray of scorn" and "thunderous flash," striking out "like a bolt of lightning," so incenses Lambert's teacher that the recalcitrant pupil is henceforth repeatedly subjected to humiliating forms of corporal punishment.

Lambert's patroness, Madame de Staël, made the decision to finance the formal education of this precocious child largely because she had discerned in him a "voyant." Even before Lambert learns to charge the electrical battery of his outer eye, he recognizes the miracles that his inner eye can perform. Reading an account of the battle of Austerlitz, he can actually hear the clatter of hoofs and the cries of soldiers, smell the gunpowder, and feel the vibrations of exploding cannon. On those occasions when Lambert brings all his powers into play, he loses consciousness of his physical existence and, according to the narrator, lives on only through the "remarkable energy of his mental powers, whose scope has been extended immeasurably" (X, 358).

The event that inspires Lambert to study the "chemistry of the will" and to draft a treatise on that subject sheds some light on the special constitution that invests him with the gift of second sight. On their way to visit the château of Rochambeau, Lambert and the narrator pause on the summit of a hill to contemplate the castle's charming surroundings. Suddenly overwhelmed by a sense of *déjà vu*, Lambert recalls that the château had once figured significantly in a

[19] For a comprehensive analysis of *Louis Lambert*, see Henri Evans, *Louis Lambert et la philosophie de Balzac* (Paris: José Corti, 1951), and Michel Lichtlé, "L'Aventure de Louis Lambert," *L'Année Balzacienne* (Paris: Garnier, 1971), pp. 127-162. I have also profited from Suzanne J. Bérard's remarks on *Louis Lambert* in "Une Enigme balzacienne: La 'Spécialité,'" *L'Année Balzacienne* (Paris: Garnier, 1965), pp. 61-82.

dream. If this dream had allowed him to traverse wide tracts of space without stirring, Lambert reasons, there must exist "internal faculties functioning independently of external physical laws" (X, 385). At last he seems to have hit upon evidence to prove that man leads two essentially separate lives—one shaped by the perceptions of the external or "corporeal" senses, the other by the latent senses of an "inner being" that is liberated from the prison of the body and galvanized into action when spirit triumphs over matter.

The narrator suggests that Lambert's views on the dual nature of human sensory perception anticipate important discoveries of a later age. Although the ideas advanced in Lambert's *Treatise on the Will* are strongly colored by Swedenborgian mysticism, they are in fact based on a concept of anatomical polarity that dates back to the eighteenth century, but that gained widespread acceptance only in the early part of the nineteenth century. The subtle fluids viewed by Lambert as the source of life and designated as will and thought also bear a striking resemblance to the electrical fluid that had figured as the soul of the universe for eighteenth-century physiologists. Lambert at first suspects that electricity may serve as the base for the fluid animating volition and ideas, but he later inclines to the view that electricity is the medium in which the will moves. Consider, for example, his speculations on the connections between electricity and the will:

> To what, then, if not to an electrical substance, can one attribute the magic by which the Will enthrones itself so majestically in the human gaze to strike down all obstacles at the bidding of genius, or by which it thunders in the voice, or insinuates itself, despite resistance, into the human frame? The current of that sovereign fluid which, under the high pressure of Thought or Feeling, flows forth in waves or subsides into a mere trickle, then marshals its forces to burst forth as lightning, is the occult agent to which we owe

> the accomplishments (be they fatal or beneficial) of art and passion.[20]

Balzac's narrator clearly entertains no doubts about the electrical qualities of will and thought. Throughout his biography of Lambert, he describes the activity of thought and the projection of the will in terms of electrical discharge.

For Lambert, both will and thought are physical realities with a life of their own; volition and ideas constitute the product of these two forces. Will and thought belong to the *être actionnel,* an inner being that Lambert depicts as "seeing, acting, perfecting, and accomplishing all things without the slightest physical effort" (X, 391). Volition and ideas—will and thought translated into action—are a part of the outer man, the *être réactionnel.*

According to Lambert, an act of the will can sever the bonds mooring the *être actionnel* to its terrestrial abode and release that inner self to soar through the vast spaces of a spiritual world. But such cosmic flights through the rarefied atmosphere of an unworldly province deplete the reserves of vital energy on which Lambert can draw. In the course of one meeting with his friend, the narrator recalls the visible effects of Lambert's mental exertions:

> He was soaring more boldly than ever through the landscape, and it seemed to me that his brow was about to burst under the efforts of his genius: his powers . . . appeared to flash from the organs appointed to project them; his eyes shot out thoughts; his uplifted hand, his

20 "Enfin, à quoi, si ce n'est à une substance électrique, peut-on attribuer la magie par laquelle la Volonté s'intronise si majestueusement dans les regards pour foudroyer les obstacles aux commandements du génie, éclate dans la voix, ou filtre, malgré l'hypocrisie, au travers de l'enveloppe humaine? Le courant de ce roi des fluides qui, suivant la haute pression de la Pensée ou du Sentiment, s'épanche à flots ou s'amoindrit et s'effile, puis s'amasse pour jaillir en éclairs, est l'occulte ministre auquel sont dus soit les efforts ou funestes ou bienfaisants des arts et des passions." (X, 396-397)

> silent trembling lips were speaking; his burning gaze was radiant; finally, his head, as if too heavy or exhausted by too eager a flight, fell forward onto his breast.[21]

The bird in flight is only one of several images that the narrator uses to express the expansion of Lambert's inner life. He also draws repeatedly on botanic metaphors to express the growth of his schoolmate's mind: Lambert is a "noble plant" that appears to be "vegetating," but in fact lives from "the heart and the brain." Attempting to convey a sense both of Lambert's great stature and of his fatal vulnerability, he summons up the image of "an oak at that stage in its development when its interior expansion bursts the tender green bark, covering it with gnarls and fissures, but at the same time advancing its majestic growth—provided that the thunder of the heavens and the axe of man spare it!" (X, 409). Lambert, however, has far more to fear from the electrical discharge of his own mind than from the thunderbolts that descend from the heavens. The concentration and projection of mental energy by the *être actionnel* have proceeded at so rapid a rate that his physical existence hangs in the balance. Although Lambert senses within himself a life so luminous that it could enlighten the world, his flights into the "spaces of thought" quickly drain the reservoir of electrical fluid at his disposal.

A passage added by Balzac to the novel a decade after its first publication in 1832 suggests that the cause of Lambert's collapse lies in his recognition that the physical pleasures of his impending marriage to Pauline de Villenoix will interfere with the "refinement of his internal sense" and with his

[21] "Il plana plus audacieusement que jamais sur le paysage, et son front me parut près de crever sous l'effort du génie: ses forces . . . semblaient jaillir par les organes destinés à les projeter; ses yeux dardaient la pensée; sa main levée, ses lèvres muettes et tremblantes parlaient; son regard brûlant rayonnait; enfin sa tête, comme trop lourde ou fatiguée par un élan trop violent, retomba sur sa poitrine." (X, 386)

"flight through spiritual worlds."[22] But Lambert's breakdown appears rather as the logical consequence of what the narrator calls "debauchery of the soul":

> He had designed for himself the most demanding life possible, and indeed the most insatiable. In order to sustain life, was he not obliged to cast constant nourishment into the abyss he had opened within him? Like certain creatures of worldly spheres, might he not die for want of a substance to satisfy his extravagant cravings?[23]

Lambert's constitution requires a prodigious supply of vital energy. His appetite for spiritual fulfillment soon assumes the character of a monomaniacal quest for knowledge as uncompromising in its aims and as fatal in its results as any of the other passions described by Balzac.

In "The Unknown Martyrs" ("Les Martyrs ignorés"), a philosophical sketch that Balzac published four years after *Louis Lambert*, an aged physician voices the conviction that thought has the power to kill. By far the most fiercely destructive of all forces, it embodies the "exterminating angel of mankind" (X, 1,149). His prescription for a long life is brief and deceptively easy to follow: "Never think" (X, 1,150).[24] Like Lambert, he identifies thought with an imponderable fluid flowing through a network of arteries and veins similar to those of the circulatory system: "A man can drain his entire fund of it through a single mental act, in

[22] This point, along with the quotations from the text of 1842, is taken from Herbert J. Hunt, *Balzac's Comédie Humaine* (London: Athlone, 1959), p. 51.

[23] "Il s'était créé la vie la plus exigeante et, de toutes, la plus avidement insatiable. Pour exister, ne lui fallait-il pas jeter sans cesse une pâture à l'abîme qu'il avait ouvert en lui? Semblable à certains êtres des régions mondaines, ne pouvait-il périr faute d'aliments pour d'excessifs appétits trompés?" (X, 406-407)

[24] The physician's definition of thought, it should be noted, is quite broad. It covers "les passions, les vices, les occupations extrêmes, les douleurs, les plaisirs" (X, 1,150).

the same way that one can drain the blood supply by opening the crural artery" (X, 1,150). Just as electricity can be stored in a Leyden jar and discharged to deliver a fatal physical blow, so the vital substance that generates thought can also be amassed and suddenly released to deal a deadly emotional shock. Thought thus places in the hands of all men a powerful weapon equally effective for both suicidal and homicidal purposes. Were the physician of "Les Martyrs ignorés" to perform an autopsy on Lambert, he would surely attribute the cause of death to the cerebral excesses of the youthful genius. Balzac himself once contemplated writing a companion piece to *Louis Lambert* which he planned to call "Ecce Homo"; the central figure of that story was to be a cretin who lived well beyond the age of one hundred.

III

The very titles of Balzac's novels and stories reflect an obsessive interest in longevity. *The Centenarian; or, The Béringhelds* (*Le Centenaire, ou les deux Béringheld*) and "The Elixir of Long Life" ("L'Elixir de longue vie") both betray the profound influence of Balzac's father, Bernard-François, a near fanatic when it came to the subject of health and old age. Although Balzac's own theory of life and duration draws on a variety of sources, it can be seen in its larger contours as the conflation of two doctrines that exercised a widespread influence on nineteenth-century thought: the Brunonian concept of excitability and vitalistic speculations on subtle fluids.[25] Nature, according to Balzac,

[25] For the specific sources of Balzac's scientific thought, see especially Muriel Blackstock Ferguson, *La Volonté dans la "Comédie humaine" de Balzac* (Paris: Georges Courville, 1935), pp. 26-47; F. Bonnet-Roy, *Balzac: Les Médecins, la médecine et la science* (Paris: Horizons de France, 1944), pp. 91-128; Moïse Le Yaouanc, *Nosographie de l'humanité balzacienne* (Paris: Maloine, 1959), pp. 153-175; and Maurice Bardèche, "Autour des 'Etudes philosophiques,'" *L'Année Balzacienne* (Paris: Garnier, 1960), pp. 109-124. The authors of these studies all agree on at least one point, namely that it is impossible to trace the scientific ideas expressed in the *Comédie humaine* to any one source. Their re-

bestows on every person a fixed sum of vital energy that, depending upon one's inclinations and priorities, can be carefully hoarded or recklessly squandered: "The amount of energy or will possessed by each one of us is diffused like sound: sometimes it is weak, sometimes strong; it varies with the octaves in its range." ("La quantité d'énergie ou de volonté, que chacun de nous possède, se déploie comme le son: elle est tantôt faible, tantôt forte; elle se modifie selon les octaves qu'il lui est permis de parcourir." X, 717)

Like John Brown's principle of excitability, Balzac's vital force paradoxically both supports life and at the same time feeds upon it. For both Brown and Balzac, intellectual stimulation, emotional strains, and physical activity deplete the stock of energy that is assigned to all men at birth and that can never be replenished.[26] But Balzac's vital force, in contrast to Brown's principle of excitability, is a ubiquitous substance permeating both organic life and inorganic matter, and as such it shares many characteristics of the ethereal fluids that preoccupied eighteenth-century physiologists. Balthazar Claës, the Flemish scientist in *The Quest for the Absolute* (*La Recherche de l'absolu*) whose passionate devotion to chemistry consumes his own reserves of vital energy, suggests that an electrical fluid, the "principle of life," resides not only in men, animals, and plants, but in minerals as well. Life, Claës maintains, is by definition a process of combustion, and its duration is determined by the pace at which this fluidic substance is expended. In rocks and metals, the rate of consumption is so slow that it exacts a barely perceptible toll and allows such inanimate objects to remain intact for centuries. But in higher forms of life, expenditure of the vital force proceeds at so rapid a rate that life spans can be measured in mere decades.

---

search further suggests that Balzac's theory of life rests on ideas that were shared by a large number of nineteenth-century scientists, philosophers, and physicians.

[26] Maurice Bardèche, "Autour des 'Etudes philosophiques,'" pp. 114-116.

For Balzac, the steady proliferation of invisible fluids in the nineteenth century seemed to run counter to the very principle that these fluids were meant to demonstrate—the sublime unity and harmony of nature. Unlike scientists of an earlier age, he was reluctant to add yet another substance to the wide variety of imponderable forces clashing in the cosmos. As a result, the vital energy coursing through the nervous system of the *Comédie humaine* does not introduce a new essence into nature, but rather absorbs all but the most extravagant subtle fluids to which eighteenth-century scientists had given their imprimatur. "Everything here on earth," Louis Lambert declares, "is produced by an *ethereal substance* that serves as the common base of various phenomena, inaccurately designated as *Electricity, Heat, Light, the Galvanic Fluid, the Magnetic Fluid, etc.*" (X, 448). The same thought is echoed by the narrator of *La Recherche de l'absolu* when he analyzes the source of Claës's fear that another scientist will beat him to the discovery of the absolute: "Learned men who were devoting their lives to science began to think, as he did, that light, heat, electricity, galvanism, and magnetism were only different effects of the same cause" (IX, 588).

Although Balzac's vital fluid supplies the illuminating power of light and possesses the radiant warmth of heat, it bears the closest resemblance to electrical and magnetic fluids. Like both of these substances it can be kept in reserve and then discharged in a flash of energy. As the medium of thought, it kindles sparks as vibrant as those emitted in electrical reactions; but as the agent of the will, it furnishes the compelling attraction exercised by magnetic forces.

Balzac's definition of life poses some disquieting questions. If thoughts, desires, and passions consume the very essence of life, is it then not wise to suppress thought, stifle desire, and smother passion, even if this means living in constant anticipation of death and turning life into a near replica of death? Or is it better to indulge one's appetites and enjoy a brief but intense life of pleasure?[27] The choice facing every character in the *Comédie humaine* receives its most concise formulation in *La Peau de chagrin*: "To kill emotions and live to an old age, or to die young, a martyr to passion" (IX, 72). It is in this same "poem" (the author bristled when he heard readers call it a novel) that Balzac shaped the perfect symbol for expressing the inverse relationship between the duration of life and the intensity of desire: the shagreen skin given to Raphaël de Valentin by an antique dealer. Every new pleasure that satisfies Raphaël's desires visibly shrinks this piece of leather which, in Balzac's own words, represents "the pure and simple expression of human life."[28]

Since life implies combustion, even those who practice moderation in all things must draw daily on the precious fund of vital energy allotted to them. Just to sustain life, man must constantly expend energy.[29] Balzac habitually described the dissipation of the life force in language borrowed from the spheres of gastronomy and finance—significantly the two areas in which he himself had the greatest difficulty exercising restraint. Lambert, we recall, is unable to curb his appetite for spiritual truth, and his quest for knowledge eventually consumes the very essence of his physical existence. César Birotteau, in the novel that bears his

[27] These questions are discussed in detail by Ernst Robert Curtius, *Balzac*, 2d ed. (Bern: Francke, 1951); by Georges Poulet, *Etudes sur le temps humain: La Distance intérieure* (Paris: Plon, 1952), pp. 122-193; and by Gretchen R. Besser, *Balzac's Concept of Genius: The Theme of Superiority in the "Comédie humaine"* (Geneva: Droz, 1969), pp. 163-193. Energy, according to Curtius, is the "magic word" that one has to know "in order to understand the whole and the true Balzac." See his "New Encounter with Balzac," in *Essays in European Literature*, by E. R. Curtius, trans. Michael Kowal (Princeton, N.J.: Princeton University Press, 1973), pp. 189-210.

[28] *H. de Balzac: Pensées, Sujets, Fragments*, ed. Jacques Crépet (Paris: Blaizot, 1910), p. 95.

[29] "Pour l'homme social, vivre, c'est se dépenser plus ou moins vite" (Balzac, "Traité des excitants modernes," *Oeuvres complètes*, ed. Marcel Bouteron and Henri Longnon, XL [Paris: Louis Conard, 1940], 180).

name, overdraws his account of vital resources and is forced to surrender to the "vague sense of exhaustion that follows strenuous mental activity" (V, 506). Having spent a sum of "nervous fluid" and "willpower" greater than that at his disposal, he must draw on the "capital of his existence." One has the choice of either prudently husbanding or impulsively disbursing that capital or "principal of life," as it is called elsewhere.

Balzac had good reason to draw his stock of metaphors for describing the economy of the life force from the language of finance. Just as the current of vital energy flowing through the human body maintains the heartbeat of the individual, so the currency that circulates through France regulates the pulse of society. Gobseck, a master in the art of economy, tells his attorney Derville: "Money is the spiritual essence of modern society" (II, 636); it represents "the total sum of human energy" (II, 629). To spend money, to buy love and power, or to gratify other passions reduces the life expectancy in the same way that more direct forms of debauchery attenuate the supply of vital energy.[30] Passion, as Balzac never grew tired of proclaiming, destroys men, and in Paris, he noted, every passion can be connected with two terms: money and pleasure—the spending of the one and the getting of the other (V, 256).

Acquisitive habits are not limited to Parisians; those residing in the provinces are equally partial to wealth, although they are generally more concerned with amassing riches than with translating them into power. Grandet, the miser par excellence of the *Comédie humaine,* hoards money with the same care that characterizes his efforts to preserve his vital energy: "He never paid any visits, wishing neither to receive nor to offer hospitality; he never made a sound and seemed intent on economizing in everything, even in muscular energy" (III, 488). To some extent, then, the

[30] Curtius maintains that money figures as the symbol of vital energy in the *Comédie humaine* (*Balzac,* p. 82).

austere habits cultivated by Grandet in his financial dealings serve him well; the crusty septuagenarian has converted his one excess, the lust for wealth, into a virtue by extending its inevitable concomitant, frugality, into all other spheres of life.

What saves many of Balzac's misers and collectors from the early death to which those ruled by an overweening passion normally succumb is utter indifference to the physical pleasures that money can buy. Masters in the arts of parsimony, continence, and sobriety, they pose as dispassionate observers of society and steer clear of emotional entanglements. These men deserve close attention largely because the pattern of their lives provides a formula for resolving the contradictions between a rich, creative existence and a long life.

The usurer Gobseck and the antiquarian of *La Peau de chagrin* are both virtuosos in the art of life. Gobseck's lawyer, Derville, dwells in detail on the orderly routine to which his client subscribes and on the care with which he avoids dipping into his reserves of vital energy for unprofitable purposes: "His every movement, from the moment of waking to his fit of coughing at night, was as regular as clockwork. . . . That man would stop short in the middle of a sentence and remain silent while a carriage passed so that he would not have to strain his voice" (II, 625). The most striking attribute of both Gobseck and the antique dealer is a smoldering and implacable gaze. The youthful eyes that sparkle in the antiquarian's icy countenance have a hypnotic influence on Raphaël, while the brilliant eyes that light up Gobseck's impassive features produce a searing effect on Derville. The narrator of *La Peau de chagrin* observes that the centenarian who bequeathes the fatal skin to Raphaël would be a hard man to deceive: he seems to possess "the gift of divining thoughts hidden in the depths of the most secretive souls" (IX, 32). One might, he further suggests, interpret the expression on his face as the luminous tranquillity of a "God who sees everything" or as the arrogant self-possession of a "man who has seen everything" (IX, 32). Gobseck takes pride in the same kind of clairvoyant vision. "My gaze," he claims, "is like that of God. I can see into your soul. Nothing is hidden from me" (II, 636).

Despite their penetrating powers of vision, Gobseck and the antiquarian share many more traits with voyeurs than with *voyants*. Both men have sublimated their passions into what the antique dealer calls knowledge and Gobseck calls power—into a kind of omniscience and omnipotence at once satanic and divine. "My only ambition," declares the antiquarian, "has been to see. To see, is that not to know?" (IX, 40). To the disconsolate Raphaël, he expounds his philosophy of life:

> I have seen everything, but calmly, without exhausting myself; I have never desired anything, but have waited for everything. I have strolled through the universe as if it were the garden of a house that belonged to me. What men call cares, loves, ambitions, failures, and sorrow are to me ideas that I translate into dreams. Instead of experiencing them, I express and interpret them. Instead of letting them consume my life, I dramatize them and enlarge upon them. I entertain myself with them as if they were novels read by the inner eye. Never having taxed myself physically, I still enjoy robust health.[31]

Gobseck makes a similar claim: "The world is mine without effort, but the world hasn't the slightest hold on me" (II,

[31] "J'ai tout vu, mais tranquillement, sans fatigue; je n'ai jamais rien désiré, j'ai tout attendu. Je me suis promené dans l'univers comme dans le jardin d'une habitation qui m'appartenait. Ce que les hommes appellent chagrins, amours, ambitions, revers, tristesse, sont pour moi des idées que je change en rêveries; au lieu de les sentir, je les exprime, je les traduis; au lieu de leur laisser dévorer ma vie, je les dramatise, je les développe, je m'en amuse comme de romans que je lirais par une vision intérieure. N'ayant jamais lassé mes organes, je jouis encore d'une santé robuste." (IX, 40)

630). Like the antiquarian, he feels only contempt for those ensnared by lust and passion, and he prefers instead to play spectator to the infinitely varied drama of human passion:

> Yesterday it was a tragedy. Some fellow, a father, gassed himself because he could not support his children. Tomorrow it will be a comedy. A young man will try to play the role of M. Dimanche, brought up to date naturally. . . . Those distinguished actors play for me alone, and yet they are incapable of deluding me.[32]

Gobseck himself recognizes the fundamental identity between his own daydreams and the visions of artists. When Derville one day interrupts his meditations and appears perplexed by his pensive mood, Gobseck informs his lawyer that he has been entertaining himself with poetic thoughts: "Do you really think," he asks, "that the only poets are those who publish verse?" (II, 628).

Balzac drew a careful distinction between two kinds of intellectual activity. The passionate desire for knowledge that shapes the ambitions of a Louis Lambert or a Balthazar Claës taxes the human body to the same degree as any form of physical excess, but the essentially passive and sober contemplative existence of Gobseck and the antiquarian yields knowledge without taking a lethal toll. It is not without reason that Balzac invested his astute financiers with the outer attributes of deities and repeatedly compared their inner lives to those of poets, novelists, and dramatists. In an act analogous to God's creation of the world and to the poet's invention of a "second nature," Balzac's financiers fashion a private universe, breathe life into its inhabitants, frame the laws that govern them, and sit back to watch the results.

[32] "Hier, une tragédie: quelque bonhomme de père qui s'asphyxie parce qu'il ne peut plus nourrir ses enfants. Demain, une comédie: un jeune homme essaiera de me jouer la scène de monsieur Dimanche, avec les variantes de notre époque. . . . Ces sublimes acteurs jouaient pour moi seul, et sans pouvoir me tromper." (II, 635-636)

IV

Few actors in the *Comédie humaine* manage to circumvent the tyrannical laws governing Balzac's universe or to achieve immunity from the dictum that everyone "exceeds his powers" (V, 260) and wears himself out "in a thousand spurts of creative will" (V, 257). One man who does cheat death, as his sobriquet Trompe-la-Mort makes clear, is the arch-criminal Jacques Collin, alias Vautrin, alias Carlos Herrera. Balzac takes pains to alert his reader to Vautrin's preternatural powers. He rarely misses an opportunity to emphasize the penetrating gaze that enables the former convict to divine the thoughts of those around him, or to hint at the formidable strength of will that constrains others to obey Vautrin's commands. At the *Maison-Vauquer*, Vautrin casts on Rastignac the "coldly fascinating gaze" characteristic of "magnetic men" (II, 1,006); when his gaze falls on Mademoiselle Michonneau, the woman who revealed Vautrin's identity to the police, it discharges a "flash of will" (II, 1,012) that makes her legs buckle.

For an explanation of the manner by which one man imposes his will on another, we need only turn to the theories advanced by the author of the *Treatise on the Will*. Louis Lambert recognizes that willpower can be "stored up by a purely contractile effort, then, by another effort, projected outward" (X, 395). Through such a discharge of energy, one man's will can invade the mind of another and establish a stronghold of influence. Lambert is only one of several theoreticians of the will in Balzac's world. In *La Peau de chagrin*, Raphaël de Valentin also composes a dense treatise on the will, a treatise he believes will not merely crown the pioneering efforts of Mesmer, Lavater, Gall, and Bichat, but also open new paths for human knowledge. Will is, in his view, a "physical force." A person who understands the principles by which it operates can overturn the laws of nature and bring about whatever changes he desires in human affairs.

Both Lambert and Raphaël would have found a kindred spirit in a German philosopher who wrote his *magnum opus* in the same decade in which they were constructing their metaphysical systems and whose work, like theirs, went almost unnoticed by contemporaries. When Arthur Schopenhauer's *The World As Will and Idea* (*Die Welt als Wille und Vorstellung*) appeared in 1819, it brought little fame to its author. Only a few philosophers read the book; virtually no one purchased it. Yet Schopenhauer was undaunted. When he began lecturing at the University of Berlin, he deliberately scheduled his class to coincide with the hour at which Hegel—then at the height of his popularity—was addressing students. Needless to say, he found himself speaking to an empty hall. He nonetheless remained confident that his work would one day find its audience and that he himself would eventually win recognition. Because Schopenhauer's work did not receive much attention until the 1850s, it is highly unlikely that the author of the *Comédie humaine* ever even heard the name of this misanthropic German, who preferred the company of his cat to that of any human being. Schopenhauer himself never referred to the French novelist in his own writings. It is therefore all the more remarkable that Balzac and Schopenhauer shared certain fundamental notions about the nature of the human will and, in addition, that both men found in animal magnetism a confirmation of their philosophical positions.

For Schopenhauer, the thing-in-itself is the will—a blind, raging impulse perpetually striving for satisfaction but never attaining it. What men call happiness is nothing more than a temporary suspension of the pain that accompanies desire, and when this happiness—at best a negative form of enjoyment—turns to boredom, the desperate attempt to gratify desire reasserts itself. Schopenhauer maps out two avenues of escape from the futile aspirations dictated by the will. The first, which is the path to salvation, lies in the Buddhist abnegation of the will and leads to nirvana; the second, which requires the elevation and transfiguration of the will into ideas, is the way of aesthetic contemplation. Reason, in Schopenhauer's view, ordinarily remains a slave to the will and serves it as an instrument for satisfying man's complicated biological needs and practical desires. But it can (at least temporarily) generate a surplus of energy that liberates it from thralldom to the will and allows it to engage in dispassionate contemplation. Then man can, by adopting an entirely disinterested point of view, become the "pure will-less subject of knowledge."[33]

Wherever Schopenhauer turned his gaze, he discovered new evidence to corroborate his thesis that nature is simply the disguise assumed by the one transcendent will. Magnetism, electricity, gravity, and chemical properties, as much as animal instinct and human desire, are "immediate manifestations of the will."[34] Not surprisingly, Schopenhauer found in animal magnetism, which he considered—from a philosophical standpoint at least—the "most significant discovery ever made," further proof that the will constitutes the thing-in-itself.[35] He flatly dismissed all theories attributing the enigmatic control exercised by mesmerists over their mediums to the action of subtle fluids. On the other hand, he willingly granted that he was not the first to recognize that the will and the will alone could account for the miracles of animal magnetism: Puységur's instructions to his disciples—"Veuillez et croyez!"—suggested that the pioneering spirits of this new medical therapy had already identified the real cause of their cures. While he declined to

[33] Arthur Schopenhauer, *Die Welt als Wille und Vorstellung, Sämtliche Werke*, ed. Arthur Hübscher, 5 vols. (Leipzig: Brockhaus, 1938), II, 209.

[34] Ibid., pp. 154-155.

[35] Schopenhauer, "Animalischer Magnetismus und Magie," in *Sämtliche Werke*, IV, 99-127. See also his "Versuch über das Geistersehn und was damit zusammenhängt," *Sämtliche Werke*, V, 239-329, for further discussion of animal magnetism.

bestow on mesmerists the power to regulate the magnetic fields and electrical currents of nature, Schopenhauer accorded to these men a metaphysical and psychological influence of impressive dimensions.

Although Balzac anticipated Schopenhauer's views by assigning to the will a central role, not only in mesmerist operations but more generally in the drama of human life, he never abandoned the belief that the will was only one of many ethereal substances—in fact perhaps the point of confluence for a variety of subtle fluids swirling in the atmosphere. Balzac also believed that men can avoid delivering themselves up to the destructive force of the will by substituting contemplation for desire; yet the most compelling figure of the *Comédie humaine* manages to retain the ability to exercise his willpower and at the same time to savor the knowledge and strength that come from renouncing desire and serenely witnessing the passions of others.

Vautrin, the last in a literary line that includes the ruthless leader of the "Band of Thirteen" and the unnamed pirate who abducts Hélène in *A Woman of Thirty* (*La Femme de trente ans*), possesses special attributes that set him apart from other men. The magnetic eyes of Vautrin and his forebears are forever divining the thoughts of others. The indomitable will of Balzac's noble outlaws effortlessly removes all obstacles in their paths. Rastignac senses that Vautrin, while assuming the inscrutable mien of a sphinx that "sees everything, knows everything, but says nothing," can probe the feelings of others and read their hearts (II, 929); Ferragus, who darts magnetic glances at his enemies, can see and foresee all thoughts (V, 45); and the pirate who seeks shelter at the home of General d'Aiglemont "charms" (Balzac underscores the verb to emphasize its double meaning) the daughter of his host with the "magnetic force" of his gaze (II, 803). These men, who share with mesmerist wizards a personal magnetism endowing them with an iron will, possess the clairvoyant vision and the herculean strength that ordinary persons can also acquire under exceptional circumstances.

Like Madame Fontaine, the undisputed oracle of the Marais who stores up her mental energy for séances with clients, Vautrin and his kinsmen can become the privileged mediums of a sublime intelligence that has "wings to cover distances" and the "all-seeing eyes of a god" (VI, 628). And like Madame de Sérizy, who is so provoked by the news of Lucien de Rubempré's suicide that she musters up the energy to snap the iron bars of his prison cell with her bare hands, they can marshal their inner resources at will and accomplish remarkable feats of strength. Dr. Bouvard, "patriarch of the doctrine of animal magnetism," supplies an explanation for this miracle:

> Under the sway of passion, which is willpower focused on a single point and brought to an immeasurable degree of brute force—as various types of electrical currents may be—man can channel all his vital energy . . . into any one of his organs.[36]

While Madame Fontaine and Madame de Sérizy have only a fixed supply of this vital power and can only mobilize it on isolated occasions, men such as Vautrin possess a nearly unlimited quantity of will and can expend it at their pleasure.

If magnetism gives these men the ability to read thoughts and to perform heroic physical labors, then it is electricity that grants them the power to immobilize the will of others. When Hélène's eyes meet the bright, sparkling gaze of the mysterious stranger with whom she later elopes, she is jolted by "the same kind of shock that one would receive . . . from touching a Leyden jar" (II, 806). The fugitive's smoldering

[36] "Sous l'empire de la passion, qui est la volonté ramassée sur un point et arrivée à des quantités de force animale incalculables, comme le sont toutes les différentes espèces de puissances électriques, l'homme peut apporter sa vitalité tout entière . . . dans tel ou tel de ses organes." (V, 1,028)

eyes can even stir up a miniature thunderstorm: the gleam of intelligence and will radiating from his visage strikes like a "flash of lightning" and overwhelms Hélène with the "force of a thunderbolt" (II, 796). So benumbing is his electrifying appearance that those around him yield without a struggle to a mysterious torpor that overcomes them in his presence. They willingly comply with his most outrageous demands. Vautrin dazes Lucien de Rubempré with the same kind of paralyzing force. He fixes on him "one of those penetrating gazes by which the will of the strong is made to enter the souls of the weak" (V, 725). This spellbinding gaze has the effect of completely checking his protégé's resistance. Like the "eye of the basilisk" and the "gaze of the serpent," it succeeds in completely captivating those who are exposed to it.

The power wielded by these titanic criminals is charged with ambivalent meaning. By granting to Vautrin, Ferragus, and the pirate both the divine faculties of somnambulist mediums and the diabolical attributes of mesmerists, Balzac betrays a divided attitude toward them. Somnambulist mediums, as the narrator of *Cousin Pons* observes, are "the chosen vessels into which God pours the elixirs that astonish mankind" (VI, 628). Such magical elixirs invest these mediums with providential powers rivaling those of prophets and saints. In the case of Vautrin, Balzac even slyly drops clues that might lead overzealous critics to identify this rebel with the Savior: the name "Trompe-la-Mort," the stories of Vautrin's sacrificial sufferings, and Jacques Collin's initials would all support such a view.[37] But more often than not, Balzac takes pains to emphasize the diabolical ends to which Vautrin and his confrères apply their powers. Drawing on the romantic interpretation of Milton's Satan, he depicts these rebels against society as fallen angels

[37] Donald Fanger suggests these analogies which, he believes, are purely ironic. See *Dostoevsky and Romantic Realism: A Study of Dostoevsky in Relation to Balzac, Dickens, and Gogol* (Cambridge, Mass.: Harvard University Press, 1965), p. 54.

and infernal geniuses who share the unlimited knowledge and power of gods and demons.[38] Like the fiendish mesmerists in the tales of Hoffmann, they use men as pawns to satisfy their own ambitions.

Unlike Gobseck and the antiquarian, Vautrin is not content with merely setting the stage for his cast of characters and passively watching the events of the tragic plot that he sets in motion. His words to Lucien—shortly before he lures the poet into a highly equivocal partnership—reveal the true scope of his aspirations:

> I want to love what I have created, to shape it, and to mold it to my purposes so that I may love it as a father loves his child. I shall ride in your carriage, my son. I shall delight in your success with women. I shall say: —I am that handsome young man! I have created the Marquis de Rubempré and placed him in the aristocratic world; his greatness is my work.[39]

In the final analysis, he takes possession of Lucien, body and soul: "That man, at once worthless and sublime, unknown yet renowned, but above all consumed with a fever for life, lived again in the graceful body of Lucien, whose soul had become his own" (V, 725).[40]

Vautrin ultimately lives up to his name "Trompe-la-

[38] For a discussion of Vautrin's satanic traits, see Besser, *Balzac's Concept of Genius*, pp. 155-157. Mario Praz considers the literary descendants of Milton's Satan in his chapter "The Metamorphoses of Satan," *The Romantic Agony*, trans. Angus Davidson, 2d ed. (London: Oxford University Press, 1970), pp. 55-94.

[39] "Je veux aimer ma créature, la façonner, la pétrir à mon usage, afin de l'aimer comme un père aime son enfant. Je roulerai dans ton tilbury, mon garçon, je me réjouirai de tes succès auprès des femmes, je dirai: —Ce beau jeune homme, c'est moi! ce marquis de Rubempré, je l'ai créé et mis au monde aristocratique; sa grandeur est mon oeuvre." (IV, 1,032)

[40] See Max Milner, "La Poésie du mal chez Balzac," *L'Année Balzacienne* (Paris: Garnier, 1963), pp. 321-335, for a description of the exceptional status that Vautrin occupies in the *Comédie humaine*.

Mort." Of all the characters in the *Comédie humaine,* he alone experiences every sensation and knows every emotion without letting passion sap his vital energy. Embracing all contradictions, he seems to figure in the minds of some critics as the exceptional being who proves the rule by which Balzac's universe operates. But facile reasoning of this kind cannot adequately explain how Vautrin acquires the superabundant supply of vital energy that allows him to usurp the powers of gods and demons. For the solution to this problem, we must turn again to a metaphysician of the will—the elderly physician in "Les Martyrs ignorés." This man exercises so authoritative an influence over one of his patients that, as he puts it, "his will, that splendid quality of man, no longer belonged to him, but to me! I could draw on it as if it were my own" (X, 1,152).

In *Le Centenaire,* one of Balzac's earliest literary efforts, the four-hundred-year-old Béringheld remains alive as long as he can find new persons willing to supply him with an undefined vital substance that he needs to sustain his existence. While Béringheld can only obtain this elixir of life by killing men, Vautrin thrives on the vital energy that he draws from living creatures. Though not a vampire in the literal sense of the term, he nonetheless feeds on the lifeblood of his victims, and through them, he achieves near immortality in Balzac's world.

V

In the vast majority of the ninety-odd novels and stories that Balzac wrote, a reader is likely to encounter the arresting gaze of a man who engages the attention of others, understands the deepest secrets of their hearts, and conquers all opposition to his own desires. Not surprisingly, a sparkling gaze and magnetic eyes can also kindle love and exert an irresistible erotic attraction. Rodolphe, the hero of a story told in *Albertus Savarus,* shoots a compelling gaze along a "current of love" in order to command the attention of the woman he loves:

> Rodolphe . . . stared at the princess and flashed at her a gaze that was firm, steady, captivating, and charged with a will permeated by the feeling we call *desire*, but expressing itself in the form of a powerful command. Did that burning gaze reach Francesca? . . . After a few minutes, she cast a glance at the door as if attracted by this current of love. Her eyes, without a moment's hesitation, met Rodolphe's gaze.[41]

Dr. Minoret tells his niece Ursule Mirouët that some women require proof of affection before love conquers them, though others, stirred by a "magnetic attraction," are possessed of it in an instant. In *The Old Maid* (*La Vieille Fille*), love strikes Suzanne with the force and speed of a thunderbolt. When the eyes of Athanase come to rest upon her, they emit an electrical spark that delivers a "blow of love" (IV, 240).[42]

Just as certain exceptional beings have at their disposal a surplus of mental energy that expresses itself as will, others possess an abundant supply of electrical and magnetic fluid that fires the passions. "How did she get the name 'Torpedo'?" Vautrin asks Rastignac when the lovely Esther Gobseck makes an appearance with Lucien at an opera ball. And Rastignac, recognizing the voice of his former

[41] "Rodolphe . . . regarda la princesse en dardant sur elle ce regard fixe, persistant, attractif et chargé de toute la volonté humaine concentrée dans ce sentiment appelé *désir*, mais qui prend alors le caractère d'un violent commandement. La flamme de ce regard atteignait-elle Francesca? . . . Au bout de quelques minutes, elle coula un regard vers la porte comme attirée par ce courant d'amour, et ses yeux, sans hésiter, se plongèrent dans les yeux de Rodolphe." (I, 799)

[42] See also Balzac, *Sténie ou les erreurs philosophiques*, ed. A. Prioult (Paris: Georges Courville, 1936), pp. 49, 53, 153. Françoise Frangi holds that the system of metaphors in Balzac's "La Duchesse de Langeais" mirrors the author's philosophical views. Her argument can, I believe, be extended to the entire range of Balzac's works. See "Sur 'La Duchesse de Langeais,'" *L'Année Balzacienne* (Paris: Garnier, 1971), pp. 235-252.

fellow lodger from the *Maison-Vauquer*, tells him that this woman has earned the name "Torpedo" (or electrical ray, as it is known today) because she is "so attractive that she would have benumbed Napoleon, and that she could benumb someone even more difficult to seduce: you!" (V, 670). Whenever Esther waves her "magic wand," Blondet remarks, she releases the purely carnal desires normally kept in check by men.

Henri de Marsay prides himself on the same kind of alluring charm and seductive grace that Esther commands. Taking a stroll one day on the Terrasse des Feuillants, he comes face to face with a ravishing young woman who, upon looking into his eyes, becomes transfixed by a shock so paralyzing that it rivets the soles of her feet to the ground. Reporting the incident to a friend, de Marsay suavely comments: "I have often produced effects of that kind. They are the result of a form of animal magnetism that becomes especially powerful when elective affinities come into play" (V, 278). But his victim, the "girl with the golden eyes," brandishes the same weapon that he takes such delight in wielding. At their first rendezvous, she presses his hand with such passionate significance that he feels a "shock from an electrical spark" pass through his frame.

These sparks of love, generated by passion and desire, are cast into the soul of the beloved, where they kindle a blaze that produces a dazzling flood of light. For Suzanne in *La Vieille Fille*, such a light disperses the dim shadows obscuring her future and grants insight into her destiny. The narrator of *Cousine Bette* recognizes that love infallibly bestows on women the gift of second sight:

> A woman in love is, by virtue of her rapport with the beloved, in the position of a somnambulist to whom the magnetizer has given the unfortunate gift of knowing as a woman (when she has ceased to serve as a mirror of the world) what she became aware of as a somnam-

bulist. Passion induces in a woman's nervous system that ecstatic state in which presentiment is as acute as the vision of seers.[43]

For some women, the clairvoyance of passion brings only anguish in its train, but for Ursule Mirouët it provides the assurance that her love for Savinien will eventually prevail. Ursule and Savinien both prophesy the future in their dreams, divine each other's thoughts even when separated by vast distances, and share the same vision of the future. It is ultimately Ursule's special talent as a medium that thwarts the designs of her rapacious relatives and brings to pass one of the rare happy endings in Balzac's *Comédie humaine*.

If Balzac was obliged to his father for an abiding interest in physiology, heredity, and macrobiotics, then it was to his mother that he owed a fascination with mystical doctrines. Laure de Balzac stirred the imagination of her son by introducing him to the teachings of Swedenborg, Saint-Martin, and Mesmer and by transmitting to him her own confidence in divination and other occult arts. Balzac himself never made a secret of his faith in mediums as mentors in both spiritual and physical matters; he did not hesitate to consult local oracles about the site of buried treasure, the cause of a painful laceration, and, more generally, about his own prospects for the future.[44] Balzac, as Gautier notes, was captivated by chiromancy, cartomancy, oneiromancy, and almost every other form of divination.[45] With Madame de Girardin, who later served as Hugo's guide to the occult

[43] "Une femme aimante est, par rapport à l'homme aimé, dans la situation d'une somnambule à qui le magnétiseur donnerait le triste pouvoir, en cessant d'être le miroir du monde, d'avoir conscience, comme femme, de ce qu'elle aperçoit comme somnambule. La passion fait arriver les forces nerveuses de la femme à cet état extatique où le pressentiment équivaut à la vision des Voyants." (VI, 340)

[44] V. S. Pritchett, *Balzac* (New York: Knopf, 1973), p. 133.

[45] Gautier, *Portraits contemporains*, p. 125.

sciences, he set out to explore the regions opened to him by spiritualism.

In *Ursule Mirouët* Balzac turned his attention to what even he designated the mystical features of mesmerism. The narrator of that novel traces the history of animal magnetism from its origins in Egypt, Chaldea, Greece, and India, through its revival in the miraculous cures performed by Jesus and his disciples, to its final rebirth in eighteenth-century Paris. Like all great discoveries, he reports, animal magnetism encountered considerable resistance from the scientific establishment and the church—two institutions that saw in its practice a formidable challenge to their own teachings. Its most outspoken advocates were persecuted and sent into exile as the result of a conspiracy spearheaded by physicians, priests, and magistrates.

Dr. Bouvard, one of the main targets of the campaign mounted against mesmerism, makes a brief appearance in *Ursule Mirouët*. Bouvard's longstanding friendship with Dr. Minoret had ended as the result of a dispute over magnetic cures. After retiring to Nemours to raise his niece Ursule, Minoret receives a note from his old friend urging him to come to Paris immediately, for Bouvard is now prepared to offer incontrovertible evidence that magnetism will soon become "one of the most important sciences" (III, 319). The letter arouses Minoret's curiosity. He sets out for Paris, where he first makes an appointment with Bouvard, then consults his former colleagues to determine whether Mesmer's disciples have in fact succeeded in acquiring influence over the Faculty of Medicine. The physicians assure him that animal magnetism, now classified with prestidigitation under the category of "amusing physics," does not pose the slightest threat to their profession. The skeptical Minoret nonetheless keeps his appointment with Bouvard. He agrees to visit a Swedenborgian mesmerist who has been credited with taming even the most rebellious will and whose reputation for inducing profound somnambulist trances is unrivaled. Minoret's doubts about the miracles of animal magnetism are completely dispelled by the performance of this mesmerist and his medium. Returning to Nemours, he broods over the "collapse of all his previous ideas on physiology, nature, and metaphysics" (III, 329).

What finally persuades Minoret to abandon his prejudices against magnetism and his indifference to religion is his inability to challenge the telepathic powers of the Swedenborgian's medium. This woman's mind, dwelling in an "invisible world" where "distances and physical obstacles have ceased to exist" (III, 322), can transport itself to Nemours in an instant to eavesdrop on Ursule and to divine her most intimate thoughts. The astonishing accuracy of the medium's pronouncements leads Minoret to recover his faith in a spiritual world and, more specifically, to convert to Catholicism. After his death, he appears to Ursule in the form of a disembodied spirit and, proving that he has learned the secrets of the Swedenborgian's art, mesmerizes his niece. Leading her soul through space and time, he allows her to witness the sordid deeds performed by Minoret-Levrault, the man who sought to cheat Ursule of her godfather's inheritance.

The marvels of animal magnetism restore Minoret's inheritance to its rightful owner and—what is even more astonishing—allow at least one Balzacian heroine to live happily ever after. As if to tone down this cheerful outcome, Balzac added a cautionary note to his tale:

> If you happen to see on the Champs-Elysées one of those charming little low carriages called *escargots* . . . and stop to admire a pretty young blond . . . gently leaning against a handsome young man—if then you are seized by a feeling of envy, remember that this handsome young couple, smiled on by God, has paid in advance its share of life's miseries.[46]

[46] "Quand, en voyant passer aux Champs-Elysées une de ces charmantes petites voitures basses appelées *escargots*, . . . vous y admirez

Balzac the novelist instinctively shied away from describing happiness and tranquillity. If the plots of his novels do not in themselves provide sufficient evidence to substantiate this view, then we need only glance at the heading for one section of *Splendeurs et misères des courtisanes*: "A boring chapter, for it describes four years of happiness."

Ursule Mirouët was not one of Balzac's most successful novels, nor did it figure among the author's favorite works. Balzac found Vautrin, the sinister man of genius with his magnetic charm and superhuman will, a far more congenial medium for his talents than Ursule Mirouët, the noble child of sweet resignation, gentle beauty, and homespun virtues. A Vautrin possesses the robust constitution and strength of will to stir up passions and to throw an entire society into disarray, while an Ursule Mirouët, with her passive disposition and clairvoyant vision, can only practice submission and occasionally use her powers to disentangle a plot. Vautrin, the self-avowed artist of the *Comédie humaine*, gives us melodrama, the *splendeurs et misères* of human existence; the story of Ursule provides a picture of life painted in pastels.

Balzac clearly favored the "poetry of evil" and endowed its leading exponent in the *Comédie humaine* with an energy, will, and passion of nearly transcendent dimensions. He himself harbored the same demiurgic aspirations that move Vautrin and cultivated in his personal life precisely those faculties so highly developed in Vautrin. The narrator of "Facino Cane" also rises to the privileged status accorded to men of will. "My powers of observation," he reports, "have taken on a clairvoyant character. I can see into a soul, but I do not neglect the body." This gift of second sight allows him to participate in the lives of those who

---

une jolie femme blonde . . . légèrement appuyée sur un beau jeune homme; si vous étiez mordu par un désir envieux, pensez que ce beau couple, aimé de Dieu, a d'avance payé sa quote-part aux malheurs de la vie." (III, 478-479)

catch his fancy. He can actually assume their identity, just as "the dervish in the *Arabian Nights* can pass into a body or soul after repeating a set formula" (VI, 66). Both Vautrin and the narrator of "Facino Cane" are invested with the most desirable traits of the *voyant* and the voyeur. Like Louis Lambert and Ursule Mirouët, they have clairvoyant powers; like Gobseck and the antiquarian, they can experience the entire spectrum of human emotions without exhausting their supply of vital energy.

Through the act of writing, Balzac believed that he could still experience—if only vicariously—the passions and desires that provide a rich existence without depleting his own store of vital energy. As he told the somewhat incredulous Théophile Gautier, unflagging dedication to writing, in conjunction with sexual abstinence, heightens the creative potential of an artist and confers special powers upon him.[47] To Madame de Berny, he confided that a regimen of hard work and constant self-denial had provided him with vast magnetic reserves, which he offered to tap in order to improve her own health.[48] But ironically the very regimen that was to prolong Balzac's life and endow him with magical powers sapped his energy and no doubt greatly shortened his life. The laws prevailing in the world of the *Comédie humaine* simply did not obtain in the world actually inhabited by Balzac.

[47] Gautier, *Portraits contemporains*, pp. 71-72.

[48] *Lettres à l'étrangère*, IV, 120.

CHAPTER 6

Masters and Slaves: The Creative Process in Hawthorne's Fiction

"He has made a slave of me with his looks. He has forced me to understand him, without his saying a word; and he has forced me to keep silence, without his uttering a threat."—Dickens, *The Mystery of Edwin Drood*

During the 1830s French magnetizers crossed the Channel and subsequently sailed the Atlantic to the United States. Both Englishmen and Americans learned the tricks of the mesmerist trade from these Gallic itinerants who were perpetually in search of new audiences for their sleeping beauties and clairvoyant maidens. A vast literature on mesmerism, ranging from household manuals outlining therapeutic procedures to learned disquisitions on magnetic and bioelectrical fluids, initiated both laymen and scholars into the secrets of those showmen.

Dr. John Elliotson, the most prominent of the English converts to the new science imported from France, originally intended to use it strictly for medical purposes. But an appetite for publicity soon led him to explore the more exotic features of mesmerism. When Elliotson opened the amphitheater of the London University College Hospital to the public for the magnetic experiments he was performing on the O'key sisters, the council of the hospital took action to stop him. Elliotson countered by tendering his resignation. Despite the views of his colleagues, he continued to use mesmerism in his medical practice and to champion its use as an anesthetic in surgical operations. His private séances and public pronouncements on the miracles of magnetism came to provide entertainment for such eminent Victorians as Dickens, Carlyle, Thackeray, and Tennyson.[1]

The so-called mesmeric mania in England was, by French standards, quite tame. Mesmerism nonetheless found its way into the novels of Bulwer-Lytton, where it mingled with alchemy and other occult sciences. It also inspired Shelley's "Magnetic Lady to Her Patient" and became a perennial topic of discussion in the correspondence between Elizabeth Barrett and Robert Browning. Harriet Martineau's *Letters on Mesmerism* created more than a literary sensation. On the advice of Bulwer-Lytton and other friends, Miss Martineau had turned to mesmerist therapy in 1844 with the hope of finding relief from an illness that had kept her an invalid for more than five years. Restored to health by a professional therapist, she gave mesmerism full credit for her dramatic recovery. *The Zoist: A Journal of Cerebral Physiology and Mesmerism,* founded by Elliotson in 1843, rejoiced in her effusions. Mesmerism, it reported, had finally become the topic of the day. Charlotte Brontë's response to Miss Martineau's proselytizing captured the dominant mood. "You ask whether Miss Martineau made me a convert to mesmerism?" she wrote James Taylor. "Scarcely; yet I heard miracles of its efficacy and could hardly discredit the whole of what was told me. I even underwent a personal experiment."[2]

[1] On Elliotson and his role in stimulating mesmerist activity in England, see Fred Kaplan, *Dickens and Mesmerism: The Hidden Springs of Fiction* (Princeton, N.J.: Princeton University Press, 1975), pp. 14-16, 20-68, and Arno L. Bader, "Those Mesmeric Victorians," *Colophon,* NS3 (1938), 335-353.

[2] For an analysis of mesmerist themes in Bulwer-Lytton's *A Strange Story,* see Robert Lee Wolff, *Strange Stories and Other Explorations in Victorian Fiction* (Boston: Gambit, 1971), pp. 265-322. Note especially the comparisons he draws between Balzac's *Louis Lambert* and Bulwer-Lytton's novel (pp. 315-320). Over a dozen references to mesmerism

In the very year when Harriet Martineau was dilating on the healing powers of mesmerism, Charles Dickens decided to try his hand at animal magnetism. Elliotson instructed him in the new art and introduced him to other authorities, among them the Reverend Chauncy Hare Townshend (whose *Facts in Mesmerism* was to serve as Poe's vademecum in things mesmeric). Dickens became fascinated by the idea that one person could cast a spell on another. Testing his gifts on Madame de la Rue, the wife of a Swiss banker living in Genoa, he discovered that he possessed a "visual ray" of extraordinary strength. For over a year he used his mesmeric powers with salutary effect—despite the protestations of his wife, Catherine—both at Madame de la Rue's bedside and at a distance. Dickens' personal experience with mesmerism came to be mirrored in his fictional world. Literary critics have investigated mesmerism to elucidate *The Mystery of Edwin Drood,* to examine the psychic control exercised by characters in *Barnaby Rudge,* and to understand the moments of insight experienced by figures in *Nicholas Nickleby, David Copperfield,* and *Little Dorrit.*[3]

---

appear in *The Letters of Robert Browning and Elizabeth Barrett Barrett: 1845-46,* ed. Elvan Kintner, 2 vols. (Cambridge, Mass.: Harvard University Press, Belknap Press, 1969). A poem of Browning's entitled "Mesmerism" is discussed by Jerome M. Schneck in "Robert Browning and Mesmerism," *Bulletin of the Medical Library Association,* 44 (1956), 443-451. Harriet Martineau's letters on mesmerism appeared in *The Athenaeum,* 23 November 1844, pp. 1,070-1,072; 30 November 1844, pp. 1,093-1,094; 7 December 1844, pp. 1,117-1,118; 14 December 1844, pp. 1,144-1,146; 21 December 1844, pp. 1,173-1,174. On her mesmerist cure see R. K. Webb, *Harriet Martineau: A Radical Victorian* (New York: Columbia University Press, 1960), pp. 226-253, and Wolff, *Strange Stories,* pp. 87-92. Charlotte Brontë's remarks on mesmerism appear in *The Brontës: Their Lives, Friendships and Correspondence,* ed. Thomas James Wise and John Alexander Symington, 4 vols. (Oxford: Shakespeare Head Press, 1932), III, 200.

[3] See Arthur J. Cox, "'If I hide my watch—,'" *Dickens Studies,* 3 (1967), 22-37, and Aubrey Boyd, "A New Angle on the Drood Mystery," *Washington University Studies,* 9 (1921), 35-85. Fred Kaplan's *Dickens*

In America, mesmerism enjoyed much the same notoriety that it had won in England and on the Continent. The Marquis de Lafayette, a charter member of the Parisian Society of Harmony, had tried as early as 1784 to establish mesmerist enclaves in the New World. In the rituals of the Shakers and in the tribal dances of American Indians he found evidence that mesmerism was not simply a figment of the European imagination. Lafayette sought without much success to enlist George Washington's support for the mesmerist cause. Mesmer himself, who had authorized the French general to disclose his secrets to Washington, was confident that the leader of the American Revolution would be "interested in the fate of every revolution that has for its object the good of humanity." Yet Washington remained politely indifferent to the petition of his French ally.[4]

Mesmerism did not take root in the American imagination until nearly half a century later, when Charles Poyen (who had learned about animal magnetism while studying medicine in Paris) toured New England with his trance-maidens.[5] Poyen at first encountered widespread resistance. American audiences seemed firmly opposed to his view that "phenomena once attributed to the action of the devil" in fact resulted from a "peculiar modification of the nervous

---

and Mesmerism gives a vivid account of the episode with Madame de la Rue (pp. 74-105) and identifies a variety of mesmerist themes in Dickens's novels.

[4] The text of Lafayette's letter to Washington on mesmerism and the correspondence between Washington and Mesmer appear in Vincent Buranelli, *The Wizard from Vienna* (New York: Coward, McCann & Geoghegan, 1975), pp. 154-155. For an account of Lafayette's mesmerist activities, see Robert Darnton, *Mesmerism and the End of the Enlightenment in France* (Cambridge, Mass.: Harvard University Press, 1968), and Ernst Benz, *Franz Anton Mesmer (1734-1815) und seine Ausstrahlung in Europa und Amerika* (Munich: Wilhelm Fink, 1976), pp. 88-93.

[5] Eric T. Carlson, "Charles Poyen Brings Mesmerism to America," *Journal of the History of Medicine and Allied Sciences*, 15 (1960), 121-132.

system and brain."[6] But Poyen was not easily discouraged. At the end of an eighteen-month lecture tour, he reflected with satisfaction that mesmerism had become "the most stirring topic of conversation among all classes of society."[7] In New England alone, at least forty men had taken up mesmerizing and were testing their skills on some two hundred mediums.

Phineas Parkhurst Quimby, whose healing powers Mary Baker Eddy was to compare with those of Christ, numbered among the spectators at Poyen's performances.[8] So impressed was Quimby by Poyen's theatrics that he closed his watchmaker's shop to become a professional mesmerist. But after nearly a decade of barnstorming, he concluded that the real agent of his cures lay in the faith of his patients and began to practice what he called "mind cures."

In 1862 Mary Baker Eddy arrived in Portland, Maine, to consult Quimby about a "serious spinal affection" that had troubled her from her youth. She provided the celebrated miracle worker with a description of her ailment and learned from him that her disease drew its strength from the unenlightened views of her physicians. After several sessions during which Quimby prescribed confidence in his methods, Mrs. Eddy recovered her health. She shortly published a statement in the *Portland Evening Courier* expressing her gratitude to the former watchmaker.[9] But four years later, soon after his death, Mrs. Eddy disputed the charge that her teachings derived from Quimby's method of healing. Ada-

[6] Charles Poyen, *Progress of Animal Magnetism in New England* (Boston: Weeks, Jordan, 1837), pp. 28-29.

[7] Ibid., p. 35.

[8] Brief accounts of Quimby's career appear in Stefan Zweig, *Die Heilung durch den Geist: Mesmer, Mary Baker-Eddy, Freud* (Vienna: Reichner, 1936), pp. 165-174, and in Bader, "Those Mesmeric Victorians," pp. 348-349.

[9] The full text of Mrs. Eddy's letter appears in Hugh A. Studdert Kennedy, *Mrs. Eddy: Her Life, Her Work and Her Place in History* (San Francisco: Farallon, 1947), p. 112.

mantly protesting that she had laid the foundations of Christian Science long before her encounter with "mind cures," she declared that Quimby's use of mesmerism disqualified him as the founder of mental healing. His name was subsequently struck from her writings. Mrs. Eddy's tirades against "malicious animal magnetism"—for her the touchstone of evil in the universe—betray the fear that opponents of her doctrines might detect the pervasive influence of animal magnetism on her own amalgamation of Christian faith healing and what she termed the science of the mind.[10]

Andrew Jackson Davis, celebrated in his own day as the "Poughkeepsie Seer," provided the decisive impulse for the American spiritualist movement. Davis obtained his introduction to animal magnetism through lectures delivered by Dr. J. S. Grimes, a professor of medical jurisprudence who had been deeply impressed by Poyen's shows. Grimes's first discourse on mesmerism generated considerable excitement in Poughkeepsie and inspired a tailor named William Levingston to test his own magnetic prowess. The experiment met with success, for his subject, the young Andrew Jackson Davis, displayed extraordinary clairvoyant powers. While on a professional tour in 1845, Davis made the acquaintance of a physician and of a minister who waxed enthusiastic over his gifts as a medium. He later appointed Dr. Lyon his personal magnetizer and the Reverend Fishbaugh his scribe for a series of lectures that he intended to dictate in a somnambulist trance. The result, eight hundred pages of misty metaphysical chatter on science, religion, love, and the spiritual world, was published in 1847 and, despite its forbidding size and price, met with nearly unparalleled suc-

[10] See especially the chapter entitled "Animal Magnetism" in *Science and Health*, 2d ed. (Boston: Armstrong, 1904), pp. 100-106. Mark Twain casts doubt on Mary Baker Eddy's authorship of *Science and Health* in a highly entertaining tirade against mental healing. See *Christian Science* (New York: Harper & Brothers, 1907).

cess. Thirty-four editions rolled from the presses in the next thirty years.[11]

The Principles of Nature, Her Divine Revelations, and A Voice to Mankind established Davis as the dean of American spiritualism. In his ponderous discourse on the origins of the universe, Davis hailed the dawning of a new era in which "the interiors of men" would be "opened" to enjoy the spiritual communion now accorded only to inhabitants of Mars, Jupiter, and Saturn.[12] Davis extended the authority of clairvoyants by declaring that they not only possess diagnostic gifts, but also have the ability to communicate with spirits from another world. The band of disciples that rallied around him published the *Univercoelum*, a journal that reported Davis's own revelations and initially devoted attention to dreams, somnambulism, and prophecy. Within a year, however, its focus shifted to social reform. Just as many of Mesmer's disciples shared the conviction that the regenerative power of the mesmerist trance signaled the possibility of restoring harmony within the body politic, so many American spiritualists believed that messages from another world foretold the removal of obstacles to social reform. The spiritualist movement and the various socialist and utopian groups that proliferated in America during the 1840s sounded much the same tone of millennial expectation and philanthropic zeal.

The doctrines Poyen brought with him from France were reshaped and infused with new meaning by American spiritualists and mental healers. The first literary reactions to spiritualism almost without exception took the form of parody and farce.[13] The "mysterious tickings" in Melville's

[11] Frank Podmore, *Modern Spiritualism: A History and a Criticism*, 2 vols. (London: Methuen, 1902), I, 168.

[12] Andrew Jackson Davis, *The Principles of Nature, Her Divine Revelations, and A Voice to Mankind*, 12th ed. (New York: Partridge and Brittan, 1855), pp. 675-676.

[13] Howard Kerr, *Mediums, and Spirit-Rappers, and Roaring Radicals: Spiritualism in American Literature, 1850-1900* (Urbana: Univer-

"Apple-Tree Table," the "disembodied Esquimaux" of James Russell Lowell's "The Unhappy Lot of Mr. Knott," and the spiritual mischief in Twain's *Huckleberry Finn* bear witness to that trend. In American literature, animal magnetism was practiced chiefly by such figures as the king and the duke, who tackle "missionarying, and mesmerizing, and doctoring, and telling fortunes" as they accompany Jim and Huck on their travels down the Mississippi.[14]

Melville, Poe, and Hawthorne were among the few American writers to extract some of the original meaning from the garbled mass of literature that had taken Mesmer's teaching as a point of departure. When the narrator of *Moby Dick* declares that Ahab "would fain have shocked . . . the same fiery emotion accumulated within the Leyden jar of his own magnetic life" into Starbuck, Stubb, and Flask, or notes that Ahab "kept his magnet at Starbuck's brain," he speaks the language of the will found in Balzac's novels.[15] It is in *Pierre; or, The Ambiguities*, however, that Melville used magnetism and electricity to greatest effect. The "electrical presentiments" and "electric insight" of the titular hero prepare the way for his encounter with the enchanting Isabel Banford. Pierre is almost deprived of consciousness when Isabel sweeps her curls over the "strange sparks" that quiver along the strings of her guitar. To his "dilated senses" Isabel appears to "swim in an electrical current"; the "vivid buckler of her brow" seems like a "magnetic plate." Isabel uses her powers to inspire in Pierre an erotic attraction that explains the "ambiguities" that figure in the subtitle of the novel:

---

sity of Illinois Press, 1972). See especially his chapters " 'Knocks for the Knockings': Humorous Literary Reactions to Spiritualism," pp. 22-54, and " 'Sperits Couldn't a Done Better': Mark Twain and Spiritualism," pp. 155-189.

[14] Mark Twain, *The Adventures of Huckleberry Finn* (New York: Harper & Brothers, 1929), p. 290.

[15] Herman Melville, *Moby Dick; or, The Whale*, 2 vols. (New York: Russell & Russell, 1963), I, 207, 266.

> For over all these things, and interfusing itself with the sparkling electricity in which she seemed to swim, was an ever-creeping and condensing haze of ambiguities. Often, in after-times with her, did he recall this first magnetic night, and would seem to see that she then had bound him to her by an extraordinary atmospheric spell—both physical and spiritual—which henceforth it had become impossible for him to break, but whose full potency he never recognised till long after he had become habituated to its sway. . . . The physical electricalness of Isabel seemed reciprocal with the heat-lightnings and the ground-lightnings nigh to which it had first become revealed to Pierre. She seemed moulded from fire and air, and vivified at some Voltaic pile of August thunder-clouds heaped against the sunset.[16]

Edgar Allan Poe, in contrast to his literary contemporaries, expressed little interest in animal magnetism as the medium of psychic control. Instead he stressed the cosmic significance of the ethereal fluids investigated by Mesmer and his colleagues.[17] For the spiritualized version of animal magnetism developed by Andrew Jackson Davis he felt little more than contempt. "There surely can*not* be 'more things in Heaven and Earth than are dreamt of' (oh, Andrew Jackson Davis!) 'in *your* philosophy,'" he sneered.[18] Poe was evidently searching for the "truth" of animal magnetism, and he found it recorded in Townshend's *Facts in Mesmerism*. "Whatever doubt may still envelop the *rationale* of

16 Herman Melville, *Pierre; or, The Ambiguities* (New York: Russell & Russell, 1963), pp. 212-213.

17 For interpretations of Poe's mesmerist tales, see Sidney E. Lind, "Poe and Mesmerism," *PMLA*, 62 (1947), 1,077-1,094; Doris V. Falk, "Poe and the Power of Animal Magnetism," *PMLA*, 84 (1969), 536-546; and Vincent Buranelli, "A Note on Poe and Mesmerism," in *The Wizard from Vienna*, pp. 219-226.

18 *The Complete Works of Edgar Allan Poe*, ed. James A. Harrison (New York: Crowell, 1902), XIV, 173. References to Poe's works will hereafter be to this edition.

mesmerism," writes the shrewd narrator of Poe's "Mesmeric Revelation," "its startling *facts* are now almost universally admitted" (V, 241). And the title of "The Facts in the Case of M. Valdemar" again reminds the reader that Poe refused to entertain fanciful psychological or spiritual interpretations of mesmerist views. He wished instead to report "authentic" case histories documenting the power of animal magnetism to provide moments of cosmic insight. In the final analysis, however, Poe's stories of suspended animation—more fantastic and indeed more grisly than most mesmerist tales—require from his readers a state of suspended disbelief.

M. Valdemar and Mr. Vankirk, the mediums of two mesmerist experiments performed by "P," are both men hovering on the brink of death. M. Valdemar, mesmerized *in articulo mortis,* remains in a state of suspended animation for nearly seven months until his physician breaks the spell to find, not the corpse of M. Valdemar, but a "liquid mass of loathsome—of detestable putridity" (VI, 166). Poe's "facts," as one critic notes, are not for the queasy.[19] Animal magnetism is also used in "Mesmeric Revelation" to sustain physical existence, this time for a Mr. Vankirk. Vankirk's voice, however, conveys considerably more information about mesmerism than Valdemar's, which produces only macabre acoustic effects. His pronouncements during the trance confirm the narrator's view that a sleep-waker (Poe borrowed the term from Townshend) perceives "matters beyond the scope of the physical organs" and that his "intellectual faculties are wonderfully exalted and invigorated" (V, 241). "When I am entranced," Vankirk declares, ". . . I perceive external things directly, without organs, through a medium which I shall employ in the ultimate, unorganized life" (V, 250).

The medium, or ether, to which Vankirk refers is identified in Poe's essay *Eureka* as electricity. It figures in that

[19] Daniel Hoffman, *Poe Poe Poe Poe Poe Poe Poe* (New York: Doubleday, 1972), p. 163.

work as the spiritual principle of the universe. To it Poe attributed the phenomena of vitality, consciousness, and thought. Since electricity can, in his view, take on the physical appearance of light, heat, and magnetism, it seems to function as the agent holding physical existence in abeyance for M. Valdemar and providing moments of psychic expansion for Mr. Vankirk.

Poe's "Tale of the Ragged Mountains" recasts once again the theme of electrical rapport between a mesmerist physician and his cadaverous patient. Dr. Templeton, who espoused Mesmer's doctrines during a visit to Paris, treats his acquaintance Bedloe for neuralgia with strong doses of morphine and mesmerism. Bedloe returns one evening from an excursion into the Ragged Mountains near Charlottesville to tell the narrator and Templeton of an eerie vision. In vivid detail he describes a journey to an Oriental city, involvement in a fracas between British soldiers and the natives there, and finally a fatal wound inflicted upon him by a poisoned arrow. After his "death," he felt a "violent and sudden shock . . . , as if of electricity" (V, 173). His soul flitted from the locus of the murder, retraced the path by which it had entered the city, and experienced a second "shock as of a galvanic battery" (IV, 173). When Bedloe concludes his account, Templeton produces a portrait of an old friend—a Mr. Oldeb—who not only bears an uncanny resemblance to Bedloe, but also died under circumstances that replicate those described in his patient's vision. Templeton had in fact been recording the events attending his friend's death at the very moment of Bedloe's vision. A week after these correspondences are brought to light, a newspaper obituary announces Bedloe's death—the result of a poisonous leech accidentally applied to the temple by his physician. It remains only for the narrator to supply one last link to this chain of coincidences: that Bedloe, minus the final "e," is but Oldeb reversed.

It is not entirely clear whether we are dealing with a case of metempsychosis, with a hypnotic suggestion planted by Templeton into Bedloe's mind, or with the revival of a memory through the influence of drugs and hypnosis. In light of Poe's other mesmerist tales, however, it seems likely that Templeton managed to revive his patient Bedloe by mesmerizing him at a distance and thereby sending a current of life-sustaining electrical fluid through his body. That Bedloe relives in his vision the passage from death to life as an electrical shock seems to support such an interpretation.

While a wide range of American authors either drew on mesmerist theories to explain abnormal mental states or poked fun at the rapping spirits summoned by mediums, few of them found in mesmerism a vehicle for expressing serious psychological insights. Nathaniel Hawthorne represents one of the exceptions, and it is to his work that we must turn for an example of the way mesmerist operations serve as metaphors for human relations.

I

Psychological domination and its inevitable concomitant, emotional bondage, constitute obsessive themes in Hawthorne's fiction. Various entries in his notebooks document an enduring interest in master-slave relationships and anticipate the controlling principle of a number of the tales and romances.[20] A passage recorded in 1842, for example, captures the essence of his later preoccupations: "A moral philosopher to buy a slave, or otherwise get possession of a

[20] Claude M. Simpson, ed., *Nathaniel Hawthorne: The American Notebooks* (Columbus: Ohio State University Press, 1972), pp. 170, 226, 237, 253. Passages from Hawthorne's works cited only by volume and page number will hereafter refer to *The Complete Works of Nathaniel Hawthorne*, ed. George Parsons Lathrop, 13 vols. (Boston: Houghton, Mifflin and Co., 1882-83). Whenever possible, however, I quote from *The Centenary Edition of the Works of Nathaniel Hawthorne*, ed. William Charvat et al. (Columbus: Ohio State University Press, 1962-). The letter "C" will precede volume and page references to that edition.

human being, and to use him for the sake of experiment" (C, VIII, 237).

The masters of Hawthorne's early tales are often diabolically shrewd, though shortsighted, scientists who sacrifice "moral slaves"—in many cases their own wives or daughters—to a quest for knowledge and power. In works written after 1850, however, the mesmerist frequently steps into the shoes of the scientist to play the role of the cold, calculating investigator. The substitution is not entirely fortuitous. Despite Hawthorne's deeply rooted aversion to the hocus-pocus of mesmerism, the philosophical claims of this occult science exercised a powerful control over his imagination. The professional mesmerists who toured New England during the 1830s at once fascinated and repelled him.[21] These men appeared to have secured a mysterious psychological power that Hawthorne found intellectually stimulating, though personally offensive. Mesmerism, as F. O. Matthiessen points out, impressed Hawthorne as a modern analogue of witchcraft and black magic.[22] By providing him with a contemporary, native version of the occult, it allowed him to add a supernatural dimension to stories set in the New England of his own day.

A study of two tales in which scientists occupy a central position can shed additional light on Hawthorne's motives for turning his attention to mesmerism. The prototype of the obsessed scientist appears in both "The Birthmark" (1843) and "Rappaccini's Daughter" (1844). Aylmer and Rappaccini conduct experiments that ultimately cause the death of their subjects: Aylmer's wife dies on the operating table, and Rappaccini's daughter perishes at the hands of her father's professional rival.

[21] For a detailed account of Hawthorne's attitude toward the mesmerist vogue in New England, see Ruth Hosmer, "Science and Pseudo-Science in the Writings of Nathaniel Hawthorne," Diss. Univ. of Illinois, 1948.

[22] F. O. Matthiessen, *American Renaissance: Art and Expression in the Age of Emerson and Whitman* (New York: Oxford University Press, 1941), p. 205.

The opening paragraph of "The Birthmark" announces that

> in the latter part of the last century . . . when the comparatively recent discovery of electricity and other kindred mysteries of Nature seemed to open paths into the region of miracle, it was not unusual for the love of science to rival the love of woman in its depth and absorbing energy. The higher intellect, the imagination, the spirit, and even the heart might all find their congenial aliment in pursuits which, as some of their ardent votaries believed, would ascend from one step of powerful intelligence to another, until the philosopher should lay his hand on the secret of creative force and perhaps make new worlds for himself. (II, 47)

Aylmer's scientific zeal is comically disproportionate to the actual goal he seeks. He directs his painstaking research at developing an operation for removing a tiny birthmark from his wife's otherwise unblemished features. Although the operation is a success, his patient dies. The narrator concludes his story by solemnly pronouncing that Aylmer "failed to look beyond the shadowy scope of time, and, living once for all in eternity, to find the perfect future in the present" (II, 69).

The fictional editor and translator of "Rappaccini's Daughter" assures his audience that his tale comes from the pen of a Frenchman and provides an elaborate account of M. de l'Aubépine's voluminous literary production—which includes such telltale works as *Contes deux fois racontées*. More importantly, however, the story he claims to render into English is set in Italy, and the names of the characters (Giacomo Rappaccini, Giovanni Guasconti, Pietro Baglioni) serve as constant reminders that we are located, not in Hawthorne's New England, but rather in Padua at some time in the remote past. No doubt Hawthorne sensed that the climate of the Old World was far more conducive to the esoteric experiments performed by Rappaccini and Baglioni.

"Rappaccini's Daughter" develops a situation analogous to that of "The Birthmark." Again Hawthorne brings to life a scientist who shows greater concern for his career than for his kin. Rappaccini, so his sinister colleague Baglioni tells Giovanni, has no reservations about sacrificing what is "dearest to him."[23] He sets his daughter Beatrice apart from all other women by nourishing her from the day of her birth with poisons and by raising her in a lethal, artificial garden of his own creation. His one concession, though not entirely unselfish, is to allow the handsome Giovanni to participate in Beatrice's tragic isolation. With the hope of purifying Beatrice of evil and neutralizing the poisons in her body, Giovanni conspires with Baglioni to produce a medical antidote for his beloved. But that antidote has a fatal effect on Beatrice and puts an abrupt end to Rappaccini's designs for creating a new Adam and Eve to inhabit his artificial paradise.

Both Aylmer and Rappaccini possess the frigid detachment characteristic of Hawthorne's unpardonable sinners. Attaching greater importance to their scientific ambitions than to moral integrity, they press other persons into the service of their cause and subject them to painful experiments. The strategies of these scientists bear an arresting resemblance to those of artists in Hawthorne's work. Like the artist, the scientist first insulates the subjects of his experiments from other men, then draws them into a sphere where they are entirely under his control, and finally uses his "art" to transform them into objects of contemplation. When Rappaccini approaches Beatrice and Giovanni to bestow on them his ambiguous paternal blessing, he seems to "gaze with a triumphant expression at the beautiful youth and maiden, as might an artist who should spend his life in achieving a picture or a group of statuary and finally be

[23] As Roy R. Male points out, Baglioni's views are colored by the professional enmity between him and Rappaccini. The tender concern that he shows for Giovanni is in fact self-serving. See *Hawthorne's Tragic Vision* (Austin: University of Texas Press, 1957), pp. 58-59.

satisfied with his success" (II, 146). Similarly, Aylmer hopes to improve nature, and when Georgiana consents to participate in his experiment, he ironically alludes to the obverse of his own intention by asserting that "even Pygmalion, when his sculptured woman assumed life, felt not greater ecstasy" (II, 53). The error of these zealots stems from what the narrator of "The Birthmark" defines as an attempt to live in eternity, that is, to translate an aesthetic ideal into reality.

Hawthorne's introductory remarks in "Rappaccini's Daughter" express the fear that his own work is only "the faintest possible counterfeit of real life." In both "The Birthmark" and "Rappaccini's Daughter," he failed to supply rational explanations for supernatural events and to enhance his narrative with the naturalistic detail that characterizes his finest works. The exotic ambience of Rappaccini's garden and of Aylmer's laboratory precluded the possibility of situating the action in a contemporary, realistic environment. Because many of his plots dictated the presence of at least one diabolical villain with supernatural powers, Hawthorne needed a modern counterpart of the obsessed scientist for the tales and romances set in New England. He found this type in the mesmerist wizard, a figure who shares the intellectual attributes of his scientists, but whose science blends the marvelous with the natural. Although the mesmerist's ability to dominate weaker personalities may derive from occult sources, it can also be ascribed to psychological acumen or to personal magnetism. Hawthorne's modern necromancers are invested with the superhuman intelligence of his scientists, but at the same time they possess a degree of psychological realism that is wanting in the portraits of the scientists.

Ethan Brand is the first of Hawthorne's New England necromancers. It has been suggested that knowledge acquired from mesmerist experiments accounts for the "vast intellectual development" that transforms Brand from a lowly laborer into a mental giant.[24] Brand experiments with mankind, "converting man and woman to be his puppets, and pulling the wires that moved them to such degrees of crime as were demanded for his study" (III, 495). The victim of one of his "psychological experiments" is a young woman whose soul is "wasted, absorbed, and perhaps annihilated" in the course of his investigation. The faculty Brand cultivates is not unlike the power that Matthew Maule and Westervelt exercise over their respective mediums in *The House of the Seven Gables* and *The Blithedale Romance*. Using mesmerism to exploit weaker personalities, Maule and Westervelt both violate the sanctity of the human heart to commit what Hawthorne termed the unpardonable sin.

When Sophia Peabody wrote Hawthorne that she was entertaining the possibility of consulting a mesmerist for her chronic headaches, he vigorously protested such a step:

> My spirit is moved to talk to thee today about these magnetic miracles and to beseech thee to take no part in them. I am unwilling that a power should be exercised on thee, of which we know neither the origin nor the consequence, and the phenomena of which seem rather calculated to bewilder us, than to teach us any truths about the present or future state of being. If I possessed such a power over thee, I should not dare to exercise it; nor can I consent to its being exercised by another. Supposing that this power arises from the transfusion of one spirit into another, it seems to me that the sacredness of an individual is violated by it; there would be an intrusion into thy holy of holies.[25]

[24] Randall Stewart, Introd., *The American Notebooks by Nathaniel Hawthorne*, ed. Randall Stewart (New Haven: Yale University Press, 1948), p. lxxv.

[25] *Love Letters of Nathaniel Hawthorne*, 2 vols. (1907; reprint ed. Chicago: The Society of the Dofobs, 1972), II, 62.

Hawthorne, as the final sentence suggests, believed that a mesmerist cure might endanger more than the integrity of Sophia's spirit. It is no accident that the mesmerists of *The House of the Seven Gables* and *The Blithedale Romance* are characterized as men of remarkable physical attractiveness, while their subjects are consistently depicted as defenseless, ethereal virgins. Hawthorne undoubtedly suspected that the psychological prowess of mesmerists derives to a great extent from their sexual magnetism. By introducing the mesmerist theme into his plots, he was able not only to anchor them in a realistic milieu, but also to add an erotic dimension missing from his scientific tales.

Mesmerism proved seductive as a literary topic in one additional sense. For Hawthorne, animal magnetism figured as a potent form of sorcery. It represented one variant of the black magic exercised by the human imagination and its products. "There is witchcraft in these little chains, and wheels, and paddles" (II, 514), Peter Hovenden breathlessly exclaims when he discovers Owen Warland's delicately wrought mechanical butterfly. For Hawthorne, statues and portraits—indeed any genuine work of art—have a profound magical significance.[26] His notebooks refer to the "indefinable spell" (X, 89) of Guido's "Cenci" and attribute occult powers to the painter. At the time Hawthorne was sitting for a portrait, he recalled that before having his first likeness painted, "there was a great bewitchery in the idea, as if it were a magic process" (C, VIII, 492-493). Many of Hawthorne's artists, but especially the sculptor and painter, produce artistic creations that weave a spell over the models and observers of the work alike.

"The Prophetic Pictures" (1837) outlines many of the similarities between artists and mesmerists. The early date of this story makes it unlikely that Hawthorne wrote it with the conscious aim of portraying an artist with mesmeric

[26] For an extensive discussion of the magic work of art, see Millicent Bell, *Hawthorne's View of the Artist* (New York: State University of New York, 1962), pp. 78-91.

gifts. Nonetheless, his description of the artist in that story anticipates the most salient features of his mesmerists and explains why the artist and mesmerist could later be fused into a single figure.

The unnamed artist of "The Prophetic Pictures" has acquired an impressive knowledge of the sciences. His singular talent for "adapting himself to every variety of character" and for capturing through his art the authentic personality of his subjects arouses the suspicion that he is more magician than painter. Before consenting to paint a portrait, he fixes his "piercing eye" on the applicant and seems to "look him through and through." His "penetrative eye" enables him to peer into the soul of his subject and to read its hidden secrets. But, "like all other men around whom an engrossing purpose wreathes itself, he was insulated from the mass of human kind . . . he did not possess kindly feelings; his heart was cold" (I, 206). His portraits of Walter Ludlow and his bride Elinor so faithfully mirror the couple's future sentiments that they become, as the title suggests, "prophetic." A sketch that the artist shows Elinor forecasts a fateful event—Walter on the verge of stabbing Elinor—and infuses the expressions of the finished portraits with a sinister meaning. The artist leaves his "creations" to embark on a long journey. Roaming through the New England wilderness, he is seized by the desire to visit his "portraits" once again and returns to see his prediction fulfilled. Standing on the threshold of the parlor, he watches Elinor and Walter gazing at his paintings. The terror on Elinor's face matches the expression of her portrait; at that very moment Walter abandons himself to "the spell of evil influence that the painter had cast upon the features" (I, 209). When the resemblance to his portrait is complete, he draws his knife to stab Elinor. Clearly relishing the role he has created for himself, the painter thwarts the very destiny that he had adumbrated in his portraits.

The painter of the prophetic pictures embodies many of the distinguishing traits of mesmerists. His ability to control the fate of others by charming them with his eye and his art are the very faculties used by Hawthorne's mesmerists to manipulate weaker intelligences. Like the mesmerist, the painter can read "other bosoms with an acuteness almost preternatural" (I, 207). Yet he too lacks the "key of holy sympathy" that would grant him the right to probe the human heart. There exists in Hawthorne's work one character who is at once mesmerist and artist, but who ultimately renounces hypnotic witchcraft and art in order to embrace the "homely witchcraft" and artfulness of domestic felicity. Holgrave, the "metamorphic hero" of *The House of the Seven Gables*, is the first of Hawthorne's full-scale portraits of the mesmerist.[27]

II

Holgrave is introduced as an "artist in the daguerreotype line." The narrator repeatedly refers to him as "the artist," perhaps not entirely in a patronizing tone, for Holgrave's unembellished images reveal the character of his subjects "with a truth that no painter would ever venture upon." Holgrave has also achieved some measure of literary fame: a sample of his narrative skill appears in his story of Alice Pyncheon. Although he has not yet reached the ripe age of twenty-two, he appears to have distinguished himself in a variety of professions ranging from country schoolmaster to peddler of perfumes. Rumors to the effect that he has delivered a series of lectures on mesmerism confirm Hepzibah's suspicion that he also practices animal magnetism. To Phoebe, Holgrave demonstrates his mesmeric gifts by putting the patriarch of the Pyncheons' hens into a deep sleep. While living at the House of the Seven Gables, this energetic jack-of-all-trades consorts with "reformers, temperance-lecturers, and all manner of cross-looking philanthropists."

[27] I borrow the phrase from Daniel Hoffman's discussion of Holgrave. See *Form and Fable in American Fiction* (New York: Oxford University Press, 1961), pp. 198-201.

In his youthful zeal, he imagines that "this age, more than any other past or future one, is destined to see the tattered garments of Antiquity exchanged for a new suit" (C, II, 180).

Holgrave's concurrent interests in art, mesmerism, and social reform suggest that some connection exists among these three vocations. In the novel that followed *The House of the Seven Gables*, Hawthorne was to develop three separate and distinct characters to represent each of Holgrave's ambitions. Coverdale, Westervelt, and Hollingsworth, the sexual and ideological rivals of *The Blithedale Romance*, can hardly be regarded as refractions of a single personality. Yet Hawthorne clearly perceived an inner affinity among the members of this seemingly incongruous triumvirate, for otherwise he could not have earlier blended their aspirations into the consciousness of a single character. Holgrave's aesthetic theories, his magical powers, and his millennial vision can shed some light on the kinship of art, mesmerism, and social reform.

Holgrave's daguerreotypes can be linked to the many mirrors, statues, and portraits that decorate Hawthorne's fictional world. Like the portraits painted by the artist of "The Prophetic Pictures," his daguerreotypes capture a likeness truer to the character of his clients than the faces they display to the world. It is clearly no accident that the subject of one daguerreotype that Holgrave takes again and again is Jaffrey Pyncheon, nor is it entirely fortuitous that the story he intends to publish in a literary magazine concerns the legend of Alice Pyncheon. Holgrave uses his art to uncover the hidden connections linking his own ancestors to the Pyncheon line. His kinship to the dispossessed Matthew Maule gives him full license to solve the mysteries of the past, but his methods still remain questionable. To Phoebe he declares that his interest in Hepzibah and Clifford stems from the impulse "to look on, to analyze, to explain matters" and to understand the enigmatic drama staged at the House of the Seven Gables over the past two centuries. He claims to be nothing but a "privileged and meet spectator" of this drama. When Phoebe reproaches him for his cold-heartedness, he defends himself by asserting that this attribute, "together with the faculty of mesmerism" (C, II, 217), is in his blood. Holgrave's manner of collecting evidence and piecing together information marks him as an artist rather than a detective. He pays close attention to the events taking place in the House of the Seven Gables and transforms them into a domestic tragedy. The house itself becomes for him a decrepit theater in which Clifford and Hepzibah pathetically struggle through a tedious fourth act. Jaffrey Pyncheon figures as one more addition to his gallery of daguerreotypes, and Alice Pyncheon plays the tragic heroine in his literary art.

When Phoebe first meets Holgrave, she finds him far too aloof for her taste. She feels only his eye and nothing of his heart. The narrator dwells in detail on the power of Holgrave's "deep, thoughtful, all-observant eyes," which contain an expression "not sinister, but questionable" (C, II, 156). And he also takes pains to point out that Holgrave's remote manner and his piercing eye are characteristic of the Maule clan:

> So long as any of the race were to be found, they had been marked out from other men—not strikingly, nor as with a sharp line, but with an effect that was felt, rather than spoken of—by an hereditary character of reserve. . . . The mantle, or rather, the ragged cloak of old Matthew Maule, had fallen upon his children. They were half-believed to inherit mysterious attributes; the family eye was said to possess strange power. (C, II, 26)

Just as Matthew Maule had once been accused of witchcraft and of exercising the "Evil Eye," so Holgrave, Maule's descendant, is thought to dabble in modern witchcraft and to possess a cold, pitiless eye.

Only one other link in the chain of generations connecting Holgrave to Matthew Maule finds mention in the novel.

The grandson of Matthew Maule not only bears the Christian name of his ancestor, but also possesses the extraordinary ocular powers of his grandfather:

> There was a great deal of talk among the neighbors, particularly the petticoated ones, about what they called the witchcraft of Maule's eye. Some said, that he could look into people's minds; others, that, by the marvellous power of this eye, he could draw people into his own mind, or send them, if he pleased, to do errands to his grandfather, in the spiritual world; others again, that it was what is termed an Evil Eye, and possessed the valuable faculty of blighting corn, and drying children into mummies with the heart-burn. (C, II, 189-190)

Although the narrator hints that the younger Matthew Maule's powers are based on nothing but idle gossip, Holgrave presents a different view in his story of Alice Pyncheon. He interprets Maule's hold over Alice as the result of mesmerist skill.

Holgrave launches his story with the report that Gervayse Pyncheon had once unexpectedly summoned Matthew Maule to the House of the Seven Gables. The invitation was extended with the hope of acquiring information about a missing deed for vast territories to the East. After some hard bargaining, Maule confided to Pyncheon that a "clear, crystal medium of a pure and virgin intelligence" —one like that of Alice Pyncheon—would supply the knowledge requisite for locating the missing document. Only after the carpenter fixed his eyes on those of Alice did Pyncheon begin to suspect that the "subtle influence" exercised by Matthew Maule over his daughter might be a form of witchcraft. Maule ostensibly mesmerizes Alice in order to use her mind as a kind of "telescopic medium" for gazing into the spiritual world. But at the same time he succeeds in converting Alice into the vessel of his own will. Alice senses that "a power . . . had laid its grasp upon her maiden soul" and that "a will, most unlike her own, constrained her to do its grotesque and fantastic bidding" (C, II, 208). As Frederick Crews rightly argues, the nature of Maule's power over Alice is "transparently sexual."[28] When Alice first sees Maule, she is impressed by his "remarkable comeliness, strength, and energy." Her submissive attitude toward him during and after the trance is entirely consonant with an unconscious erotic attraction on her part. In her waking state, Alice is convinced that her own sphere is "impenetrable" and that she is immune to Maule's influence. But after shedding the protective shell of consciousness, she succumbs to Maule's will and carries out his bidding in all matters. His control over her ultimately brings about her death.

Just as the sudden and mysterious deaths in the Pyncheon family can be traced to a hereditary illness, and as Old Maule's prophecy derives from a secret knowledge of this physical defect in the Pyncheon line, so the notorious "witchcraft of Maule's eye" can be explained through the sexual and psychological vulnerability of the Pyncheon women to Maule's male descendants. Hawthorne generally provided an alternative, rational explanation for supernatural attributes and marvelous occurrences. Mesmeric control hovers somewhere between the natural and the supernatural. It is at once the psychosexual control of the magnetic personality and the witchcraft of the evil eye. Mesmerism was also especially well suited to the genre that Hawthorne favored. The romance, by Hawthorne's own definition, weds the real to the fantastic: it stimulates the reader's imagination, yet remains within the bounds of the plausible.

The pairing of mesmerist with medium, emblematic of the master-slave relationship, allowed Hawthorne to hint

[28] Frederick Crews, *The Sins of the Fathers: Hawthorne's Psychological Themes* (New York: Oxford University Press, 1966), p. 180.

at the strength of erotic ties, but at the same time to preserve the innocence of the women bound by those ties. Early tales such as "The Birthmark" and "Rappaccini's Daughter" prefigure the relationship between mesmerist and medium by matching a manipulative male scientist with a defenseless female subject. But since such experiments as Aylmer's and Rappaccini's require the consent of their subjects, only wives and daughters—who remain blameless in their acquiescence—qualify as victims. By shifting his focus from scientific experimenters to mesmerist wizards, Hawthorne was able to add a sexual and psychological component to the relationship between diabolical sorcerer and vulnerable maiden. The virginal women in Hawthorne's fiction are receptive to mesmerist influence in part because of their ethereal physical constitutions, but more importantly because of a subconscious attraction to the mesmerist. Overtly they resist enslavement—Hawthorne repeatedly assures his readers that they retain their purity throughout the period of bondage. At the same time, the language used to describe their rapport with the magnetizer is charged with sexual innuendo. Crews maintains that "when Hawthorne . . . takes extraordinary pains to emphasize the asexuality of a girl, he is preoccupied with the general sexuality of women."[29] The very fact that Hawthorne's fair-haired maidens are susceptible to the mesmerist's influence indicates some kind of repressed sexual element in their character.

The episode that follows Holgrave's narration of "Alice Pyncheon" reveals the covert sexuality of Hawthorne's mediums. Holgrave has inherited the penetrating eye of his ancestors, and even though he has sublimated its power into other channels, he still retains a degree of mesmeric control over the Pyncheons. While narrating his story to Phoebe, he mimics the gestures Matthew Maule had used to hypnotize Alice and unwittingly induces a trance in Phoebe.

[29] Crews, *The Sins of the Fathers*, p. 217.

She in turn leans toward him and seems "almost to regulate her breath by his." Holgrave realizes that only a slight increase in the concentration of his will and a wave of the hand are required to consummate his control over her. Even Phoebe's "natural magic" is no match for the black magic of the Maules.

The passive strain in Phoebe's personality, which accounts for her physical predisposition to mesmeric influence, is introduced into the novel through floral imagery. She is an "earthly rosebud," a sister of the garden flowers blossoming on the Pyncheon lands. Such symbolic props require emphasis not only because they underscore Phoebe's docility, but also because they define her relationship to Holgrave. As the caretaker of a small plot on the Pyncheon estate, Holgrave —"either out of love or curiosity"—tends flowers and vegetables. In keeping with his plebeian origins, he acts as laborer and servant to the aristocratic Pyncheons. But Holgrave also checks and controls the growth in the garden, and, like his forebears, he plays master as well as slave. His role as gardener is thus informed by the same kind of ambiguity that characterizes his initial response to Phoebe. When he first meets her, it is not clear whether curiosity or love will dominate his emotions. But once he resists the urge to mesmerize her and relinquishes "the opportunity of acquiring empire over the human spirit," the ethic of love conquers the passion of curiosity.

It should be noted in passing that Hepzibah, the only other female Pyncheon in Hawthorne's romance, endures a painful enslavement that functions as a comic counterpart to Alice Pyncheon's humiliating bondage.[30] Hepzibah

[30] John Caldwell Stubbs suggests that the relationship between Hepzibah and Clifford functions as a tragicomic pendant to the sentimental love affair between Phoebe and Holgrave. By inviting a comparison between the two couples, Hawthorne mitigated the essential banality of his plot. See *The Pursuit of Form: A Study of Hawthorne and the Romance* (Urbana: University of Illinois Press, 1970), pp. 101-119.

greets Holgrave, the first customer to patronize her cent shop, with the mournful complaint that her presence behind the counter constitutes the fulfillment of Maule's curse. And, in fact, the shop bell, which tinkles "as if it were bewitched," appears to be a well-disguised agent of Matthew Maule's sorcery. Hepzibah is an "enslaved spirit"; the shop bell is a "talisman" to which she owes "obedience." It wreaks havoc with her nerves and brings a severe "crisis" upon her. Only through Phoebe's intercession is Hepzibah eventually released from her bondage to this demonic instrument of Maule's curse.

Holgrave's refusal to hypnotize Phoebe paves the way for the resolution of various tensions within the novel. The symbolic union of Holgrave and Phoebe occurs at twilight, a moment when the beams of the ascending moon and the rays of the descending sun strike a perfect balance. The harmonic blending of moonlight and sunshine figures as the setting for the preliminary reconciliation of black magic and natural magic, coldness and warmth, isolation and sympathy, plebeianism and aristocracy. By renouncing psychological control for the redeeming power of love, Holgrave takes a tentative but decisive step toward eradicating the curse of the past. At the same time his utopian projects suffer a grave setback. Now he is convinced that "moonlight, and the sentiment in man's heart, responsive to it, is the greatest of renovators and reformers. And all other reform and renovation . . . will prove to be no better than moonshine!" (C, II, 214). Yielding to Phoebe's charm, he first gives up the mesmerist powers that helped him to unravel the mysteries of the past and then abandons the grand schemes that connected him to the future. Rooted entirely in the present, he has lost those qualities that might have transformed him into the inspired reformer or the visionary artist. D. H. Lawrence sneered at the cheerful outcome of the novel. "The new generation," he grumbled, "is having no ghosts or cobwebs. It is setting up in the photography line, and is going to make a sound financial thing of it."[31]

The figure of the mesmerist in Hawthorne's works commands attention because he is essentially cast from the same mold as the social reformer and the romantic artist. In Clifford's words, mesmerism is one of many "harbingers of a better era" and "messengers of the spiritual world." Holgrave's interest in mesmerism is inextricably bound up with his concern for radical reform and his fascination with futurity. At the same time, he has an equally fanatical, though less abstract, interest in the past. His concern with the House of the Seven Gables is motivated by the desire to impose order upon the past and thus to divine its meaning. His daguerreotypes, his stories, his dramatization of life expose a compulsive need to isolate persons and events from their normal contexts, to transform them into objects of aesthetic contemplation, and finally to use them as mediums for grasping the significance of the past.

The artist of "The Prophetic Pictures" apostrophized art as a means of bringing the past and the future into "the narrow strip of sunlight, which we call Now" (I, 207). Holgrave's art, in keeping with this definition, functions as a revelatory medium of the past and a prophetic guide to the future. When he finally resists the impulse to hypnotize Phoebe, he not only renounces mesmerism, but also substitutes the domestic arts for the fine arts and henceforth devotes his attention to preserving tradition rather than pressing for change. As he confesses to Phoebe with a sigh and a troubled smile:

> The world owes all its onward impulse to men ill at ease. The happy man inevitably confines himself within ancient limits. I have a presentiment, that, hereafter, it will be my lot to set out trees, to make fences—perhaps, even, in due time, to build a house for another

[31] D. H. Lawrence, *Studies in Classical American Literature* (New York: Viking, 1923), p. 104.

generation—in a word, to conform myself to laws, and the peaceful practice of society. (C, II, 306-307)

III

The narrator of *The Blithedale Romance,* like Holgrave, vows to steer clear of art and social reform after dabbling in both enterprises. In his final confession to the reader, Miles Coverdale declares that he has given up writing poetry and laid aside the utopian schemes that drew him to Blithedale. Coverdale is not the only character in the novel to suffer a setback. Hollingsworth's project for reforming criminals founders on his personal need for rehabilitation, and Westervelt, deprived of a medium, presumably loses his livelihood as a mesmerist. Coverdale, Hollingsworth, and Westervelt, the defeated trio of *The Blithedale Romance,* all commit what Hawthorne called the unpardonable sin. In the notebooks the unpardonable sinner is defined as a fiendish investigator who pries into the "dark depths" of the human heart, "not with a hope or purpose of making it better, but from a cold philosophical curiosity." The sin is nothing less than the "separation of the intellect from the heart" (C, VIII, 251).[32] Coverdale attempts to fathom the secrets of his friends at Blithedale; Hollingsworth hopes one day to probe the minds of criminals; Westervelt seeks to gather information about a spiritual realm from the Veiled Lady. All three men regard those around them as mere instruments for their ends.

Philanthropy is the overweaning ambition dominating Hollingsworth's life. Although Coverdale concedes that he is not the most objective judge of the man, the events at Blithedale bear out his view that Hollingsworth and his acolytes have "no heart, no sympathy, no reason, no conscience" and that they "will keep no friend, unless he make

[32] For a detailed discussion of Hawthorne's unpardonable sinners, see Donald A. Ringe, "Hawthorne's Psychology of the Head and Heart," *PMLA*, 65 (1950), 120-132.

himself the mirror of their purpose" (C, III, 70).[33] The philanthropist falls prey to the unpardonable sin by devoting himself to his ostensibly altruistic, but covertly self-serving, designs for criminal reform. Westervelt proposes an even grander scheme for shaping the future of mankind. His discourse in the village hall, as Coverdale recalls, alluded to "a new era that was dawning upon the world; an era that would link soul to soul, and the present life to what we call futurity, with a closeness that should finally convert both worlds into one great, mutually conscious brotherhood" (C, III, 200).

Coverdale himself seems to lack the intense drive that impels Hollingsworth and Westervelt to realize their lofty plans. His disparaging remarks about the Blithedale project make it clear that he sets no great store by utopian dreams, and the languid tone of his narrative suggests that his own poetry is without vitality and imagination. Yet he also takes on precisely those traits that appear so repellent in Hollingsworth and Westervelt. He confesses to the same "cold tendency, between instinct and intellect" that regulates the lives of his rivals and declares that his icy intellect is responsible for "unhumanizing" his heart.[34]

Like Holgrave, Coverdale recoils from experience and disengages himself from those around him in order to play the dispassionate observer. As Zenobia so aptly puts it, he continually speculates on how to "turn the affair into a ballad" (C, III, 33). Although Coverdale chooses a different genre to render his perception of events at Blithedale, he

[33] I disagree here with Ringe, who claims that "the dangers of too great a reliance on heart alone are exemplified in the character of Hollingsworth" ("Hawthorne's Psychology of the Head and Heart," p. 121).

[34] All three figures are also associated with images of death. Coverdale takes refuge in an "aerial sepulchre"; if Priscilla were to give Hollingsworth her love, it would be like "casting a flower into a sepulchre"; and Westervelt's speech is compared to a "current of chill air, issuing out of a sepulchral vault."

eventually succeeds in transforming life into art. Filtered through his consciousness, every episode at Blithedale takes on a theatrical coloring. Hollingsworth, Zenobia, and Priscilla figure as protagonists in his "private theater." Coverdale is fascinated by the "play of passions" among them; he reflects on the various intrigues that have kept them so long on his "mental stage"; and he views himself alternately as chorus and as spectator of this drama.[35] For him, the residents of Blithedale are nothing more than potential mediums for solving the mysteries that constitute the substance of his melodramatic narrative. In much the same fashion, both Hollingsworth and Westervelt exploit Zenobia and Priscilla, using them to further their own exalted plans. Hollingsworth spurns Zenobia for Priscilla once he discovers that Old Moodie has disinherited the one daughter and bequeathed his entire fortune to the other. Westervelt uses Zenobia's influence to put Priscilla on the stage as his "Veiled Lady," a genuine medium for his fraudulent art and millennial histrionics.

The recurrent pattern of exploitation and manipulation within the framework of human relations at Blithedale has led one critic to call Hawthorne's romance a "drama of masters and slaves."[36] The master-slave relationship is introduced early in the novel, during the first meeting between the dark temptress Zenobia and her blonde rival Priscilla. When the latter catches sight of Zenobia, she kneels before her in rapt silence. Coverdale suspects that the desire to become Zenobia's "slave" motivates Priscilla's presence at Bithedale. Priscilla's vulnerability lets her half-sister give

[35] For a discussion of Coverdale's role as a chorus, see Terence Martin, *Nathaniel Hawthorne* (New York: Twayne, 1965), pp. 153-155. On the imagery of masks and veils, see Hyatt H. Waggoner, *Hawthorne: A Critical Study* (Cambridge, Mass.: Harvard University Press, Belknap Press, 1963), pp. 188-208, and Frank Davidson, "Toward a Re-evaluation of *The Blithedale Romance*," *New England Quarterly*, 25 (1952), 374-383.

[36] Stubbs, *The Pursuit of Form*, p. 120.

free rein to sadistic impulses, and Zenobia seizes every opportunity to commit gratuitous acts of cruelty. Witness, for example, the scene in which she decks out Priscilla with flowers, but at the same time mockingly places "a weed of evil odor and ugly aspect" in the midst of the blossoms.

As Hawthorne observed in a notebook entry, a person who appears to be master "must inevitably be at least as much a slave, if not more, than the other. All slavery is reciprocal" (C, VIII, 253). Just as Priscilla, the pale flower, droops when Zenobia prospers, so Zenobia fades when Priscilla flourishes. On one occasion Coverdale perceptively characterizes Priscilla as a "gentle parasite," but on the whole the metaphors that dominate his descriptions of her tend to the floral variety. He watches her "budding and blossoming"; he cannot resist the temptation "to take just one peep beneath her folded petals"; he finds her "lovely as a flower." Such descriptions heighten and intensify the strain of passivity associated with Priscilla, but at the same time they operate within the sinister dialectic that Hawthorne used to define the master-slave relationship.[37] Moodie informs Coverdale that Priscilla's love for Zenobia "grew, and tended upward, and twined itself perseveringly around this unseen sister; as a grape-vine might strive to clamber out of a gloomy hollow among the rocks, and embrace a young tree, standing in the sunny warmth above" (C, III, 186). His image echoes a brief description of the foliage that borders on Coverdale's hermitage at Blithedale:

> It was a kind of leafy cave, high upward in the air, among the midmost branches of a white-pine tree. A wild grape-vine, of unusual size and luxuriance, had twined and twisted itself up into the tree, and, after wreathing the entanglement of its tendrils around almost every bough, had caught hold of three or four neighboring trees, and married the whole clump with

[37] Peter Murray was the first to point out Priscilla's stifling effect on Zenobia. See "Mythopoesis in *The Blithedale Romance*," *PMLA*, 75 (1960), 591-596.

> a perfectly inextricable knot of polygamy. . . . A hollow chamber, of rare seclusion, had been formed by the decay of some of the pine-branches, which the vine had lovingly strangled with its embrace, burying them from the light of day in an aerial sepulchre of its own leaves. (C, III, 98)

Coverdale, who later reveals his infatuation with Priscilla, sits in the hollow "vine-encircled heart of the tall pine." It serves him as a celestial refuge for his terrestrial investigations. The "seemingly impervious mass of foliage" surrounding his retreat is emblematic of the tangled relations from which he so artfully attempts to escape. Coverdale is situated at the heart of the matter, but he nonetheless remains isolated and unattached.

This dense mass of foliage with its "inextricable knot of polygamy" often appears as impenetrable to the reader as it does to Coverdale. The nearly insistent use of such vague terms as "influence," "sympathy," and "sphere" to define the psychology of the characters does little to illuminate the disconcertingly elusive nature of the bonds between them. It was Hawthorne's weakness for the last two substantives that Henry James was to find highly questionable and to regard as "a sort of specialty" with writers far less talented than Hawthorne.[38]

Roy Male, however, has set forth persuasive arguments for exploring the hidden meaning that informs Hawthorne's concept of sympathy.[39] Eighteenth-century inquiries into the nature of electricity and magnetism, he observes, invested the term "sympathy" with new vitality. Galvani's discovery of animal electricity and Mesmer's theory of animal magnetism seemed to demonstrate the existence of a magnetic or electrical current that maintains the pulse of the entire universe and beats to the rhythm of the human heart.

Hawthorne used both electricity and magnetism as syno-

[38] Henry James, *Hawthorne* (New York: Collier, 1966), p. 106.

[39] Roy R. Male, Jr., "Hawthorne and the Concept of Sympathy," *PMLA*, 68 (1953), 138-149.

nyms for human sympathy. In *The Scarlet Letter,* Hester, Dimmesdale, and Pearl link hands to forge an "electric chain" (V, 186). The narrator of *The House of the Seven Gables* describes the warmth of Phoebe's hand and notes that the act of touching it assures one a place "in the whole sympathetic chain of human nature" (C, II, 141). Finally, the search for the unpardonable sin causes Ethan Brand to lose his hold on "the magnetic chain of humanity" (III, 495). Sympathy, like electricity and magnetism, appears as a kind of vital current flowing around all those who submerge themselves in the great mass of humanity. Communicated by touch or by a clasp of the hand, it links men into one grand chain of brotherhood and connects them with the source of life. In *The House of the Seven Gables* the narrator states that "the sympathy or magnetism among human beings is more subtle and universal, than we think; it exists, indeed, among different classes of organized life, and vibrates from one to another" (C, II, 174). Hawthorne's current of sympathy bears all the earmarks of the "universally diffused" and "incomparably subtle" magnetic fluid that Mesmer used to cure his patients. Although Hawthorne carefully studied the effects of this ethereal fluid, he branded any attempt to isolate it, to subject it to rigorous investigation, or to take advantage of its powers as a violation of nature. His greatest scorn is reserved for the self-styled mesmerist, Westervelt, who prides himself on the "chemical discovery" of this fluid and uses it to establish communication with the spiritual world.

Both Westervelt and Hollingsworth are endowed with prodigious magnetic attractiveness. Westervelt, a practitioner of animal magnetism, maintains a powerful hold over Priscilla, just as he presumably once ruled over Zenobia. Even Coverdale, who is initially repelled by the artificiality of his appearance, finds that a part of his own nature "showed itself responsive to him." Hollingsworth, the "man of iron, in more sense than one," seems invested with an equally compelling form of magnetism. Priscilla and Zenobia are both drawn to this blacksmith turned altruist, and Coverdale too allows that he is sensitive to the man's magnetic personality. When Hollingsworth attempts to persuade him to join his cause, Coverdale feels as if the philanthropist had caught hold of his heart and were "pulling it towards him with an almost irresistible force." "Had I but touched his extended hand," he declares, "Hollingsworth's magnetism would perhaps have penetrated me with his own conception of all these matters" (C, III, 134). Like Westervelt, Hollingsworth possesses a "tremendous concentrativeness" and an "indomitable will."

Coverdale himself can boast no more than "a feeble degree of magnetism," and his attempt to draw other persons (including literary critics) into his sphere meets with little success. Much of recent criticism has in fact centered on Coverdale's limitations as a narrator.[40] He stands accused of a long roster of misdemeanors, among them coldness, clumsiness, distortion, and self-deception. Although the bulk of these charges can be substantiated without great difficulty, it is not impossible to look at Coverdale with a sympathetic eye. As much as he lacks the personal magnetism of Hollingsworth and Westervelt, he dispenses an admirable portion of sympathy, receiving virtually none in return.

Coverdale's analytic detachment is generally argued on the strength of his own words about the "cold tendency" that "unhumanizes his heart." But Coverdale's admission is framed by two equally important statements concerning his role at Blithedale and his attitude toward his companions:

> With the power, perhaps, to act in the place of destiny, and avert misfortune from my friends, I had resigned

[40] See especially William Van O'Connor, "Conscious Naivëte [*sic*] in *The Blithedale Romance*," *Revue des Langues Vivantes*, 20 (1954), 37-45; Frederick C. Crews, "A New Reading of *The Blithedale Romance*," *American Literature*, 29 (1957), 147-170; and Kelley Griffith, Jr., "Form in *The Blithedale Romance*," *American Literature*, 40 (1968), 15-26.

> them to their fate. That cold tendency, between instinct and intellect, which made me pry with a speculative interest into people's passions and impulses, appeared to have gone far towards unhumanizing my heart.
>
> But a man cannot always decide for himself whether his own heart is cold or warm. It now impresses me, that, if I erred at all, in regard to Hollingsworth, Zenobia, and Priscilla, it was through too much sympathy, rather than too little. (C, III, 154)

The two paragraphs contrast the consciousness of the experiencing self with the thoughts of the narrating self. Coverdale invites the reader to share the view, espoused by his experiencing self, that he is nothing but a dispassionate observer. But Coverdale the narrator carefully avoids identifying with the ideas to which he had earlier subscribed. While still at Blithedale, Coverdale believed that he could assume the role of destiny, and he sensed that a "cold tendency" had "unhumanized his heart." The words "perhaps" and "appeared" are qualifications which, as the second part of the passage suggests, reflect Coverdale's retrospective interpretation of his thoughts. The narrator harbors no illusions about the flaws in his past perceptions. "Now"—at the moment of narration—he endorses a radically different hypothesis about his behavior. He seems to have bestowed "too much sympathy, rather than too little" on his friends. Coverdale consistently guards against equating his present persuasions with the convictions of his experiencing self. In addition, he cautiously qualifies views attributed to his experiencing self, rendering them almost without exception as tentative judgments.

Coverdale's narrating consciousness appears to be the more reliable index of the part he played at Blithedale. When Coverdale prefaces his remarks with such phrases as "it now appears to me" or "the more I consider myself as I was then," he dissociates himself from his experiencing self and renders his thoughts from the perspective of the moment of narration. In retrospect he believes that he possessed too much sympathy, and he refers to the "sympathetic impulse" that often controlled him in "those more impressible days." Reflecting on the past, Coverdale observes that Zenobia should have been able to appreciate "that quality of the intellect and heart" that compelled him to "live in other lives" and to try "by generous sympathies, by delicate intuitions" (C, III, 160) to learn the secret of the Blithedale community. As much as Coverdale distances himself from his friends in order to master their secrets and to control their destinies, he ultimately becomes the slave of the characters in his story. He refers to them as "goblins of flesh and blood"; upon his return to Blithedale he recognizes the danger of renewing his "thralldom" to them. By the time he leaves Blithedale, his individual life is "attenuated of much of its proper substance"; he feels "listless, worn-out with emotion . . . and sympathy for others." Coverdale's evolution from master to slave echoes Hawthorne's maxim that all slavery is reciprocal.

By his own admission, Coverdale insulates and does violence to his characters in much the same way that Westervelt isolates and abuses Priscilla. As Crews points out, both Coverdale and Westervelt are showmen and snoopers.[41] They remove their subjects from a normal environment and transport them, in Westervelt's words, to a realm where "the limitations of time and space have no existence." For Westervelt this signifies a spiritual region; for Coverdale it constitutes an aesthetic space. The hopes of both men are shattered by Hollingsworth's marriage to Priscilla.

The parallels between Coverdale and the mesmerist Westervelt are compelling, but they explain only one facet of the narrator's personality. Coverdale also delivers himself up to his friends, becomes totally absorbed in their lives, and emerges drained of all sympathies and emotions. Just as he is master and slave to his characters, so he shares the char-

[41] Crews, *The Sins of the Fathers*, p. 206.

acteristics of mesmerist and medium. In *The Marble Faun,* Hawthorne drew an analogy between artists and mediums. While sculpting a bust of Donatello, Kenyon gives up "all pre-conceptions about the character of his subject" and allows his hands to work "uncontrolled, with the clay, somewhat as a spiritual medium, while holding a pen, yields it to an unseen guidance other than that of her own will" (C, IV, 271). Hawthorne appears to have held a dualistic conception of the creative process that accords with his psychology of the head and the heart. The mesmerist stands as a model for the coldly intellectual artist, while the medium represents the divinely inspired artist. In the tradition established by the German Romantics, Hawthorne held that the true artist surrenders himself to the divine sympathy of nature and becomes the vessel of a higher spiritual force. He achieves his finest results by yielding to the influence of impalpable powers.

There exist as many similarities between Coverdale and the mesmerist Westervelt as between Coverdale and the medium Priscilla. During his illness at Blithedale, Coverdale becomes "something like a mesmerical clairvoyant." He is highly receptive to the influence of his companions; his delicate health endows him with a subtle "species of intuition" that allows him to hear conversations in other rooms and to divine the identity of persons hidden from his view. In the final chapter of the novel he too removes the veil by confessing his secret love for Priscilla. But Coverdale possesses mere mortal sympathies and lacks what is designated in "The Great Stone Face" as "sublimity and stateliness, the grand expression of a divine sympathy" (III, 430). He appears as a peculiar hybrid form of the mesmerist and medium, acquiring neither the truth of the psychological artist nor the insights of the visionary artist. Lacking the eye and the will of the coldly arrogant mesmerist, he also fails to attain the calmly receptive attitude of the inspired medium.

IV

Despite his moral reservations about mesmerism, Hawthorne showed little reluctance to turn to the power of animal magnetism for his literary needs. Mesmerism appealed to his imagination for a number of reasons. Master-slave relationships dominate Hawthorne's tales and romances, and the pairing of mesmerist with medium replicates the alliance between master and slave. At Westervelt's performance in a village hall, one spectator comments on the miraculous power of "wizards" over "maidens." He cites examples of the astonishing ability of the mesmerist to control the will and the passions of his medium:

> Settled grief was but a shadow, beneath the influence of a man possessing this potency, and the strong love of years melted away like a vapor. At the bidding of one of these wizards, the maiden, with her lover's kiss still burning on her lips, would turn from him with icy indifference; the newly made widow would dig up her buried heart out of her young husband's grave, before the sods had taken root upon it; a mother, with her babe's milk in her bosom, would thrust away her child. (C, III, 198)

The wizard's mesmeric influence figures here as a form of psychological and sexual control over his medium.

The psychological terrain of mesmerism was largely unexplored in Hawthorne's day. As a result, the baffling power of the mesmerist was often more readily associated with witchcraft than with hypnotic control. Mesmeric control constituted for Hawthorne a mingling of psychic influence with magnetic powers, and it thus represented for him a kind of natural supernaturalism. Evidence for Hawthorne's conscious fusion of mastery and mystery appears in a sequence of verbs uttered by Zenobia at Eliot's pulpit. She tells Hollingsworth: "I am awake, disenchanted, disenthralled" (C, III, 218). Zenobia is no longer subject to Hollingsworth's hypnotic influence; his magical spell has been broken; she is his slave no more. Just as Priscilla is liberated from bondage to Westervelt, so Zenobia is released from enslavement to Hollingsworth. For Hawthorne magnetic influence is analogous to the fascination exercised by men who are ruled by the head rather than the heart. The mesmerist stands as model for a large class of men in Hawthorne's fiction who impose their will upon weaker personalities and attempt to draw converts and disciples into their sphere.

Hawthorne borrowed from the rhetoric of mesmerism not only to describe the laws of human psychology, but also to define the sympathetic bond between man and nature. The subtle and universal fluid that he viewed as the animating force of the universe resembles the magnetic fluid that Mesmer identified as the agent of health. It too can be communicated from one individual to another by a mere touch of the hand. Although Hawthorne condemned human efforts to harness the power of this fluid, he seemed to rejoice in its regenerative qualities. By clasping the hand of a person in harmony with nature and mankind, Hawthorne's coldly speculative heroes can regain their hold on the chain of human sympathies.

Many of Hawthorne's characters can be neatly divided into two groups. Critics traditionally refer to the dichotomy of the head and the heart when they seek a concise formula for classifying Hawthorne's heroes. Two different parts of the human anatomy—the eye and the hand—are equally appropriate emblems for those who isolate themselves from the mass of humanity and those who possess a common bond with mankind. All of Hawthorne's scientists, reformers, and artists have the penetrating eye of the astute observer and the detached spectator. Rooted entirely in futurity, these perceptive observers are often misguided utopian dreamers or fraudulent schemers who seek to master nature, society, or individual human destinies through science, social reform, or art. As long as they cling to their visionary ideals, they remain isolated from others and insulated from reality. They lack the divine sympathy and warmth of those who clasp hands to form the magnetic chain of humanity.

Finally, Hawthorne's artists can be defined in terms of their qualities as mesmerists or as mediums. In *The Marble Faun,* Hilda reflects on the shortcomings of paintings by artists who draw inspiration from direct examination of nature. She believes that they cultivate "a keen intellectual perception, and a marvellous knack of external arrangement" instead of a "live sympathy and sentiment" (C, IV, 338-339) which would serve them better. The probing eye alone cannot provide revelations. The artist as mesmerist represents the coldly sober, but keenly perceptive, observer. He ruthlessly sacrifices everything to an artistic performance that is essentially a sham. The authentic artist subordinates his own will to an invisible current of sympathy vibrating through the universe. As the vessel of this higher force, he becomes a spiritual medium invested with the power to communicate life to his creations.

CHAPTER 7

From Science Fiction to Psychoanalysis: Henry James's "Bostonians," D. H. Lawrence's "Women in Love," and Thomas Mann's "Mario and the Magician"

"Hypnosis has something positively uncanny about it."—Freud, *Group Psychology and the Analysis of the Ego*

One of Charcot's most significant contributions to the study of neuroses, Freud declared, had been to replace the "demon of priestly imagination" with a "psychological formula."[1] Freud overstated the actual situation—Charcot's recent death had no doubt quickened Freud's sense of his mentor's accomplishments. Charcot was only the most recent in a line of figures who had taken the burden of evil from the devil and placed it squarely on the shoulders of man. By carrying Charcot's insights to their logical conclusion, Freud was able to locate both the diabolical and the divine within the human psyche.

Deviations from normal behavior have been interpreted in a variety of ways through the ages. In pagan traditions, as in their spiritualized variants, madness is generally viewed as literal possession by a god or a demon. It is the divine breath that rouses men to speak in tongues and the demon

[1] Sigmund Freud, *Collected Papers*, trans. Joan Riviere, 4 vols. (New York: Basic Books, 1959), I, 22.

within that dictates demented behavior. In the literature inspired by mesmerism, amateur scientists and psychologists usurped the powers of gods and demons to become the agents of good and evil. Having mastered the secrets of a cosmic fluid, they were able to control the human mind. These men of science, who possessed powers at once satanic and divine, could take advantage of that fluid to establish a mental rapport with other people. They could turn the men around them into instruments of their own will or into mediums of a higher intelligence.

Mesmerists of the nineteenth century were in turn divested of their powers by modern science and psychoanalysis. At the time animal magnetism enjoyed its greatest popularity, it had secured a certain degree of scientific respectability. But because the assumptions under which it operates no longer find widespread acceptance, mesmerists of the past century are now more likely to be regarded as wizards with magical powers than as scientists and psychologists. By the same token, the science fiction of mesmerism has become for us less science than fiction.

Just as literary critics are no longer obliged to resort to the divine breath or to cosmic fluids when speaking of the creative process, so twentieth-century authors need refer neither to demons nor to mesmerists when describing the sources of irrational behavior. Psychoanalysis, as Tzvetan Todorov observes, has replaced the literature of the fantastic.[2] Perhaps the best example of how mesmerism came to be stripped of its magical powers and the human psyche revealed as the sole agent of magnetic miracles appears in Henry James's *Bostonians*. James's novel replaced the animal magnetism of Mesmer's imagination with a psychological formula. With the publication of *The Bostonians* in 1886, the nineteenth-century tradition of the mesmerist novel came to an end.

[2] Tzvetan Todorov, *The Fantastic: A Structural Approach to a Literary Genre*, trans. Richard Howard (Ithaca, N.Y.: Cornell University Press, 1975), pp. 160-161.

Animal magnetism nonetheless found its way into modern literature—on the one hand despite psychoanalysis, on the other because of it. D. H. Lawrence, one of Freud's most vocal opponents, developed "psycho-somatic" theories that relied heavily on the basic tenets of mesmerism and mysticism. The nearly insistent use of magnetic and electrical metaphors in *Women in Love* to describe erotic attraction and psychological domination echoes the diction used by Hoffmann, Balzac, and Hawthorne, but deepens its mystical component. In reaching back to a mode of thought that had lost much of its vitality, Lawrence at times ran the risk of challenging his readers' credulity. If his mesmerist metaphors are not entirely convincing, it is in part because he deliberately shunned even the standard formulations of psychoanalysis. Hypnosis, the psychoanalytic counterpart of mesmerism, could in Lawrence's day serve as a viable literary theme. Mesmerism itself had received the deathblow.

Between the two great wars of our century, one subject that commanded the attention of many writers was the relationship between the leader and the masses. For Thomas Mann (as for Freud and other students of mass psychology), hypnosis remained a topic of deep and continuing fascination. It promised to explain the spell that dictators seemed to weave over the masses. Cipolla, the unsavory hypnotist of Mann's *Mario and the Magician* (*Mario und der Zauberer*) figures as one of the "legitimate heirs" to the mesmerist tradition. He represents the last (and clearly the most sinister) of the literary progeny to which animal magnetism gave birth.

I

Although Leon Edel dismisses "Professor Fargo" as one of the "recurrent potboilers" written by Henry James and asserts that the story requires "no critical attention,"[3] an

[3] Leon Edel, Introd., *The Complete Tales of Henry James*, ed. Leon Edel, 12 vols. (London: Rupert Hart-Davis, 1962-64), III, 10. Cornelia

analysis of *The Bostonians* can scarcely pass over this first installment of James's views on "mediums, and spirit-rappers, and roaring radicals."[4] Both "Professor Fargo" and *The Bostonians* are the final expressions of a peculiarly American blend of mesmerist romance and social criticism —a tradition launched by Hawthorne's *Blithedale Romance* and sustained in its course by Howells's *Undiscovered Country.*

The trio of impoverished barnstormers who roam the New England countryside in "Professor Fargo" includes Colonel Gifford, a "famous lightning calculator and mathematical reformer," his unnamed deaf-mute daughter, and the titular villain of the tale—a man who bills himself as an "infallible waking medium and magician, clairvoyant, prophet, and seer."[5] The story of their adventures, filtered through the consciousness of a narrator who frankly confesses his lack of faith in mesmerist wonders, focuses on Fargo's plot to secure control over Gifford's daughter. Like his literary predecessor Miles Coverdale, James's narrator makes no attempt to rescue the heroine of his story from the designs of an evil showman. Despite his sympathy for Gifford's plight and his revulsion at Fargo's methods, he remains throughout the impassive observer—fascinated by the events he witnesses, yet incapable of intervening in them.

The narrator's description of Fargo draws special attention to the mountebank's "impudent eyes," eyes that have

---

Pulsifer Kelley also finds the story devoid of "artistic merit": see *The Early Development of Henry James,* rev. ed. (Urbana: University of Illinois Press, 1965), p. 168. S. Gorley Putt is to my knowledge the only critic who has probed beneath the surface of the story. He finds in it a "freshness of observation" and a vibrant expression of James's "horror of American vulgarity." See *A Reader's Guide to Henry James* (London: Thames and Hudson, 1966), pp. 43-45.

[4] Henry James, *The Bostonians* (New York: Dial, 1945), p. 3. All parenthetical page references are to this volume; the New York edition of James's works does not include *The Bostonians.*

[5] Henry James, "Professor Fargo," in *The Complete Tales of Henry James,* III, 261; hereafter cited as *Complete Tales.*

"peeped into stranger places than even lions' mouths" in their attempt to "pierce the veil of futurity."[6] In addition to his many other occult gifts, the professor is endowed with what he calls "great magnetism" and prides himself on his power as a "healing medium." But Fargo also uses his magnetic prowess for less salutary aims. The narrator—again much like Coverdale in his fondness for eavesdropping—is the sole witness of a scene that should have alerted him to Fargo's evil intentions. While taking a stroll across the cemetery of the village in which the mesmerist troupe performs, he surreptitiously observes an exchange between Fargo and Gifford's daughter. The girl's eyes remain fixed on Fargo's face throughout the interview; the professor seems to hold her "spellbound" by wielding some kind of power "best known to himself." Even after hearing Fargo expatiate to some local worthies on the mysterious influence he exercises over other persons, the narrator is not inclined to interfere with the professor's plans. "I can do all sorts of things," Fargo boasts. "I can find out things. I can make people confess. . . . I can make 'em in love—what do you say to that? I can take 'em out of love again. . . . It's a free gift. It's magnetism, in short. Some folks call it animal magnetism, but I call it spiritual magnetism."[7]

Fargo's spiritual magnetism so bewitches Gifford's daughter that the frail young girl does not hesitate for a moment when faced with the choice of remaining with her father or forming an alliance with Fargo. She turns to the professor and drops before him on her knees. "I have often wondered," the narrator later muses, "how far, in her strangely simple mood and nature, her consciousness on this occasion was a guilty one."[8] And he adds that he has never properly settled the question in his own mind. It may strike the reader that the word one might normally expect in the narrator's reflections on the girl's moral character would

[6] *Complete Tales*, III, 261-262. [7] Ibid., p. 286.

[8] Ibid., p. 297.

be "conscience." The use of the term "consciousness" appears, however, to be both deliberate and meaningful in its context. Does the girl, by responding to Fargo's personal and sexual charm, consciously obey his commands and thus forfeit her moral purity; or has she, as the victim of mesmerist powers, temporarily lost the faculty of consciousness and thus managed to preserve her innocence? By ending his story on an ambiguous note, the narrator betrays his own desire to defend the girl's virtue by placing the blame for her action on an occult power. Once a confirmed skeptic, he now finds it convenient to declare his faith in spiritual magnetism.

In *The Bostonians* James returned to the principal theme of "Professor Fargo" by placing at the center of his work a contest of will between two people competing for the attention of a young woman.[9] Although animal magnetism, spiritualism, and clairvoyance figure significantly in the novel, they are no longer used to explain the behavior of characters or to account for the subtle chemistry at work between them. Yet the images and metaphoric vehicles for expressing the influence of one person over another are drawn largely from the language of witchcraft and mesmerism.

Before examining descriptions of psychic control in *The Bostonians,* we must first consider a problem that has repeatedly drawn the attention of James's critics: the extent of Hawthorne's influence on *The Bostonians.*[10] *The Blithe-*

[9] Edmund Wilson has stated the theme in bolder terms. "The subject of *The Bostonians,*" he writes, "is the struggle for the attractive daughter of a poor evangelist between a young man from the South who wants to marry her and a well-to-do Boston lady with a Lesbian passion for her." See "The Ambiguity of Henry James," *Hound and Horn,* 7 (1934), 385-406.

[10] See especially Marius Bewley, "James's Debt to Hawthorne (I): 'The Blithedale Romance' and 'The Bostonians,'" *Scrutiny,* 16 (1949), 178-195, reprinted in Marius Bewley, *The Complex Fate: Hawthorne, Henry James and Some Other American Writers* (London: Chatto and Windus, 1952), pp. 11-30. In a letter to the editors of *Scrutiny,* Leon

dale Romance and *The Bostonians* share a number of themes, among them, feminism, social reform, and mesmerism. Hawthorne's cast of characters seems also to serve as a model for the principal actors in James's novel.[11] Both Zenobia and Olive Chancellor exercise an authoritative influence over younger women—the power they exert is, in each instance, thwarted by males who figure as their ideological rivals. Hawthorne's portrait of "Professor" Westervelt is painted in the same tawdry colors as James's picture of Selah Tarrant; the unsavory grin and grotesque teeth (Westervelt's are artificial, Tarrant's "carnivorous") of the two mesmerist frauds belie the lofty spiritual aims to which they claim allegiance. Eager to secure wealth and fame, they do not hesitate to exploit the seemingly preternatural gifts of mediums. Basil Ransom functions as the counterpart of Hollingsworth, the "man of iron" who rescues Priscilla from Westervelt's clutches. And finally, Verena Tarrant, the eloquent and docile heroine of *The Bostonians*, partakes of both Zenobia's histrionic talents and Priscilla's submissive nature.

The list of comparisons between *The Blithedale Romance* and *The Bostonians* is extensive. Yet critics have overlooked some points that not only set the parallels between the two novels into sharp relief, but also allow the

---

Edel challenged Bewley's arguments and claimed that, in limiting his focus to comparisons between *The Blithedale Romance* and James's novel, Bewley had failed to search for influence "in depth." His letter and Bewley's reply appear in *Scrutiny*, 17 (1950), 53-60. For more recent comparisons of the two novels, see Robert Emmet Long, "The Society and the Masks: *The Blithedale Romance* and *The Bostonians*," *Nineteenth-Century Fiction*, 19 (1964), 105-122; Martha Banta, *Henry James and the Occult: The Great Extension* (Bloomington: Indiana University Press, 1972), pp. 90-100; and Howard Kerr, *Mediums, and Spirit-Rappers, and Roaring Radicals: Spiritualism in American Literature, 1850-1900* (Urbana: University of Illinois Press, 1972), pp. 56-65, 190-222.

[11] Bewley, *The Complex Fate*, pp. 11-30.

reader to appreciate the thirty years separating them. It may seem nothing more than coincidence that Hawthorne describes the residents of Blithedale as a "knot of dreamers," while James characterizes the feminist audience gathered in South Boston as a "knot of reformers." But consider the following passage from *The Bostonians*: "Ransom could see that, according to a phrase which came back to him just then, oddly, out of some novel or poem he had read of old, she was the cynosure of every eye" (228). If we now turn to *The Blithedale Romance*, to a passage inspired by Miles Coverdale's thoughts on the relationship between Priscilla and Zenobia, then it might be possible to refresh Ransom's memory: "A brilliant woman is often an object of the devoted admiration . . . of some young girl, who perhaps beholds the cynosure only at an awful distance, and has as little hope of personal intercourse as of climbing among the stars of heaven."[12]

Such artful allusions to Hawthorne's novel suggest that James was quite sensitive to the language of his literary model and that he consciously adopted words and phrases from it. Yet James, as noted in an earlier chapter, also candidly criticized what he considered the defects of Hawthorne's style; he also expressed irritation at the New Englander's "predilection for a small number of vague ideas which are represented by such terms as 'spheres' and 'sympathies.' "[13] James's aversion to the word "sympathy" appears all the more strange when one considers the frequency with which he uses that very noun and its variants in *The Bostonians*. On the other hand, he was clearly not so much finding fault with the substantive itself as with the "vague ideas" linked to it. And these ideas furnished the target for a more severe indictment of *The Blithedale Romance*:

[12] Nathaniel Hawthorne, *The Blithedale Romance and Fanshawe*, ed. William Charvat et al. (Columbus: Ohio State University Press, 1964), pp. 32-33.

[13] Henry James, *Hawthorne* (New York: Collier, 1966), p. 106.

> The portion of the story that strikes me as least felicitous is that which deals with Priscilla, and with her mysterious relation to Zenobia—with her mesmeric gifts, her clairvoyance, her identity with the Veiled Lady, her divided subjection to Hollingsworth and Westervelt, and her numerous other graceful but fantastic properties—her Sibylline attributes, as the author calls them. Hawthorne is rather too fond of Sibylline attributes—a taste of the same order as his disposition . . . to talk about spheres and sympathies.[14]

Despite his objections to Priscilla's "Sibylline attributes" and to the "mysterious relationship" between Zenobia and Priscilla, James seems—at first blush in any case—to have introduced precisely the "least felicitous" elements of Hawthorne's plot into his own work. Verena, in the opinion of nearly every character in *The Bostonians*, possesses some kind of marvelous "gift." James judiciously left it to the reader to determine whether this gift is what Miss Birdseye identifies as "genius," what Selah Tarrant enthusiastically describes as something "inspirational," what Olive reverently terms a "divine" faculty, or what Dr. Prance sardonically dismisses as "the gift of the g——." This precious endowment, whether oracular or oratorical in nature, appears to derive from a source entirely outside Verena's command. "It isn't *me*," she insists at her first speaking engagement in Boston. And Selah Tarrant, a "mesmeric healer" who is said to be "very magnetic," heartily endorses her declaration. Transmitting Tarrant's own feelings about his psychic powers, the narrator notes: "When he just calmed her down by laying his hand on her a few moments, it seemed to come" (46). But Olive Chancellor's reflections offer the reader a quite different view of Tarrant's magnetic assistance: "The girl had virtually confessed that she lent herself to it only because it gave him pleasure, and that anything else would do as well, anything that would make her

[14] Ibid., p. 119.

quiet a little before she began to 'give out' " (99). Thus James with one stroke effectively eliminated the possibility of attributing Verena's inspired discourses to the agency of an occult power. Her gift, however miraculous it may seem, is nothing more than a natural talent for eloquent speech—a talent that takes on special intensity when reassurance and support are at hand.[15]

While Verena possesses the same "graceful" and "fantastic" properties ascribed to Priscilla, James naturalized her "Sibylline attributes" and humanized her divine powers. But how is one to explain the "conscious tyranny" exercised by Olive over Verena and the "irremediable hold" obtained upon her by Ransom? The spell that both Olive and Ransom cast on Verena allows them to enthrall "the young prophetess" as effectively as Zenobia and Westervelt held the "Veiled Lady" in bondage.

After her first interview with Olive, Verena feels as if she has been "seized," and we learn that she gives herself up "as we do whenever a person in whom we have perfect confidence proposes, with our assent, to subject us to some sensation" (67). Verena is at first "drawn" to Olive, then falls "under her influence," and is finally "completely under the charm." "The fine web of authority, of dependence" woven by Olive about her protégée becomes "as dense as a suit of golden mail." But Olive fails to shield Verena from the assaults of a "chivalrous Southerner," a man whose strength of will rivals her own admirable "concentration of purpose." Basil Ransom's magnificent eyes with their "smouldering fire," his "magical touch," and his nearly arrogant self-confidence allow him to undermine Olive's influence and to take possession of Verena. His words to Verena have the unmistakable flavor of magical incantations: "Come out with me, Miss Tarrant; come out with me.

[15] Kerr, incidentally, points out that Verena's career as a feminist orator is modeled on that of Cora Hatch, a young woman whose inspirational speaking James himself had had occasion to hear. See Kerr, *Mediums, and Spirit-Rappers, and Roaring Radicals*, pp. 197-203.

Do come out with me," he pleads; "Give me the day, dear Miss Tarrant, give me the day," he later murmurs; and finally, shortly before spiriting Verena away from Boston's Music Hall, where a crowd has gathered to hear the "red-haired young *improvisatrice*," he whispers softly in her ear: "Come away, come away."

Although James draws repeatedly on the vocabulary of necromancy and mesmerism to depict Verena's subjugation to Olive and Ransom, Verena's devotion to her two friends is in the final analysis neither magical nor magnetic.[16] The girl's psychological disposition provides a far more plausible explanation of her eager capitulation to the demands of others. From Hawthorne, James had picked up some pointers for suggesting the vulnerability of his heroine. Like Priscilla, Verena is a "passive maiden"; her submissive nature is persistently underscored by floral imagery. Clutching a leather strap hanging from the roof of a streetcar, she has the appearance of "some blooming cluster dangling in a hothouse." Verena's mother is dimly aware that her daughter has "the sweetest flower of character" that has ever "bloomed on earth." Olive regards Verena as "a flower of the great Democracy," and the narrator, not to be outdone, observes that Verena blossoms "like the flower that attains such perfection in Boston."

In less florid language, the narrator gives some insights into Verena's personality:

16 For a discussion of analogies between the plot of *The Bostonians* and the archetypal pattern of fairy tales, see W. R. Martin, "The Use of the Fairy-Tale: A Note on the Structure of *The Bostonians*," *English Studies in Africa*, 2 (1959), 98-109. David Bonnell Green briefly considers the language of sorcery in James's novel: see "Witch and Bewitchment in *The Bostonians*," *Papers on Language and Literature*, 3 (1967), 267-269. I cannot agree with Martha Banta's view that James made "adroit use of the nomenclature of vampirism" in *The Bostonians*. Words such as "influence," "charm," and "spell" are only remotely connected with the theme of intellectual vampirism. See Martha Banta, *Henry James and the Occult*, pp. 97-100.

> Artlessly artful facilities . . . were not a part of her essence, an expression of her innermost preferences. What *was* a part of her essence was the extraordinary generosity with which she would expose herself, give herself away, turn herself inside out, for the satisfaction of a person who made demands of her. (319)

It is in Verena's nature, we learn, to be "easily submissive, to like being overborne." Just as the narrator divests Verena's "gift" of its supernatural aura by tracing its origin to a natural talent for rhetoric, so he strips the power wielded by Olive and Ransom of all mystery by depicting it as purely psychological.

Priscilla's fate was happier than Verena's. In *The Blithedale Romance*, Hollingsworth helped Priscilla cast off her veil and thus break the spell binding her to Westervelt. But for Verena, Ransom's personal and sexual magnetism assumes so overpowering a character that she is deprived of the power to shape her destiny. Shortly before Ransom leaves the Music Hall with Verena, the narrator reports that the gallant Southerner "perceived, tossed upon a chair, a long, furred cloak, which he caught up, and, before she could resist, threw over her." This gesture, fraught with symbolic meaning, is prefigured by two other episodes in the novel. Fearing that Verena may succumb to the blandishments of Matthias Pardon or to the charms of two Harvard undergraduates, Olive takes the girl aside, flings over her the folds of her mantle, and seeks to extract from her a promise never to marry. An invitation from Mrs. Burrage to spend a fortnight in New York elicits the same response from Olive: she prepares to throw her cloak over Verena. The gesture, in both contexts, betokens an effort to place a shield between Verena and the outside world and at the same time to take full possession of the girl. By draping a long cloak over Verena—covering her "from head to foot" with it—Ransom signalizes both his victory over Olive and his conquest of Verena. But for Verena, one form of tyranny has supplanted another. She leaves the Music Hall in tears, and the narrator expresses his trepidation that "with the union, so far from brilliant, into which she was about to enter, these were not the last she was destined to shed."

In *The Bostonians,* James hoped to produce a new breed of mesmerist satire by crossing the anti-spiritualist, anti-reform satire of the 1850s with a modern version of the mesmerist romance.[17] His discussion of *The Blithedale Romance* expressed disappointment with the absence of satire in Hawthorne's novel. "The quality," he observed, "is almost conspicuous by its absence."[18] The first book of *The Bostonians,* on the other hand, offers little more than social satire; the narrator directs his urbane wit at feminism, mesmerism, communal utopianism, and nearly all the other strange types of radical activity that flourished in nineteenth-century New England. Only in the second book does the narrator introduce the central theme of the novel—the conflict between Olive and Ransom—and, in order to depict this conflict, he abandons the satirical mode for psychological analysis.[19] Once he has probed the minds of "various queer specimens of the reforming genus"[20] and revealed the vulgarity, self-deception, and naiveté attending their efforts,

[17] Kerr, *Mediums, and Spirit-Rappers, and Roaring Radicals,* p. 191.

[18] James, *Hawthorne,* p. 82.

[19] Alfred Habegger, "The Disunity of *The Bostonians,*" *Nineteenth-Century Fiction,* 24 (1969), 193-209. Habegger points out that the two parts of the novel form a unified whole in that they are both concerned with the "American sexual malaise." The first part directs attention to the public aspects of this theme, the second to its private features. On the cultural, political, and social questions raised by the novel, see Lionel Trilling, introduction to *The Bostonians* (London: John Lehmann, 1952), pp. vii-xv, reprinted in Lionel Trilling, *The Opposing Self* (New York: Viking, 1955), pp. 104-117; Irving Howe, *Politics and the Novel,* 2d ed. (New York: Avon, 1957), pp. 186-203; and Clinton Oliver, "Henry James As a Social Critic," *Antioch Review,* 7 (1947), 243-258.

[20] James, *Hawthorne,* p. 82.

he turns his attention almost exclusively to the tug of war between Olive and Ransom over Verena.

Both Miles Coverdale, the narrator of *The Blithedale Romance*, and the unnamed narrator of "Professor Fargo" left their readers suspended between a natural and a supernatural explanation for the romantic intrigue described in their stories.[21] The narrator of *The Bostonians* also carefully guides the reader's response to his story, but he presents only one possible solution to the mysterious relations among his characters. Despite his use of metaphors pointing to the influence of witchcraft and mesmerism in determining Verena's subjection to Olive and Ransom, the narrator makes it abundantly clear—first by satirizing the claims of mesmerists and spiritualists, then by punctuating his narrative with psychological insights—that a quite natural explanation can account for Verena's receptivity to the affluent Bostonian and her impoverished cousin. Olive's "charm" and Ransom's "spells," like Verena's "gifts," are in the end no more satanic and no more divine than human nature.

II

"I stick to the solar plexus," Lawrence announced peevishly in his *Fantasia of the Unconscious*.[22] Anticipating Nabokov's characterization of Freud as the Viennese witch doctor, Lawrence designated doctors in general, and psychoanalysts in particular, as the "medicine-men of our decadent society" (198). His profound contempt for students of Freud stemmed from the belief that their doctrines aimed at subverting the

[21] The narrators of *The Blithedale Romance* and "Professor Fargo," it should be added, both have a covert interest in the young women who yield to the compelling attraction of mesmerist wizards. Their interpretations of the relations between mesmerist and medium may thus be colored by a desire to protect the integrity of the medium.

[22] D. H. Lawrence, *Fantasia of the Unconscious and Psychoanalysis and the Unconscious* (London: Heinemann, 1971), p. 5. Page references for both essays are to this edition and will hereafter be incorporated into the text.

moral faculty in man. By consistently tracing neuroses to unadmitted incestuous drives, psychoanalysts, he charged, had shown incest to be a part of normal sexuality. The lesson to be drawn from Freud's theories, Lawrence reasoned, was that men must indulge their "incest-craving" in order to preserve their mental health. In Lawrence's view, incest is a mentally derived idea that lacks a biological basis; Freud's concept of the unconscious (which includes incest drives) therefore amounts to nothing more than a "cellar in which the mind keeps its own bastard spawn." Lawrence, by contrast, was in search of the "true unconscious," a pristine psychic space yet to be invaded by the "huge slimy serpent of sex" that Freud had discovered lurking in the dark cavern of the unconscious mind.[23]

In *Psychoanalysis and the Unconscious* (1921) and again in *Fantasia of the Unconscious* (1922), Lawrence placed the psychometaphysical doctrines expressed in his novels into a theoretical framework. The foreword to *Fantasia of the Unconscious*, an essay that restates and extends themes sounded in the earlier study of the unconscious, betrays Lawrence's keen resentment of the critical response to his first attempt at dethroning Freud. The "generality of readers," he warns, had best leave his book alone; the "generality of critics" would be wise to cast it, without a moment's hesitation, into the wastebasket. But the "limited few"—to whom Lawrence addresses his remarks—will find that "the whole thing hangs inevitably together."

The limited few were perhaps smaller in number than even Lawrence himself had expected. Reviewers of the two works had little patience with Lawrence's "pollyanalytics." What scant attention they did give the books took the form of good-humored indulgence or outright ridicule.[24] Judging

[23] On Lawrence's dispute with Freud, see Frederick J. Hoffman, *Freudianism and the Literary Mind* (Baton Rouge: Louisiana State University Press, 1945), pp. 149-180.

[24] Philip Rieff, Introd., *Psychoanalysis and the Unconscious and Fantasia of the Unconscious*, by D. H. Lawrence (New York: Viking, 1960), pp. vii-viii.

from the limited use of the essays in contemporary discussions of Lawrence's fiction, it appears that even the novelist's admirers, with a few notable exceptions, are somewhat embarrassed by the huffy tone and inflated rhetoric of the two works.[25] Yet Lawrence's views on the unconscious (however opaque they may appear) should not be lightly dismissed. The flaws of a psychological theory inevitably color the description of character, and one key to the many passages that have exasperated readers of Lawrence's novels lies in an understanding of the ideas expressed in *Psychoanalysis and the Unconscious* and in *Fantasia.*

"I am not a scientist," Lawrence conceded in his critique of psychoanalysis. He even went so far as to profess "no scientific *exactitude,* particularly in terminology" (234). One can only wonder then why he chose to express his intuitive insights within a conceptual framework so closely resembling that of a textbook on anatomy. In *Psychoanalysis and the Unconscious,* for example, Lawrence presents for his readers a chart dividing man into four quarters. The diaphragm figures as a dividing line between two lower centers of consciousness (the solar plexus and the lumbar ganglion) and two upper centers of consciousness (the cardiac plexus and the thoracic ganglion). An imaginary vertical line separates the sympathetic plexus system of the human body from its two voluntary ganglionic centers. These four nerve centers generate a "lovely polarized vitalism" to control, during the first twelve to fourteen years of life, what Lawrence called

[25] John Middleton Murry, in the opinion of most critics, exceeds the limits of sober judgment when he calls *Fantasia of the Unconscious* Lawrence's "greatest book" (*Son of Woman: The Story of D. H. Lawrence* [London: Jonathan Cape, 1931], p. 171). F. R. Leavis, who sees the "triumphant reign of intelligence" in Lawrence's *Psychoanalysis and the Unconscious,* surely loses his credibility on this point when he calls the work a "serene and lucid essay" (*D. H. Lawrence: Novelist* [London: Chatto & Windus, 1955], p. 147). Mary Freeman is one of the few critics to make more than passing reference to the two works (*D. H. Lawrence: A Basic Study of His Ideas* [Gainesville: University of Florida Press, 1955], pp. 127-157).

dynamic consciousness and dynamic creative relationships.

Lawrence's predilection for seeing all things in terms of polar opposites considerably facilitates the task of understanding his anatomy of consciousness. The solar plexus, the primal affective center of Lawrence's system, serves as the point of departure for his discussion. This "magnetic or dynamic centre of first-consciousness" is the source of all knowledge and being. From the moment of conception, a "lovely, suave, fluid, *creative* electricity" flows from the solar plexus of the new unit of life to a corresponding nerve center in the mother. The child comes to know its mother through a form of "magnetic interchange." But from the lumbar ganglion the newly born infant asserts its will to establish a separate identity, and a negative current vibrating from mother to child swiftly sunders connections between them. The establishment of these dual circuits constitutes for Lawrence the very essence of creative development. At the two upper centers of consciousness the same process takes place. From the cardiac plexus issues a vital current of love that is checked in its course by the countervailing force of the thoracic ganglion. Within every individual there is, then, a fourfold polarity; between individuals the polarity is eightfold.

Both sympathetic and voluntary modes of consciousness should, according to Lawrence, act in unison. There must be a "twofold passionate flux of sympathetic love" and a "twofold passional circuit of separatist realization." To stress either one of these modes to the exclusion of the other is to hinder creative activity and to court "corruption." Lawrence himself recognized the difficulty of attaining an ideal balance between the two activities: "We either love too much, or impose our will too much, are too spiritual or too sensual" (42).

To complicate matters further, Lawrence's anatomical scheme includes four deeper centers of consciousness (the hypogastric plexus, the sacral ganglion, the cervical plexus, and the cervical ganglion) that spring into being during puberty and develop new fields of "passional relationships." These four organs set up electrical circuits and magnetic fields similar to those of the organs operating on the first plane of psychic activity. Consider, for example, Lawrence's description of erotic attraction and sexual union:

> Without sight or scent or hearing the powerful magnetic current vibrates from the hypogastric plexus in the female, vibrating on to the air like some intense wireless message. And there is immediate response from the sacral ganglion in some male. . . . The male enters the magnetic field of the female. He vibrates helplessly in response. There is established at once a dynamic circuit. . . . There is one electric flow which encompasses one male and one female. . . .
>
> This circuit of vital sex magnetism, at first loose and wide, gradually closes and becomes more powerful, contracts and grows more intense, until the two individuals arrive into contact. (183)

The most apt metaphors for describing sexual congress, as Lawrence himself points out, are drawn from the language of meteorology. When male and female come into contact, there is a "lightning flash," a "thunder of sensation," and finally a release of tension. And just as a thunderstorm purifies the atmosphere, so coition relieves the "electrical accumulation" in the nerves to produce an entirely "new state of blood." This altered mental and physiological state in turn arouses the desire for a radically different polarized connection—not one between man and woman, but between man and men. Once sexual energy has been released, the male shifts his attention to daytime activities, to a collective purpose, while the female, who exists for Lawrence only "in the twilight, by the camp fire," presumably awaits the return of nightfall. Without the invigorating power of sexual fulfillment man must inevitably drift into sterility; without the sober satisfaction attending collective activity, there can be nothing but anarchy.

Although the heady combination of physiology and mysticism in Lawrence's essays on the unconscious may have perplexed his contemporaries, it would not have greatly troubled readers of an earlier generation. Lawrence's concept of anatomical polarity, his circuits of passional interchange, and his vital magnetic and electrical fluids fit squarely into the frame of eighteenth-century psychology and physiology. Like the scientists of that century, he saw a direct correlation between physiological and mental processes on the one hand and the laws governing electricity and magnetism on the other. Lawrence, however, placed special emphasis on the mystical component in these doctrines and added an explicitly sexual dimension to the magnetic or electric interchange between individuals.

It is in *Women in Love* more than in any of his other novels that Lawrence deployed the rhetoric of his psychological theories. The sexual rapport between characters in that work is persistently described in terms of electrical tensions and magnetic attractions. Such phrases as "electrical vibrations," "magnetic domination," "shocks of invisible fluid lightning," and "passional electrical energy" ring in the reader's ear with an almost deadening monotony.[26] As

[26] The repetitiousness and the incantatory tone of Lawrence's prose has been noted by many literary critics. Even F. R. Leavis, Lawrence's most eloquent champion, takes exception to the "jargon" in some passages of *Women in Love* (*D. H. Lawrence*, p. 148). I have profited especially from discussions of Lawrence's style in Mark Schorer, "*Women in Love* and Death," *Hudson Review*, 6 (1953), 34-47; Robert B. Heilman, "Nomad, Monads, and the Mystique of the Soma," review of *D. H. Lawrence: The Failure and the Triumph of Art*, by Eliseo Vivas, *Sewanee Review*, 68 (1960), 635-659; and William H. Gass, "From Some Ashes No Bird Rises," review of *Phoenix* and *Phoenix II*, by D. H. Lawrence, *New York Review of Books*, 1 August 1968, pp. 3-4. Lawrence himself apologized for the "continual, slightly modified repetition" found in his work, but pointed out that "every natural crisis in emotion or passion or understanding comes from this pulsing, frictional to-and-fro, which works up to culmination" ("Foreword to *Women in Love*," in *Phoenix II: Uncollected, Unpublished and Other Prose Works by D. H. Lawrence*, ed. Warren Roberts and Harry T. Moore [London: Heinemann, 1968], pp. 275-276).

W. H. Auden pointed out, Lawrence was far more interested in "states" than in "individuals," and the sheer repetition of scenes suggesting (though not always explicitly depicting) the state of sexual arousal, for example, seems to have exhausted his lexicon of adjectives.[27] The wholesale repetition of electrical and magnetic metaphors must, however, be distinguished from the infinitely tedious litany of abstract adjectives that Lawrence used in his prose. The electrical and magnetic metaphors, which have become a trademark of Lawrence's style, acquire an added dimension of meaning when considered in concert with his psychological theories.

Of the four major characters in *Women in Love*, Gerald is most abundantly endowed with electrical energy. He is described as "attractive"; his blood seems "fluid and electric"; he gives off an "electric power"; and a "fierce electric energy" flows through his body.[28] The list of his electrical and magnetic attributes could be greatly extended, but the exercise would hardly prove fruitful. The meaning of such attributes becomes clear only through an understanding of their power, and we must therefore examine Gerald's relations with others.

The London courtesan Minette, who finds fulfillment only in violence, becomes the "passive substance" of Gerald's will. For Gerald, man's will is the absolute, "the only absolute." In one of the many emblematic scenes in the novel, the strength of Gerald's magnetic power is shown in vivid detail. On the way home, the Brangwen sisters see him ride a red Arab mare up to a railway crossing. When the mare bolts at the sound of sharp blasts issuing from a passing locomotive, Gerald ruthlessly holds her in check, using "white magnetic domination" to coerce his mount into "unutterable subordination." Gerald emerges from the struggle

[27] W. H. Auden, "Some Notes on D. H. Lawrence," *The Nation*, 26 April 1947, pp. 482-484.

[28] D. H. Lawrence, *Women in Love* (London: Heinemann, 1971), pp. 53, 57, 389. Page numbers in the text refer hereafter to this edition of the novel.

with his will "bright and untarnished." The mare's instincts, on the other hand, have been perfectly curbed: after the contest with Gerald, her breathing is no longer a "roar," but sounds "automatically."

What Gerald has accomplished with the mare is the perfect analogue of what he has achieved in managing the mines and the lives of the colliers who work them. He seeks nothing more than the "pure fulfillment of his own will in the struggle with the natural conditions." To achieve this end he introduces a mechanical perfection into the operation of the mines. Whether he is making love, taming a horse, or presiding over the mines, Gerald aims only at imposing his will and thus moves, in accordance with Lawrence's psychological typology, closer to chaos and dissolution. By substituting the mechanical principle for the organic, Gerald takes a decisive step toward "pure organic disintegration and pure mechanical organisation" (223).

Gerald's disease is what Lawrence, in his *Fantasia*, called the "ghastly white disease of self-conscious idealism." It is no accident that the narrator of *Women in Love* repeatedly remarks on Gerald's northern beauty and white fairness, that Birkin views his friend as a messenger of the "universal dissolution into whiteness and snow," and that Gerald finds his death among snowflakes whose whiteness and geometrical perfection mock his own aspirations.[29] "It is the death of all life to force a pure *idea* into practice" (81), Lawrence proclaimed in his *Fantasia*. Investing the figure of Gerald with all the traits of idealism, or self-conscious will, that he himself found so repellent, Lawrence moved his character through an atmosphere tainted with corruption and death. Even the locus of Gerald's death is the symbolic analogue of his mental life; frozen in the snows of abstraction, Gerald becomes one with the element that he cultivated in his mental life.

[29] Julian Moynahan, *The Deed of Life: The Novels and Tales of D. H. Lawrence* (Princeton, N.J.: Princeton University Press, 1963), p. 86.

The inverse of Gerald's will to dominate is the desire to be overpowered, "to yield everything to dissolution," as one critic puts it.[30] Gudrun, the one figure in the quartet of major characters who has made the greatest advances on the road to sensuality and corruption, is obsessed by that desire and initially feels drawn to Gerald as a result of it. She is "magnetised" by Gerald's "arctic" manner; his beauty casts a "spell" on her; at times she feels "almost mesmerised" by him; and she thrills at his "magnetic domination" of the Arab mare. Gudrun is attracted not simply to Gerald, but to the world he has created. The "half-automatised colliers," whose voluptuousness resembles that of "machinery, cold and iron," arouse in her a strange nostalgic desire—a desire later unmasked as literal *nostalgie de la boue*. The chapter "Sketch-Book" opens with a description of Gudrun seated on a gravelly shoal, staring at some aquatic plants:

> What she could see was mud, soft, oozy, watery mud, and from its festering chill, water-plants rose up, thick and cool and fleshy, very straight and turgid. . . . She could feel their turgid fleshy structure as in a sensuous vision, she *knew* how they rose out of the mud, she *knew* how they thrust out from themselves, how they stood stiff and succulent against the air. (111)

While Gudrun is absorbed in the plants, Gerald rows toward her "magnetically" to send an "electrical vibration" through her veins. Although Gudrun and Gerald have not yet sealed their diabolical blood compact, they establish at that moment a tacit bond of recognition. Approaching dissolution from two entirely different avenues, they are inexorably drawn to one another.

Gerald and Gudrun stand at opposite ends of Lawrence's spectrum of organic decay and cultural decline. In one of many passages of pure doctrine inserted into the novel,

[30] Schorer, "*Women in Love* and Death," p. 42.

Birkin sets forth a typology of decadence that matches views advanced in Lawrence's essays. He contrasts Nordic "ice-destructive knowledge" and "universal dissolution into whiteness and snow" with the "mindless progressive knowledge through the senses" and "mystic knowledge in disintegration" of the African races (245-247). Gerald, the man of self-conscious will, is an exponent of the former culture; Gudrun, the woman of self-conscious senses, represents the latter. Gerald's faith in pure mechanism leads him down the path of the Arctic races to disintegration; Gudrun's regressive primitivism takes her to the same goal via the African route.[31]

Even before Gerald drifts off into his Alpine sleep, Gudrun has destroyed him by locating the fatal flaw in his will. As Gerald himself confesses to Birkin, there is something about Gudrun that withers his consciousness, blights his vision, and shrivels his soul as if it had been "struck by electricity." The "tremendous flashing interchange" that, according to Lawrence, normally takes place in erotic encounters annihilates rather than renews Gerald's being.

Ursula and Birkin, on the other hand, establish "a rich new circuit" and release "a new current of passional electric energy." From the start Birkin has sought to chart a course that will avoid both the Nordic and the African paths to dissolution:

> There was another way, the way of freedom. There was the paradisal entry into pure, single being, the individual soul taking precedence over love and desire for union, stronger than any pangs of emotion, a lovely state of free proud singleness, which accepted the obligation of the permanent connection with others, and

[31] On the destructive tendencies embodied in the figures of Gerald and Gudrun, see Stephen J. Miko, *Toward "Women in Love": The Emergence of a Lawrentian Aesthetic*, Yale Studies in English, no. 177 (New Haven: Yale University Press, 1971), pp. 238-243.

> with the other, submits to the yoke and leash of love, but never forfeits its own proud individual singleness, even while it loves and yields. (247)

This is the ideal to which Birkin would educate Ursula. But Ursula clings tenaciously to the notion of a love that implies at once complete surrender and perfect possession. "Why drag in the stars?" she asks herself when Birkin speaks of an "equilibrium, a pure balance of two single beings: —as the stars balance each other" (139). But both she and Birkin find at least one moment of ideal equipoise. In the chapter "Excurse," Ursula becomes an "essential new being" after sexual union; she is left "quite free, . . . free in complete ease," and Birkin is "upheld immemorially in timeless force" (310).

Women in Love nonetheless closes on a discordant note. Although Birkin and Ursula have set up what is identified in *Fantasia* as a "dynamic polarized flow of vitalistic force or magnetism or electricity," Birkin lacks a social space in which to engage in the collective activity that constitutes man's second greatest need. After attaining a perfect union with Ursula, his thoughts turn almost automatically to the idea of being free, "in a free place, with a few other people." Without a community in which to fulfill his drive for "purposive activity," Birkin seeks the next best alternative, "eternal union with a man." At the end of the novel, he has yet to consummate such a union, but his faith in its vital importance remains unshaken.

In *Fantasia,* Lawrence declared that his metaphysic was informed by the substance of his novels and poems, and that the novels and poems were in turn shaped by experience alone. His own science, he proudly stated, proceeded solely on the basis of living experience and intuition. Yet some of Lawrence's "scientific" insights clearly derived from his wide and varied readings as well as from experience. William York Tindall, who has identified some of the sources for Lawrence's vitalistic theories, points to the many similarities that exist between ideas expressed in the Hindu philosophy known as Yoga and Lawrence's mystical doctrines.[32] Lawrence became acquainted with Yoga largely through secondhand sources: James M. Pryse's *Apocalypse Unsealed* and Mme Blavatsky's *Secret Doctrine* served as his introduction to this physical and mental discipline. Mme Blavatsky, it should be noted, was a prominent member of the spiritualist movement in America until she broke away from it to found her own Theosophical Society in 1875. For many years a disciple of Mesmer, she amalgamated his views into her own mystical program. Lawrence's concept of a dynamic cosmic power that vibrates from one pole of being to another was no doubt modeled on Mme Blavatsky's description of *Fohat,* an electrical life force that shares the most salient characteristics of both Mesmer's fluid and the Yogic Kundalini.

Although it is difficult to define precisely the sources of Lawrence's mysticism, it is clear that his psychology of consciousness can be traced to eighteenth-century theories of vital energy and anatomical polarity. The passional energy flowing through the universe is for Lawrence a cosmic power, ultimately governed by the sympathetic and voluntary poles of the sun and moon. At once magnetic and electric in nature, it is also the key to physical and mental health. But for Lawrence, the circuits of interchange between individuals take precedence over a rapport between man and the universe. And these circuits are charged with a sexual power that was unrecognized (or at least not explicitly acknowledged) by the magnetizers of an earlier generation.

The polemic waged by Lawrence against Freud was, from the start, futile. The significance of *Fantasia* and of *Psychoanalysis and the Unconscious* rests today not on their insights into human behavior, but on their ability to cast light

[32] William York Tindall, *D. H. Lawrence & Susan His Cow* (New York: Cooper Square, 1972), pp. 124-161.

on Lawrence's own philosophical position. To the twentieth-century reader, whose views have been irrevocably colored by Freudian psychoanalysis, Lawrence's psychology remains unpersuasive. Both admirers and detractors of his work have little patience with passages in the novels that dilate on vital energy, mystic conjunction, and blood consciousness. The sources of such excesses can be traced directly to Lawrence's writings on the unconscious. Although Lawrence can be credited with revitalizing eighteenth-century views, he reshaped those views in such a way that they remain anachronistic to any reader who does not share a partiality for mystical thought.

III

"I have fallen into the hands of the occultists," Thomas Mann candidly avowed in an essay describing his brief foray into the world of mediums and ectoplasmic spirits.[33] Mann's essay, which bears the intriguing title "An Experience in the Occult" ("Okkulte Erlebnisse"), serves not only as a guide to the "most questionable" of Hans Castorp's adventures on the magic mountain, but also reveals the novelist's own ambivalent attitude toward the supernatural. Despite his natural skepticism, Mann accorded the occult a position somewhere near the middle of the spectrum where science shades off into metaphysics. For him it constituted a kind of "empirical-experimental metaphysics."

Mann described the occult as "bizarre," "treacherous," and "disreputable." Yet he could not rid himself of a desire to witness the so-called *Materialisations-Phänomene* that enjoyed wide public acclaim in Munich during the 1920s. Obtaining an invitation to a séance posed little difficulty for him. At the home of Dr. Albert Freiherr von Schrenck-Notzing, Munich's renowned master of ceremonies for spir-

[33] Thomas Mann, *Gesammelte Werke*, 2d ed. (Frankfurt a.M: Fischer, 1970), X, 136. Subsequent references to Mann's work will be to this edition.

itualist gatherings, he became acquainted with the unearthly antics of spirits. There he saw at firsthand the disembodied human limbs and self-propelled objects that occultists dignified with the name of teleplasmic and telekinetic phenomena. Willi S., Schrenck-Notzing's psychic prodigy, had some difficulty warming up for the performance attended by Mann. But after falling into a "magnetic" trance, he succeeded in summoning his ethereal helpmate Minna to the séance.[34] Minna discharged her duties faithfully. After ringing bells, pressing buttons, and tapping out indecipherable messages on a typewriter, she provided a suitable finale by displaying to the audience her forearm and hand.

"What did I in fact see?" Mann asked himself after returning from his journey into occult regions. He ruled out the possibility of fraud and declared it sheer sophistry to question the authenticity of the events he had witnessed. Drawing on the views of Schrenck-Notzing and his associates —views cast in high-sounding technical jargon, but not far removed from those of the early mesmerists and spiritualists —he spoke of a teleplasmic substance that forms the basis of organic life. This substance streams out from mediums (who possess what Mann calls ideoplasmic powers) to give palpable form to their unconscious thoughts and wishes. As implausible as the theory seems, there remains little doubt that Mann found some truth in it. The fact that Dr. Krokowski, the tendentious psychoanalyst of *Der Zauberberg*, sponsors similar ideas only gives added emphasis to the vulgar and unappetizing features of spiritualism. Events at the séance over which Krokowski presides clearly suggest that the spirits invoked by mediums are genuine messengers from another world. How is one, after all, to explain the attire of the ghost conjured up by the company at Berghof? The specter of Joachim Ziemssen makes its appearance in

[34] For photographs of Willi S., see A. Freiherr von Schrenck-Notzing, *Materialisations-Phänomene: Ein Beitrag zur Erforschung der mediumistischen Teleplastie*, 2d ed. (Munich: Ernst Reinhardt, 1923).

military dress modeled on uniforms and helmets that were yet to be designed for German soldiers of the First World War.[35]

In the concluding paragraphs of his essay on the occult, Mann categorically stated that he would never again attend another session at Schrenck-Notzing's establishment. But he immediately qualified this statement by conceding that the first séance had so whetted his appetite that he might well venture another visit or two. In fact Mann attended three séances in all, though after the publication of his essay, he never again returned to Schrenck-Notzing's salon.[36] In later years the man who often referred to himself as the "magician" turned his attention from the gifts of mediums to the powers of hypnotists.

Shortly after the end of the Second World War, Mann reviewed his literary career and, in passing, identified the principal theme of *Mario und der Zauberer* (1930). That highly political tale, he observed, explores the psychology of fascism and the problem of freedom (XI, 672).[37] While Mann's critics have defined the principal political and ethical issues raised by *Mario und der Zauberer*, they have, for the most part, disregarded the psychological dimensions of the story and have consequently failed to explain why Mann chose a magician with hypnotic powers to play the central role in it.[38]

[35] On this point see Hermann J. Weigand, *Thomas Mann's Novel "Der Zauberberg"* (New York: Appleton-Century, 1933), pp. 143-144.

[36] Hans Bürgin and Hans-Otto Mayer, *Thomas Mann: Eine Chronik seines Lebens* (Frankfurt a. M.: Fischer, 1965), p. 61.

[37] A decade earlier, Mann had referred to the work as "a tale with moral and political implications." See the preface to *Stories of Three Decades*, trans. H. T. Lowe-Porter (New York: Knopf, 1936), p. viii.

[38] Henry Hatfield first called attention to the political message of Mann's story and to its significance for understanding the structure of the text: see "Thomas Mann's *Mario und der Zauberer*: An Interpretation," *Germanic Review*, 21 (1946), 306-312. For less balanced interpretations that focus mainly on political aspects of the work, see Eugen Imhof, "Thomas Mann: 'Mario und der Zauberer,'" *Der Deutsch-*

For all his seemingly preternatural powers, the hypnotist Cipolla is not an artist. The gifts of this "charlatan and mountebank" who seems to have stepped out of the eighteenth century are more closely aligned with the hocus-pocus and humbug ("fauler Zauber") that Mann linked to fascist leaders than with the delightful roguery associated with some of Mann's artists. Cipolla in addition embraces precisely those attitudes that Mann viewed as the essence of fascism: the showman's anti-intellectual bias and his celebration of irrational forces mark him as an exponent of totalitarian ideology.[39]

Let us now turn, however, to the views of the German tourist who narrates the story in which Cipolla makes his appearance. *Mario und der Zauberer* divides quite neatly into two sections; in the very first paragraph of his account the narrator provides the link connecting these two parts:

> The atmosphere of Torre di Venere remains unpleasant in the memory. From the first moment the air of the place made us uneasy, we felt irritable, on edge; then at the end came the shocking business of Cipolla, that dreadful being who seemed to incorporate, in so fateful and so humanly impressive a way, all the particular evilness of the situation as a whole.[40]

---

unterricht, 4 (1952), 59-69; Harry Matter, "'Mario und der Zauberer': Die Bedeutung der Novelle im Schaffen Thomas Manns," *Weimarer Beiträge,* 6 (1960), 579-596; Dietrich Schuckmann, "Thomas Manns Novelle 'Mario und der Zauberer' im Literaturunterricht der 12. Klasse," *Deutschunterricht,* 16 (1963), 26-44; and J. P. Stern, *Hitler: The Führer and the People* (Glasgow: Fontana/Collins, 1975), pp. 66-67.

[39] In his "Rede über Lessing," Mann identified these two traits as the most salient characteristics of fascist thought (IX, 244-245).

[40] "Die Erinnerung an Torre di Venere ist atmosphärisch unangenehm. Ärger, Gereiztheit, Überspannung lagen von Anfang an in der Luft, und zum Schluss kam dann der Choc mit diesem schrecklichen Cipolla, in dessen Person sich das eigentümlich Bösartige der Stimmung auf verhängnishafte und übrigens menschlich sehr eindrucksvolle Weise zu verkörpern und bedrohlich zusammenzudrängen schien." (VIII, 658)

Descriptions of the Italian resort town and of the German family's unpleasant experiences in the Grand Hotel and on the beach take up the first quarter of the text and set the stage for Cipolla's "entertainment." The strident tone of provincial nationalism prevailing on the beach anticipates Cipolla's patriotic outburst on the grandeur of Italy; the shabby treatment to which the narrator and his family are subjected prepares the way for Cipolla's contemptuous attitude toward his audience. Even the detailed reflections on atmospheric conditions in Torre di Venere form a prelude to Cipolla's performance. The blazing Italian sun, which "arrogantly" beats down on natives and tourists alike, imposes what the narrator calls a "reign of terror." On Cipolla's arrival in Torre di Venere, the sun suddenly disappears behind the clouds as if to make way for its human counterpart. For the narrator, Cipolla personifies the oppressive tensions with which the atmosphere of Torre di Venere is charged.

Cipolla's superhuman hypnotic powers become immediately apparent. Before the magician's actual performance begins, one impetuous youth makes the fatal error of challenging his authority. Cipolla delivers a pointed lecture on volition, orders the fellow to stick out his tongue at the audience, turns his "piercing gaze" on him, and snaps his whip through the air. Without a moment's hesitation the youth carries out Cipolla's command. Such spellbinding theatrical feats, in combination with a glib eloquence and fawning servility, enable the hypnotist to gain a hold over the rest of his audience. The first half of Cipolla's act draws largely on a variety of routine magical tricks: that repertoire marks the magician as little more than an astute mathematician, a cardsharp, and a master of parlor games. Only when provoked does he summon up his mesmerist powers. But after the intermission, Cipolla's "tricks" take on a decidedly sinister tone. A sturdy young man loses the power to raise his arm; another is reduced to a state of "military somnambulism"; a third joins, against his will, a company of dancing "automatons" that Cipolla has set in motion on the stage.

Cipolla himself never tires of proclaiming that he—and not his victims—assumes the "suffering, receptive, and performing part" during the proceedings. Acting in obedience to what he calls the common will, he miraculously carries out directives that have been devised in secret by members of the audience. Yet he never relinquishes the role of the leader and reminds his audience that, in the *Führer*, will becomes obedience and obedience will.

The narrator repeatedly punctuates his account of Cipolla's performance with comments on the audience's responses and with reflections on his own growing sense of uneasiness as the evening progresses. The hour is late; the narrator's children—although delighted by the show—are dozing off; Cipolla's tone becomes increasingly offensive. There is every reason to return home. And yet, yielding to his children's pleas, the narrator decides to stay "for the moment, for a little while longer, just a few minutes more." The sequence of temporal phrases suggests that, against his own better judgment, he succumbs more than once to the temptation to linger. The entire audience seems to share the narrator's ambivalent feelings toward Cipolla, and yet not a person leaves the room. "Were we under the sway of a fascination that emanated from this man who earned his bread in so strange a manner; a fascination which he gave out independently of the program—even between the tricks —and which paralyzed our will?" (VIII, 695), the narrator wonders. As reluctant as he is to admit this possibility and as often as he manufactures new explanations for his failure to leave at the intermission, it seems clear that he too falls under Cipolla's spell.

In addition to the psychological and possibly occult overtones of Cipolla's powers, there exists in the relationship between the hypnotist and his subjects a distinctly erotic strain. Signora Angiolieri, an attractive Italian woman who served as companion to Eleonore Duse before marrying a meek, physically unimpressive man, proves especially vulnerable to Cipolla's influence. Ignoring her husband's entreaties to resist the magician's commands, she marches toward Cipolla without once faltering in her course. Powers "stronger than either reason or virtue" triumph over connubial loyalties.

The greatest humiliation, however, is reserved for Mario, an unassuming youth whose profession as waiter—a man trained both to obey and to serve—takes on special significance. Laboring under the delusion that the grotesque hunchback is his beloved Silvestra, Mario plants a kiss on Cipolla's cheek. What the audience witnesses represents, in the narrator's words, a "public display of timid and deluded passionate rapture." Mario strikes out at his oppressor at the moment when he becomes conscious of the public degradation to which Cipolla has subjected him. As one critic correctly points out, Mario's injured sense of dignity impels him to act, to fire the fatal shots at the tyrant.[41] Despotic control is cast off not through a conscious act of will, but through an instinctive desire to recover a sense of personal integrity.

The title *Mario und der Zauberer* is somewhat misleading, for Mann's story tells us far more about his narrator's impressions of Torre di Venere and his personal response to Cipolla than about either the young assassin or his victim. The major part of the text examines the relationship between Cipolla and his audience as the narrator perceives it. While this highly sensitive narrator is unable (or unwilling) to define the exact nature of his own fascination with Cipolla, he identifies precisely the source of the magician's power to subdue others in the audience. "This proud cripple," he observes, "was the most powerful hypnotist I had ever come across in my life" (VIII, 696). But in the opinion of at least one expert in mass psychology, the narrator's inability to walk out on Cipolla's performance stems also from hypnotic influence.

In an essay entitled "Group Psychology and the Analysis

[41] Hatfield, "Thomas Mann's *Mario und der Zauberer*," p. 312.

of the Ego," Sigmund Freud cites a key passage from Gustave Le Bon's *Psychology of Crowds* (*Psychologie des foules*): "An individual immersed for some length of time in a group in action soon finds himself . . . in a special state, which much resembles the state of 'fascination' in which the hypnotized individual finds himself in the hands of the hypnotizer."[42] Le Bon, as Freud notes, explained the mental state of fascination by pointing to the "mutual suggestion" of individuals within a group and to the "prestige" of the group's leader. Freud had no quarrel with Le Bon's analogy between group formation and the bond that develops between a hypnotist and his subject—in fact he considered it accurate to state that the two phenomena are identical. He also adopted Le Bon's view that contagion, the commerce that takes place among members of a group, and suggestion, the relation between members of a group and their leader, constitute the two main traits of closely knit groups. But Freud moved beyond Le Bon's descriptive observations to study the etiology of group behavior and to provide an analytic interpretation of group psychology.

A group, Freud writes, consists of "*a number of individuals who have put one and the same object in the place of their ego ideal* [what Freud was later to call the superego] *and have consequently identified themselves with one another in their ego.*"[43] The moral conscience of a group is externalized in its leader, a figure who represents the "dreaded primal father." The leader awakens in his subjects that part of their "archaic heritage" that once rendered them compliant to their parents. The members of a group are, then, held together as a cohesive social unit by a common libidinal tie inhibited in its aims. The emotional bond joining the group to its leader in turn fosters emotional bonds within the group. Contagion thus derives from suggestion, and the source of suggestion itself lies in a "mys-

[42] Sigmund Freud, *Standard Edition of the Complete Psychological Works*, trans. and ed. James Strachey, 24 vols. (London: Hogarth, 1953-74), XVIII, 75-76.

[43] Ibid., p. 116.

terious power" which, as Freud notes, is widely identified as "animal magnetism." Such magnetism derives its strength, both in hypnotic relations and in group formations, from the fact that suggestibility is actually an "irreducible, primitive phenomenon, a fundamental fact in the mental life of man."[44] The predisposition for suggestibility, which has survived in the collective unconscious mind, has its roots in the early history of the family.

If Freud's discussion of the genesis of suggestibility in mental life is not entirely convincing, his analysis of mass psychology does not in any way suffer from the highly speculative nature of his metapsychological thought. His observation that the individual submerged in a group forfeits the power to exercise his own moral conscience and yields to "the attraction of the increased pleasure that is certainly obtained from the removal of inhibitions" provides a succinct explanation for the remarkable behavior of both the narrator and the audience in *Mario und der Zauberer*.[45] The narrator concedes that his own critical faculties were mysteriously paralyzed during Cipolla's performance. Although he does not have an opportunity to experience the great sense of relief and pleasure attending compliance with the magician's most outrageous demands, he confesses that he too was infected by the general devil-may-care attitude that contaminated the audience. His statement, "Nothing mattered any longer," starkly underlines the abandonment of normal ethical standards. Cipolla's dazzling feats give rise to "a kind of dissolution, a kind of festive, helter-skelter abandon, a drunken abdication of critical resistance." Cipolla assumes, to a greater or lesser extent, the role of the moral conscience for the individuals in his audience. The spectators thus come to support forms of regressive behavior that their own private consciences would not tolerate.

Freud's analysis of group formation and Mann's fictional treatment of the same subject bring strikingly similar insights to bear on the psychological mechanisms operating

[44] Ibid., p. 89.

[45] Ibid., p. 85.

in the attitude of a group toward its leader. Although it is likely that Mann knew of Freud's essay, there is to my knowledge no evidence that he had actually read it.[46] That Mann's story appears to highlight features of Freud's theories should, however, come as no great surprise. The novelist himself pointed out in "Freud and the Future" ("Freud und die Zukunft") that affinities between ideas expressed in his own work and the findings of psychoanalytic inquiry had existed long before he became acquainted with the writings of his Viennese contemporary. "It would indeed be too much to say that I came to psychoanalysis," Mann noted with characteristic modesty. "It came to me" (IX, 482). Freud's disciples, he added, had long recognized the connections between his own early works and the theories that their mentor was developing. In *Mario und der Zauberer,* Mann's latent sympathy with psychoanalysis becomes manifest.

Mann's story of hypnotic control may, however, have drawn inspiration from more than just a latent sympathy with psychoanalysis. In the 1920s, the German film industry was producing what Siegfried Kracauer has called a "procession of tyrants."[47] Those tyrants resembled in many ways the *Massenhypnotiseur* that Mann had consciously sought to portray in *Mario und der Zauberer.* Cipolla's cinematic cousins include such fiendish personalities as Dr. Caligari and Dr. Mabuse—men who use hypnosis to satisfy their craving for power. *The Cabinet of Dr. Caligari (Das Kabinett des Dr. Caligari*), as it was first conceived by the authors of the screenplay, attempted to expose the brutality

[46] Although Mann owned an edition of Freud's collected works, he made no annotations in the margins of the essay on group psychology. I am grateful to Henry Hatfield for examining Mann's library in Zurich.

[47] Siegfried Kracauer, *From Caligari to Hitler: A Psychological History of the German Film* (Princeton, N.J.: Princeton University Press, 1947), p. 77. See also Lotte Eisner, *The Haunted Screen* (London: Thames and Hudson, 1969), and Roger Manvell and Heinrich Fraenkel, *The German Cinema* (London: J. M. Dent & Sons, 1971), pp. 11-49.

of authoritarian rule. Caligari, a mad psychiatrist who converts a somnambulist into the instrument of his will, was to serve as a symbol of despotism. The filmed version of the script, however, introduced a radical change that subverted the authors' intentions. Robert Wiene, the director, added an opening and closing sequence that presented Caligari's evil deeds as nothing more than the paranoid fantasies of a madman. Francis, the young man who tells the tale of Caligari's crimes and whose retrospective narrative constitutes the film's plot, is in reality the inmate of an asylum. Laboring under the delusion that the asylum's director is mad, he has invented the entire story of Caligari as a justification for his own confinement. Yet one portion of the film's message remains intact despite Wiene's recasting of the plot: the link between tyranny and hypnotic control.

Fritz Lang's *Dr. Mabuse, The Gambler* (*Dr. Mabuse, Der Spieler*), filmed two years later in 1922, showed the use of hypnosis on a grand scale. Mabuse, a man of many disguises, has more than one victim. A power-hungry criminal, he manipulates the commodities market, runs a counterfeiting ring, and uses his hypnotic powers to coerce others into carrying out his bidding. Even Dr. Wenk, the foxy public prosecutor, is unable to resist Mabuse's powerful gaze. Mabuse, like the Caligari of Francis's imagination, is eventually trapped by the forces of good and goes mad. The reign of terror he launches ends with his capture.

A decade later, shortly before fleeing the real tyranny of Nazi Germany, Lang directed a sequel to the film. In *The Last Will of Dr. Mabuse* (*Das Testament des Dr. Mabuse*), the titular villain hatches, from the madhouse, a diabolical plot to control the world. Using the director of the asylum and a gang of criminals as his agents, he manages to throw mankind into an "abyss of terror." Lang later reported that he had made the film as "an allegory to show Hitler's process of terrorism."[48] That Goebbels banned the film before

[48] Cited in Kracauer, *From Caligari to Hitler*, p. 248.

it could be shown in Germany suggests that the portrayal of Mabuse hit uncomfortably close to home.

If we now turn from fiction, theory, and cinematic documents to historical fact, Mann's tale, Freud's essay, and Lang's films seem to take on a nearly prophetic character. The man whose party was to drive Mann and Lang out of Germany and Freud from Austria possessed, in exaggerated form, nearly all the principal traits assigned by these three men to leaders. Friends, associates, and supporters of Adolf Hitler repeatedly drew attention to the Führer's magnetic personality, the hypnotic quality of his eyes, and his ability to cast a magical spell on those who surrounded him.[49] Large crowds were especially receptive to Hitler's electrifying rhetoric and mesmerizing gaze.

That Hitler deliberately sought to draw people under his influence by riveting his gaze upon them is evident from the testimony of dozens of witnesses. He scheduled his speeches for late in the evening when physical and mental resistance to his impassioned oratory was at its lowest point. For an hour or two he would deliver a soporific lecture on historical and philosophical questions. When his audience had been lulled into a semiconscious state, Hitler would deliver his real message. At a military conference in 1945, Hitler explicitly acknowledged his use of hypnotic persuasion: he announced to his colleagues that he in-

[49] Gerhard Ritter calls attention to these traits in his introduction to *Hitlers Tischgespräche im Führerhauptquartier: 1941-42*, comp. Henry Picker (Bonn: Athenäum, 1951), pp. 14-15. See also Walter C. Langer, *The Mind of Adolf Hitler: The Secret Wartime Report* (New York: Basic Books, 1972), pp. 44-49, and Joseph Nyomarkay, *Charisma and Factionalism in the Nazi Party* (Minneapolis: University of Minnesota Press, 1967), pp. 9-15. For documentation on this aspect of Hitler's personality, see Rudolph Binion, *Hitler among the Germans* (New York: Elsevier, 1976), pp. 118-127. Professor Binion generously shared his extensive knowledge of the Führer's legendary magnetic powers with me.

tended that very day to "hypnotize" the Norwegian fascist leader Vidkun Quisling.[50]

Finally we may turn to the testimony of Hitler's associates to learn what kind of role the Führer played in their psychic lives. After a quarrel with Hitler, Goebbels wrote in his diary that his falling out with the Führer had deprived him of his "inner self." Göring echoed this view when he declared: "I have no conscience. Adolf Hitler is my conscience."[51] Hitler seems to have exercised his powers with equal success on individuals and on the masses.

Like Mann's Cipolla, Hitler also promoted an image of himself as the instrument of a higher power. For Cipolla the inner voice that dictates his actions is the communal will; for Hitler it was both that and divine providence. Following his course with the "precision and security of a sleepwalker," he promised the German people to carry out the mission thrust upon him by fate: "fulfillment of Germany's destiny."[52]

While Hitler's alleged animal magnetism and his oratorical gifts alone are obviously insufficient to explain his rise to power, they can enlarge our understanding of the tremendous appeal that he exercised on individuals and groups alike. The Führer's magical powers naturally became more effective as the legend that he was endowed with those powers gained currency. Although it is difficult to determine how much these powers rested on Hitler's genuinely hypnotic gaze and to what extent they stemmed from his audience's eagerness to believe that he possessed them, the fact

[50] *Hitlers Lagebesprechungen: Die Protokollfragmente seiner militärischen Konferenzen, 1942-45*, ed. Helmut Heiber (Stuttgart: Deutsche Verlags-Anstalt, 1962), p. 862.

[51] *Das Tagebuch von Joseph Goebbels: 1925-26*, ed. Helmut Heiber (Stuttgart: Deutsche Verlags-Anstalt, n.d.), p. 60. Hermann Rauschning reported Göring's statement: see his *Gespräche mit Hitler* (Zurich: Europa, 1940), p. 77.

[52] Langer, *The Mind of Adolf Hitler*, p. 29.

remains that Hitler consciously exploited hypnosis in order to maintain his position as leader of the German people.

IV

"How have I been able to live so long outside nature," asks the narrator of Gérard de Nerval's *Aurélia*, "without identifying myself with it? Everything lives, everything moves, everything corresponds; the magnetic rays, emanating from myself or from others, cross the infinite chain of created things unimpeded; the network covering the world is transparent, and its slender threads communicate themselves by degrees to the planets and stars. Captive now upon earth, I commune with the chorus of the stars who share in my joys and sorrows!" ("Comment . . . ai-je pu exister si longtemps hors de la nature et sans m'identifier à elle? Tout vit, tout agit, tout se correspond; les rayons magnétiques émanés de moi-même ou des autres traversent sans obstacle la chaîne infinie des choses crées; c'est un réseau transparent qui couvre le monde, et dont les fils déliés se communiquent de proche en proche aux planètes et aux étoiles. Captif en ce moment sur la terre, je m'entretiens avec le choeur des astres, qui prend part à mes joies et à mes douleurs!")[53] These joyous effusions are suddenly arrested by a chilling thought: "If electricity, which is the magnetism of physical bodies, can be forced in a direction imposed on it by laws, then hostile and tyrannical spirits may be able to enslave the intelligences of others and make use of their divided strength for purposes of domination." ("Si l'électricité, . . . qui est le magnétisme des corps physiques, peut subir une direction qui lui impose des lois, à plus forte raison des esprits hostiles et tyranniques peuvent asservir les intelligences et se servir de leurs forces divisées dans un but de domination.")[54]

[53] Gérard de Nerval, *Oeuvres*, ed. Albert Béguin and Jean Richer, 2 vols. (Paris: Gallimard, 1966), I, 403.

[54] Ibid., pp. 403-404.

In the course of his monologue, Nerval's narrator sounds the two dominant themes of mesmerist literature. His vision of a "vast conspiracy between every living creature to reestablish the world in its original harmony" renews faith in the organic unity of nature and in man's ability to recover that unity. Joining the chorus of Romantic voices proclaiming the perfect harmony of nature, he sees in magnetism a vehicle for securing a sense of communion and continuity in the chain of creation. The mystical experience he describes came to figure as the source of artistic inspiration for writers from Novalis to Hawthorne. Magnetism, with its partner electricity, made it possible to communicate with the entire universe—to attain that exalted mental state considered highly conducive to poetic invention.

The magnetic and electric qualities of mystical experience and inspiration were not unknown to earlier writers. Good poets, Socrates told Ion the rhapsode, "compose their beautiful poems not by art, but because they are inspired and possessed." When the Muse takes hold of poets, a divinity, "like that contained in the stone which Euripides calls a magnet," moves within them and endows them with a magnetic power to attract other men.[55] Socrates' remarks were echoed many centuries later in Shelley's words on poetry: "The sacred links of that chain have never been entirely disjoined, which descending through the minds of many men is attached to those great minds, whence as from a magnet the invisible effluence is sent forth, which at once connects, animates and sustains the life of all."[56] For some nineteenth-century writers, the discovery of animal magnetism turned the spiritual magnetism of poetry into a physical reality.

The doctrine of inspiration, both in its pagan and in its

[55] *The Dialogues of Plato*, trans. B. Jowett, 2 vols. (New York: Random House, 1937), I, 289.

[56] "A Defence of Poetry," in *The Complete Works of Percy Bysshe Shelley*, ed. Roger Ingpen and Walter E. Peck, 10 vols. (New York: Gordian Press, 1965), VII, 124.

Platonic form, was later absorbed into the mysteries of the Christian religion. There, it was the "divine spark" that represented the presence of God's qualities in man. The Romantics, as noted earlier, mined the rich vein of Christian mysticism for words to describe the creative process. Many of them, however, transformed the divine spark that kindles flames of love into an electrical spark that generates bolts of lightning. Again, an example from Shelley is apposite. In his view, each of Dante's words is "as a spark, . . . pregnant with a lightning which has yet found no conductor."[57] The magnetic and electrical metaphors for expressing the gift of divine visitation prepared the way, in a sense, for the associations between mesmerism and creative consciousness.

For Kleist, Hoffmann, Balzac, and Hawthorne, as for Nerval, mesmerism came to be associated with both divine influence and demonic power—in many cases an ambiguous combination of the two. Enslavement and domination, as Nerval's narrator notes, are the goals of men who have arrogated powers once controlled solely by the gods or by nature. Sandy, the "Laird of Cockpen" in George du Maurier's *Trilby*, gives a telling portrait of one such mesmerist figure: "He's a bad fellow, Svengali—I'm sure of it! He mesmerized you; that's what it is—mesmerism! I've often heard of it, but never seen it done before. They get you into their power, and just make you do any blessed thing they please—lie, murder, steal—anything!"[58] The same could be said of Hoffmann's Count S——i, Balzac's Vautrin, and Hawthorne's Westervelt. (Kleist's Wetter vom Strahl at first seems to belong with this infernal trio, but in the last analysis, he does not consciously wield his power over Käthchen.) Eros, passion, and the will to power are the prime movers of the mesmerist intrigues that these men set into motion.

[57] Ibid., p. 131.

[58] George du Maurier, *Trilby* (New York: Harper & Brothers, 1895), p. 75.

If it is true, as Denis de Rougemont has argued, that in our own century passion has been transplanted from private life into the public arena, then the transference of mesmerist powers from suitors and seducers to political tyrants becomes quite logical.[59] In twentieth-century literature, hypnosis represents a tool for establishing master-slave relationships not merely between men and women, but also between the leader and the masses. These two varieties of mesmerist control appear in Lawrence's *Women in Love* and Mann's *Mario and the Magician.* The political demagogue who figures significantly in the history as well as in the literature of our century inherited his traits from the mesmerist and the man of will who dominated the literary landscape of the nineteenth century. If the range of his influence exceeds that of his literary predecessors, his ruthless character and lust for power remain unchanged.

[59] Denis de Rougemont, *Love in the Western World,* trans. Montgomery Belgion, rev. ed. (New York: Harper & Row, 1974), pp. 267-271.

Appendix

Mesmer's Propositions

Mesmer's twenty-seven propositions on animal magnetism outline the essential points of his doctrines. They were published in his *Mémoire sur la découverte du magnétisme animal* in 1779.

1. Il existe une influence mutuelle entre les corps célestes, la terre et les corps animés.

2. Un fluide universellement répandu, et continué de manière à ne souffrir aucun vide, dont la subtilité ne permet aucune comparaison, et qui, de sa nature, est susceptible de recevoir, propager et communiquer toutes les impressions du mouvement, est le moyen de cette influence.

3. Cette action réciproque est soumise à des lois mécaniques inconnues jusqu'à présent.

4. Il résulte de cette action des effets alternatifs qui peuvent être considérés comme un flux et un reflux.

5. Ce reflux est plus ou moins général, plus ou moins particulier, plus ou moins composé, selon la nature des causes qui le déterminent.

6. C'est par cette opération, la plus universelle de celles que la nature nous offre, que les relations d'activité s'exercent entre les corps célestes, la terre et ses parties constituantes.

7. Les propriétés de la matière et du corps organisé dépendent de cette opération.

8. Le corps animal éprouve des effets alternatifs de cet agent, et c'est en s'insinuant dans la substance des nerfs qu'il les affecte immédiatement.

9. Il se manifeste, particulièrement dans le corps humain, des propriétés analogues à celles de l'aimant; on y distingue des pôles également divers et opposés, qui peuvent être communiqués, changés, détruits et renforcés; le phénomène même de l'inclinaison y est observé.

10. La propriété du corps animal qui le rend susceptible de l'influence des corps célestes et de l'action réciproque de ceux qui l'environnent, manifestée par son analogie avec l'aimant, m'a déterminé à la nommer magnétisme animal.

11. L'action et la vertu du magnétisme animal, ainsi caractérisées, peuvent être communiquées à d'autres corps animés ou inanimés. Les uns et les autres en sont cependant plus ou moins susceptibles.

12. Cette action et cette vertu peuvent être renforcées et propagées par ces mêmes corps.

13. On observe à l'expérience l'écoulement d'une matière dont la subtilité pénètre tous les corps sans perdre notablement de son activité.

14. Son action a lieu à une distance éloignée, sans le secours d'aucun corps intermédiaire.

15. Elle est augmentée et réfléchie par les glaces, comme la lumière.

16. Elle est communiquée, propagée et augmentée par le son.

17. Cette vertu magnétique peut être accumulée, concentrée, transportée.

18. J'ai dit que les corps animés n'en étaient pas également susceptibles: il en est même, quoique très rares, qui ont une propriété si opposée, que leur seul présence détruit tous les effets de ce magnétisme sur les autres corps.

19. Cette vertu opposée pénètre aussi tous les corps; elle peut être également communiquée, propagée, accumulée, concentrée et transportée, réfléchie par les glaces et propa-

gée par le son, ce qui constitue non seulement une privation, mais une vertu opposée positive.

20. L'aimant, soit naturel, soit artificiel, est, ainsi que les autres corps, susceptible du magnétisme animal, et même de la vertu opposée, sans que ni dans l'un ni dans l'autre cas son action sur le feu et l'aiguille souffre aucune altération, ce qui prouve que le principe du magnétisme animal diffère essentiellement de celui du minéral.

21. Ce système fournira de nouveaux éclaircissements sur la nature du feu et de la lumière, ainsi que dans la théorie de l'attraction, du flux et du reflux, de l'aimant et de l'électricité.

22. Il fera connaître que l'aimant et l'électricité artificielle n'ont, à l'égard des maladies, que des propriétés communes avec une foule d'autres agents que la nature nous offre, et que, s'il est résulté quelques effets utiles de l'administration de ceux-là, ils sont dus au magnétisme animal.

23. On reconnaîtra par les faits, d'après les règles pratiques que j'établirai, que ce principe peut guérir immédiatement les maladies des nerfs et médiatement les autres.

24. Qu'avec son secours, le médecin est éclairé sur l'usage des médicaments, qu'il perfectionne leur action, et qu'il provoque et dirige les crises salutaires, de manière à s'en rendre le maître.

25. En communiquant ma méthode, je démontrerai, par une théorie nouvelle des maladies, l'utilité universelle du principe que je leur oppose.

26. Avec cette connaissance, le médecin jugera sûrement l'origine, la nature et les progrès des maladies même des plus compliquées; il en empêchera l'accroissement et parviendra à leur guérison sans jamais exposer le malade à des effets dangereux et à des suites fâcheuses, quels que soient l'âge, le tempérament et le sexe. Les femmes, même dans l'état de grossesse, et lors des accouchements, jouiront du même avantage.

27. Cette doctrine, enfin, mettra le médecin en état de bien juger du degré de santé de chaque individu, et de le préserver des maladies auxquelles il pourrait être exposé. L'art de guérir parviendra ainsi à sa dernière perfection.

Index

Abrams, M. H., *Natural Supernaturalism*, 67n
abreaction, compared with magnetic crisis, 15-16; used in cathartic method, 39
Academy of Sciences (Bavaria), 10
Academy of Sciences (Berlin), 10
Academy of Sciences (Paris), 12, 17n, 21; investigates animal magnetism, 16; Charcot's association with, 33-34; denounced by Hugo, 158
Agrippa, Cornelius, 61
Albrecht, Hans, on Kleist, 101n
All-Tier, see Ritter, Johann Wilhelm
animal electricity, Galvani's discovery of, 58-59
animal gravity, 8
animal heat, 23
animal magnetism, *see* Mesmer: theory of animal magnetism
Animist Society of Harmony (Ostend), 25
animists, replace animal magnetism with faith and will, 25-26
Anna O. (Breuer's patient Bertha Pappenheim), treated by cathartic method, 37; case history, 39-40
Anstett, Jean-Jacques, *La Pensée religieuse de Friedrich Schlegel*, 76n
Arnim, Achim von, 76n; interest in electricity and magnetism, 75
Artelt, Walter, *Der Mesmerismus in Berlin*, 76n; on mesmerism in Germany, 76n
asthenic disease, 56, 57. *See also* Brown, John
Auden, W. H., on D. H. Lawrence, 249
Aurélia, see Nerval, Gérard de

Baader, Franz von, on an internal sense, 46
Bachelard, Gaston, *La Terre et les rêveries de la volonté*, 143n
Bader, Arno L., on mesmerism, 190n, 193n
Bailly, Jean-Sylvain, 21
Balzac, Anne Laure (Mme de), 184
Balzac, Bernard-François, 166, 184
Balzac, Honoré de
general: x, xi, xiv, 81, 156, 232, 270; personal magnetism and strength of will, 152-54; theory of vital force, 166-69; analysis of metaphorical language, 169-70; significance of money, 170-71; and Schopenhauer, 175-77; interest in the occult, 184-85; belief that writing prolongs life, 188
works: *Albertus Savarus*, 181-82; *The Centenarian*, 166, 181; *César Birotteau*, 169-70; *Cousin Pons*, 178-79; *Cousine Bette*, 183-84; "Ecce Homo," 166; "The Elixir of Long Life," 166; *Eugénie Grandet*, 170-71; "Facino Cane," 187; "Gobseck,"

Balzac, Honoré de (*cont.*)
170-73, 180, 188; *History of the Thirteen*, 177, 183; *Lost Illusions*, 178, 182-83; *The Old Maid*, 182-83; *La Peau de chagrin*, 169, 171-75, 180, 188; *The Quest for the Absolute*, 167-68, 173; *Splendeurs et misères des courtisanes*, 187; *Sténie*, 182n; "The Unknown Martyrs," 165, 181; "A Woman of Thirty," 177-78
Louis Lambert: 168, 169, 173, 188, 190n; hero's mental powers, 160-64; views on will and thought, 161-63; quest for knowledge, 165-66; *Treatise on the Will*, 174-75
Ursule Mirouët: 178, 182; clairvoyance of passion, 184; mystical features of animal magnetism, 185-86; heroine contrasted with Vautrin, 187-88
Vautrin (character in *La Comédie humaine*): preternatural powers, 174, 177-80; significance of sobriquet Trompe-la-Mort, 179-81; as exponent of "poetry of evil," 187
Banta, Martha, *Henry James and the Occult*, 236n, 240n
baquet, 24, 25, 159; description of, 13-14
Barbarin, Chevalier de, 29; replaces magnetic fluid with will and prayer, 25-26
Bardèche, Maurice, on Balzac, 166n, 167n
Barrucand, Dominique, *Histoire de l'hypnose en France*, 23n, 33n
Bastien und Bastienne, *see* Mozart, Wolfgang Amadeus
Baudelaire, Charles, on Balzac, 153
Béguin, Albert, *L'Ame romantique et le rêve*, 77n
Bell, Millicent, *Hawthorne's View of the Artist*, 206n
Benz, Ernst, *Franz Anton Mesmer und seine Ausstrahlung in Europa und Amerika*, 24n, 192n
Bérard, Suzanne J., on *Louis Lambert*, 161n
Bergasse, Nicolas, 19
Berlin, University of, 75, 156, 175
Berliner Abendblätter, 87
Bernfeld, Siegfried, on Helmholtz and Freud, 43n
Bernheim, Hippolyte Marie, 6, 30, 32, 36, 42; visits Liébeault's clinic, 33; challenges Charcot's views, 33-34; consulted by Freud, 38; views on posthypnotic amnesia, 41
Berny, Laure (Mme de), 188
Besser, Gretchen R., *Balzac's Concept of Genius*, 169n, 180n
Bewley, Marius, on *The Blithedale Romance* and *The Bostonians*, 235n, 236n
Bicêtre, 35
Bichat, Xavier, 174
Binion, Rudolph, *Hitler among the Germans*, 266n
Bittel, Karl, *Mesmer und sein Problem*, 7n
Blanchard, Marc, on Balzac, 153n
Blavatskaya, Elena Petrovna (Mme Blavatsky), 254
Blithedale Romans, The, *see* Hawthorne, Nathaniel
Bloch, Marc, *The Royal Touch*, 5n
Böckmann, Paul, on Kleist's "Über das Marionettentheater," 115
Böhmer, Auguste, 57n

Bollnow, Otto Friedrich, on Hoffmann, 139n
Bonnet-Roy, F., on Balzac, 166n
Bostonians, The, see James, Henry
Bouvard et Pécuchet, see Flaubert, Gustave
Boyd, Aubrey, on Dickens, 191n
Brahm, Otto, on *Die Wahlverwandtschaften*, 78n
Braid, James, 3; introduced to animal magnetism, 31; publishes study on hypnosis, 32
Breuer, Josef, 28, 29, 36, 42, 43; cathartic method, 37-40; *Studies on Hysteria*, 38-40
Brontë, Charlotte, 190, 191n
Brown, Ford Madox, 55
Brown, John, 58n; medical theories, 55-56; *Elementa Medicinae*, 56; influence in Germany, 56-58; principle of excitability, 166-67
Browning, Elizabeth Barrett, 190, 191n
Browning, Robert, 190; "Mesmerism," 191n
Bulwer-Lytton, Edward, 190
Buranelli, Vincent, *The Wizard from Vienna*, 7n, 192n, 197n
Burckhardt, Sigurd, on Kleist, 116n, 117n
Bürgin, Hans, *Thomas Mann*, 257n
Buzancy, 27
Byron, George Gordon, Lord, 62

Cabinet of Dr. Caligari, The, 264-65
Cagliostro [Giuseppe Balsamo], x, 158
Carlson, Eric T., on Charles Poyen, 192n
Carlyle, Thomas, 190
cathartic method, 29, 42; developed by Breuer, 37-40; used by Freud, 40-41
Catherine II (the Great), empress of Russia, 56
Charcot, Jean-Martin, 6, 32, 37, 42, 230; lectures on hypnosis and hysteria, 33; studies hypnosis, 34-35; influence on Freud, 35-36
Chasles, Philarète, on Balzac, 153
Chateaubriand, François-René de, 156
Chertok, L., *Naissance du psychanalyste de Mesmer à Freud*, 44n
chimney-sweeping, 39
Christian Science, 4, 6; anticipated by Barbarin, 26; and Mary Baker Eddy, 193-94
Cohen, I. Bernard, *Franklin and Newton*, 49n
Cohn, Dorrit, on Kleist, 96n, 108n
Coleridge, Samuel Taylor, 50
Comédie humaine, La, see Balzac, Honoré de
concentration technique, used by Freud, 40-41
Constant, Benjamin, 156
Corday, Charlotte, 159
Così fan tutte, see Mozart, Wolfgang Amadeus
Court de Gébelin, Antoine, 23
Cox, Arthur J., on Dickens, 191n
Crews, Frederick, 212, 213, 225; *Out of My System*, ix; on *The Blithedale Romance*, 223n; *The Sins of the Fathers*, 212n, 213n, 225n
crisis, magnetic, 45, 54
Crosby, Donald H., on Kleist, 101n

Curtius, Ernst Robert, *Balzac,* 169n, 170n; "New Encounter with Balzac," 169n

Daemmrich, Horst, *The Shattered Self,* 140n
Dahmen, Hans, *E.T.A. Hoffmanns Weltanschauung,* 122n; on Schubert and Hoffmann, 123n
Dante, Alighieri, 159, 270
Darnton, Robert, 20; *Mesmerism and the End of the Enlightenment in France,* 7n, 12n, 21n, 158n, 192n
Darwin, Erasmus, 62
Davidson, Frank, on *The Blithedale Romance,* 219n
Davin, Félix, on Balzac, 154
Davis, Andrew Jackson, 197; develops powers as medium, 194; publishes *The Principles of Nature,* 194-95
de la Rue, Madame, 191
Deleuze, Joseph Philippe François, 159
De planetarum influxu, see Mesmer, Franz Anton
Deslon, Charles, 19; defends Mesmer, 17; establishes mesmerist practice, 17-18; submits to investigation by royal commission, 21-22
Dickens, Catherine, 191
Dickens, Charles, x, 190; experiments with animal magnetism, 191
Docteurs modernes, Les, see Radet, Jean Baptiste
Dr. Mabuse, The Gambler, 265
Dumas, Alexandre, 156, 158
du Maurier, George, *Trilby,* 270
Dyer, Denys, on Kleist, 101n

Eddy, Mary Baker, consults Quimby, 193; denounces Quimby and animal magnetism, 194. *See also* Christian Science
Edel, Leon, 232, 235n, 236n
Edison, Thomas Alva (in *L'Eve future*), 63
Eichendorff, Joseph Freiherr von, 141; *Geschichte der poetischen Literatur Deutschlands,* 141n
Eichner, Hans, *Friedrich Schlegel,* 76n
Eisner, Lotte, *The Haunted Screen,* 264n
electricity, as model for animal magnetism, 14; and Leyden jar, 50-51; used for public entertainment, 51-52; as agent of life, 52-53; used in shock therapy, 53-55; as source of vital power, 55-60; as soul of universe, 58-59; in *Frankenstein,* 60-63; in *L'Eve future,* 63; in *Heinrich von Ofterdingen,* 66; significance for Kleist, 90-92; in Hoffmann's works, 127-29; in *Louis Lambert,* 162-64; and *passim. See also* galvanism, Leyden jar, subtle fluids
electrotherapy, 43; practiced by Freud, 36; used by physicians, 53-54
Elementa Medicinae, see Brown, John
Elementa Physiologiae, see Haller, Albrecht von
Elisabeth von R. (Freud's patient), 41
Ellenberger, Henri, 14; *The Discovery of the Unconscious,* 4n, 14n, 15n
Elliotson, John, experiments with animal magnetism, 189-90; in-

structs Dickens in mesmerist methods, 191
Ellis, J. M., *Kleist's "Prinz Friedrich von Homburg,"* 116n, 118n
Erb, Wilhelm, 36
Euripides, 269
Evans, Henri, *Louis Lambert et la philosophie de Balzac*, 161n
L'Eve future, *see* Villiers de l'Isle-Adam, Auguste de
excitability, 56, 166-67
"Experience in the Occult, An," *see* Mann, Thomas

Falk, Doris V., on Poe and mesmerism, 197n
Fanger, Donald, *Dostoevsky and Romantic Realism*, ix, 179n
Fantasia of the Unconscious, *see* Lawrence, D. H.
Ferguson, Muriel Blackstock, *La Volonté dans la "Comédie humaine" de Balzac*, 166n
Fichte, Johann Gottlieb, 47, 75, 76n
Fishbaugh, Reverend (scribe to Andrew Jackson Davis), 194
Flaubert, Gustave, *Madame Bovary*, xi, xii; *Bouvard et Pécuchet*, xii
Fliess, Wilhelm, 37
Fludd, Robert, 5
fluidists, endorse use of magnetic fluid, 25-26
Ford, Ford Madox, 55
Fraenkel, Heinrich, *The German Cinema*, 264n
Frangi, Françoise, on Balzac, 182n
Frankenstein, see Shelley, Mary
Franklin, Benjamin, 12, 21, 50, 61, 63, 120n; serves as member of royal commission, 21-23; experiments with electricity, 52
Franklinism, 54
free association, 38, 42
Freeman, Mary, *D. H. Lawrence*, 245n
Freemasons, 12, 19
Freud, Sigmund
general: xiii, 6, 28, 29, 30, 34, 111, 141n, 230, 232, 254, 255, 266; influence on literary criticism, ix; studies with Charcot, 35-36; uses electrotherapy, 36-37; experiments with hypnosis, 37-39; disenchantment with hypnosis, 40-42; sources for his language, 42-44; denounced by Lawrence, 243-44
works: *Autobiographical Study*, 37; *Studies on Hysteria*, 38-40; "Project for a Scientific Psychology," 43; "Group Psychology and the Analysis of the Ego," 262-64
Fricke, Gerhard, *Gefühl und Schicksal bei Heinrich v. Kleist*, 83n
Friedrich Wilhelm II, king of Prussia, 75

Gall, Franz Joseph, 174
Galvani, Luigi, 63, 65, 129, 221; discovery of animal electricity, 58-59; influence on German scientists, 59
galvanism, 74; Ritter's views on, 59-60; Mary Shelley's views on, 62; Novalis's views on, 63-69
Garland, Mary, *Kleist's "Prinz Friedrich von Homburg,"* 93n
Garrison, Fielding H., *An Introduction to the History of Medicine*, 57n
Gass, William H., on *D. H. Lawrence*, 248n

Gautier, Théophile, on Balzac, 152, 153n, 184, 188; "Avatar," 159-60; "Jettatura," 160
Gearey, John, *Heinrich von Kleist*, 97n
Girardin, Delphine (Mme de), 159, 184
Gluck, Christoph Willibald, 8
Gode-von Aesch, Alexander, *Natural Science in German Romanticism*, 59n, 125n
Goebbels, Joseph, 265-67
Goethe, Johann Wolfgang von, 66, 67, 77; *Die Wahlverwandtschaften*, 78-79; on subtle fluids, 79
Goldsmith, Margaret, *Franz Anton Mesmer*, 4n, 7n, 24n
Göring, Hermann, 267
Grabo, Carl, *A Newton among Poets*, 62n
Graham, James, 54
Green, David Bonnell, on *The Bostonians*, 240n
Griffith, Kelley, Jr., on *The Blithedale Romance*, 223n
Grimes, J. S., 194
"Group Psychology and the Analysis of the Ego," *see* Freud, Sigmund
Guillain, Georges, *J.-M. Charcot*, 34n
Guillotin, Joseph-Ignace, 21

Habegger, Alfred, on *The Bostonians*, 242n
Haller, Albrecht von, 55
Hardenberg, Friedrich von, *see* Novalis
Hardenberg, Prince Karl August von, 156
Hartley, David, 50
Hatch, Cora, 239n
Hatfield, Henry, 264n; on Mann, 257n, 261n
Hauffe, Friederike, 77
Hawthorne, Nathaniel
general: xi, xiv, 196, 200, 232, 269, 270; master-slave theme in his works, 200-201, 227; interest in animal magnetism, 201, 212, 227; animal magnetism and sexuality, 205-206, 227; mesmerism and art, 206, 227-29
works: "The Birthmark," 201-204, 213; "Ethan Brand," 204-205, 222; "The Great Stone Face," 226; *The Marble Faun*, 226, 229; "The Prophetic Pictures," 206-208, 216; "Rappaccini's Daughter," 201-204, 213; *The Scarlet Letter*, 222
The Blithedale Romance: 205, 206, 209, 233, 243; theme of unpardonable sin, 217-19; role of narrator, 218-19, 223-25; master-slave relationships, 219-20; concept of sympathy, 221-22; magnetic personalities, 222-23; narrator's evolution from master to slave, 225-26; artist as mesmerist and medium, 226; influence on *The Bostonians*, 235-38, 240-41
The House of the Seven Gables: 205, 206, 222; characterization of Holgrave, 208-10; Maule's mesmerist powers, 210-12; master-slave relationships, 212-13; relationship of medium to mesmerist, 212-14; Holgrave's renunciation of mesmerism, 215-17
Hawthorne, Sophia Peabody, 205
Haydn, Franz Joseph, 8

Haym, Rudolf, 69-70; *Die romantische Schule,* 70n
Haywood, Bruce, on Klingsohr's *Märchen,* 64n
Hegel, Georg Wilhelm Friedrich, 67, 142n, 175
Hegener, Johannes, *Die Poetisierung der Wissenschaften bei Novalis,* 64n, 65n
Heilman, Robert B., on D. H. Lawrence, 248n
Heine, Heinrich, 156; on Hoffmann, 120; *Die Bäder von Lucca,* 120n
Heinrich von Ofterdingen, see Novalis
Helbling, Robert E., *The Major Works of Heinrich von Kleist,* 104n
Hell, Maximilian, 9-10
Helmholtz, Hermann, 43
Helmont, Johann Baptist van, 5
Hemsterhuis, Frans, on the *organe moral,* 47
Hermann, Helene, on Kleist, 101n
Hillman, Robert G., on the Nancy-Salpêtrière controversy, 32n
Hitler, Adolf, 265; alleged magnetic powers, 266-68
Hoffman, Daniel, *Poe Poe Poe Poe Poe Poe Poe,* 198n; *Form and Fable in American Fiction,* 208n
Hoffman, Frederick J., *Freudianism and the Literary Mind,* 244n
Hoffmann, Ernst Theodor Amadeus
general: x, xi, xiv, 80, 120, 180, 232, 270; sources of information on mesmerism, 122-23; language of mesmerism in his works, 123; obsession with eyes and optical instruments, 123-24; description of transitions from blindness to insight, 124-26, 150-51; views on creative process, 125-27; characters' changes in perception, 127-29; *Serapionsbund,* 128; significance of *Kristall,* 134-35, 142-45; ambivalent attitude toward mesmerism, 149-50; popularity in France, 156-57
works: "The Contest of the Singers," 125, 128-29; "The Deserted House," 124, 130; "Don Juan," 129-30; *Fantastic Sketches in the Style of Callot,* 129; "The Jesuit Church in G.," 143; *Kater Murr,* 129; "The Magnetizer," 122, 130-35, 150; *Master Flea,* 124, 148; "Master Martin the Cooper and His Apprentices," 146n; "The Mines of Falun," 142-43; "Nutcracker and the King of Mice," 128; "The Pledge," 122; *Princess Brambilla,* 124, 144, 147; "Ritter Gluck," 147; "The Uncanny Guest," 122, 133-35, 138, 150
The Golden Pot: 123, 124, 130, 134; ambiguity of perception, 136-37; magnetism and electricity, 137-39; analysis of formulaic language, 140-41; pattern of plot, 141-42; suicide of protagonist, 145-46; role of reflection and knowledge, 146-48; significance of death, 148-49; narrator's role, 149-50
Hogg, Thomas Jefferson, 62n
Holz, Hans Heinz, *Macht und Ohnmacht der Sprache,* 90n
Horace, *Ars poetica,* 7-8
Hosmer, Ruth, on Hawthorne and mesmerism, 201n

House of the Seven Gables, The, see Hawthorne, Nathaniel
Howe, Irving, on *The Bostonians*, 242n
Howells, William Dean, *The Undiscovered Country*, 233
Hubbs, V. C., on Kleist, 116n
Hughes, H. Stuart, *Consciousness and Society*, 43n
Hugo, Léopoldine, 159
Hugo, Victor, 156, 184; interest in animal magnetism and spiritualism, 158-59
Hull, Clark L., on hypnosis, 29
Humboldt, Alexander von, 59
Humboldt, Wilhelm von, 75
Hunt, Herbert J., *Balzac's Comédie Humaine*, 165n
Hutcheson, Frances, on the moral sense, 47
hydrotherapy, 43
hypnosis, early medical use of, 4-5; and James Braid, 31-32; Freud's interest in, 35-36; Freud's experiments with, 37-42; and *passim*
hypnotic anesthesia, 26
hysteria, 15, 29, 42; studied by Charcot, 32, 34-35; Freud's interest in, 35-36; studied by Freud and Breuer, 38-40

Ide, Heinz, *Der junge Kleist*, 90n
Illuminism, 156
Imhof, Eugen, on *Mario and the Magician*, 257n
Ion, 269
irritability, 55

Jaffé, Aniela, on Hoffmann, 139n
James, Henry
 general: on Balzac, 154; on Hawthorne, 221; "Professor Fargo," 232-35
 The Bostonians: 231, 233; analysis of imagery, 235; influence of *The Blithedale Romance*, 235-38; psychological explanations for magnetic powers, 238-43; social satire, 242-43
Jean Paul [Johann Paul Friedrich Richter], 75, 76n; on Schelling, 72
Jesus of Nazareth, 4, 185, 193
Jones, Ernest, 35; *The Life and Work of Sigmund Freud*, 35n
Journal du Magnétisme, 158
Jussieu, Antoine-Laurent de, 23

Kanter, Fritz, *Der blidliche Ausdruck in Kleists "Penthesilea,"* 101n
Kaplan, Fred, *Dickens and Mesmerism*, 190n, 191n, 192n
Käthchen of Heilbronn, see Kleist, Heinrich von
Kellaway, Peter, on electric fish, 53n
Keller, Marie-Luise, on Kleist, 101n
Kelley, Cornelia Pulsifer, *The Early Development of Henry James*, 233n
Kennedy, Hugh A. Studdert, *Mrs. Eddy*, 193n
Kepler, Johann, 50
Kerner, Justinus, *Franz Anton Mesmer aus Schwaben*, 74n, 77n; his views on Mesmer, 76-77; *The Seeress of Prevorst*, 77
Kerr, Howard, *Mediums, and Spirit-Rappers, and Roaring Radicals*, 195n, 196n, 236n, 239n, 242n
"King's Evil," 4-5
Kleist, Ewald Georg von, 50-51

Kleist, Heinrich von
general: xi, xiv, 67, 80, 270; meteorological metaphors in his work, 82-84, 87-90; shift in interest from electricity to animal magnetism, 84-85; analogical thought, 85-87; interest in animal magnetism, 105-106; moments of recognition in his works, 118-19; problem of knowledge, 119-20
works: *Amphitryon*, 88; *The Battle of Arminius*, 88; "The Betrothal in Santo Domingo," 82, 84, 94; "Essay on the Sure Way of Finding Happiness," 92; "Event of the Day," 87; "The Foundling," 83-84, 94; "The Marquise of O . . . ," 83-84, 92, 94, 108; "On the Gradual Formation of Thoughts during Speech," 90-92, 96, 111, 120; "On the Marionette Theater," 115; "Saint Cecilia; or The Power of Music," 88, 89, 95; "The Stylus of God," 87; "The Very Latest Educational Scheme," 90, 91-92
Käthchen of Heilbronn: 112, 114-20 *passim*, 138; significance of Wetter vom Strahl's name, 102-103; theme of magnetic attraction, 103-104; Schubert's influence, 104-106; theme of mental rapport, 106-107, 109-110; divine and diabolical elements, 107-108; problem of knowledge, 108-112
Penthesilea: 84, 90, 92, 103, 105, 106, 112, 114-20 *passim*; meeting of protagonists, 92-93; analysis of imagery, 94-95, 100-102; electrical reactions, 94-99; problem of knowledge, 99
Prince Friedrich of Homburg: 118-20 *passim*; meteorological metaphors, 87-88; theme of somnambulism, 112-13; merging of dream and reality, 113-15; analysis of dramatic conflict, 116-18
Klingsohr's *Märchen*, *see* Novalis
Koch, Friedrich, *Heinrich von Kleist*, 83n
Koreff, David Ferdinand, 122, 123n; renews French interest in mesmerism, 156
Kornmann, Guillaume, 19
Kotzebue, August von, *Das neue Jahrhundert*, 57-58
Kracauer, Siegfried, 264; *From Caligari to Hitler*, 264n, 265n
Kreutzer, Hans Joachim, *Die dichterische Entwicklung Heinrich von Kleists*, 86n
Kuhn, Thomas S., *The Structure of Scientific Revolutions*, 50n

Lafayette, Marie-Joseph, Marquis de, 12, 192
Lafontaine, Charles, 31
Lang, Fritz, *Dr. Mabuse, The Gambler*, 265; *The Last Will of Dr. Mabuse*, 265-66
Langer, Walter C., *The Mind of Adolf Hitler*, 266n, 267n
Last Will of Dr. Mabuse, The, *see* Lang, Fritz
Lavater, Johann Kaspar, 174
Lavoisier, Antoine-Laurent de, 21
Lawrence, D. H.
general: 232; on Hawthorne, 215-16; *Studies in Classical American Literature*, 216n; contempt for psychoanalysis, 243-44; sources for his vitalistic theories, 253-54
Fantasia of the Unconscious:

Lawrence, D. H. (*cont.*)
243, 250, 253, 254; reception by critics, 244-45; as key to novels, 245
Psychoanalysis and the Unconscious: 254; as key to novels, 245; polarity and human anatomy, 245-47; magnetic and electrical interchange, 247-48
Women in Love: 232, 271; analysis of metaphorical language, 248-49; magnetic and electrical qualities of characters, 249-51; theme of dissolution, 251-52; theme of equilibrium, 252-53

Leavis, F. R., *D. H. Lawrence*, 245n, 248n

Le Bon, Gustave, *Psychology of Crowds*, 262

Leibbrand, Werner, *Die spekulative Medizin der Romantik*, 57n, 59n

Lessing, Gotthold Ephraim, 67

Levingston, William, 194

Le Yaouanc, Moïse, *Nosographie de l'humanité balzacienne*, 166n

Leyden jar, 91, 161, 166, 178; as model for *baquet*, 14, 43, 54; invention of, 50-51; used for electrical demonstrations, 51-52; and electric torpedo, 53; used by Galvani, 58. *See also* electricity, galvanism

Lichtlé, Michel, on *Louis Lambert*, 161n

Liébeault, Ambroise Auguste, 30, 36; treats patients with animal magnetism, 32-33; visited by Bernheim, 33; visited by Freud, 38

Liebig, Justus von, 70

Lilienstern, Rühle von, 92

Lind, Sidney E., on Poe and mesmerism, 197n

London University College Hospital, 189

Long, Robert Emmet, on *The Blithedale Romance* and *The Bostonians*, 236n

Lott, Frans van der, 53

Louis XV (king of France), 51

Louis XVI (king of France), 4, 21, 90

Louis Lambert, see Balzac, Honoré de

Lovenjoul, Charles de, on Balzac, 154n

Lowell, James Russell, "The Unhappy Lot of Mr. Knott," 196

Lyon, Dr. (physician to Andrew Jackson Davis), 194

Mabille, Pierre, *Le Miroir du merveilleux*, 80

McGlathery, James M., on Hoffmann, 145n

MacKay, A. T., on Jean Paul and animal magnetism, 76n

Macpherson, James, 56

Madame Bovary, see Flaubert, Gustave

Magic Mountain, The, see Mann, Thomas

Magnétiseur, Le, see Soulié, Frédéric

Magnétisomanie, Le, 157

Magnus, Albertus, 61

Male, Roy R., *Hawthorne's Tragic Vision*, 203n; on Hawthorne, 221

Maniquis, Robert M., on the *Mimosa pudica*, 53n

Mann, Thomas
general: 232, 266; *The Magic Mountain*, 255; "An Experience

in the Occult," 255-57; "Freud and the Future," 264
Mario and the Magician: 232, 267, 271; theme of fascism, 257-58; links between its two parts, 258-59; Cipolla's powers, 259-61; problem of group psychology, 261-64
Manvell, Roger, *The German Cinema*, 264n
Marble Faun, The, see Hawthorne, Nathaniel
Marc, Julia, 148
Marcus, Adalbert Friedrich, 57n, 122, 123n
Maria Theresa (empress of Austria), 9, 11
Marie Antoinette (queen of France), 18
Mario and the Magician, see Mann, Thomas
Martin, Marietta, *Le Docteur Koreff*, 156n
Martin, Terence, *Nathaniel Hawthorne*, 219n
Martin, W. R., on *The Bostonians*, 240n
Martineau, Harriet, *Letters on Mesmerism*, 190-91
Martini, Christian Ernst, 87
Matt, Peter von, *Die Augen der Automaten*, 126n
Matter, Harry, on Mann, 258n
Matthiessen, F. O., on Hawthorne, 201
Maximilian III Joseph (elector of Bavaria), 10
Maxwell, William, 5
Mayer, Hans-Otto, *Thomas Mann*, 257n
Mead, Richard, 43
medical faculty (University of Paris), 12, 17n, 21; refuses to pronounce judgment on animal magnetism, 17
medical faculty (University of Vienna), 8, 37; denies Mesmer recognition, 11
Medical Society (Lyons), 26
Melville, Herman, "The Apple-Tree Table," 195-96; *Moby Dick*, 196; *Pierre*, 196-97
Mémoire sur la découverte du magnétisme animal, see Mesmer, Franz Anton
Mémoires d'un médecin, see Dumas, Alexandre
Mérimée, Prosper, 156
Mesmer, Franz Anton
general: xiii, 25, 27, 28, 40, 42, 43, 50, 56, 75, 129, 157, 158, 159, 174, 184, 197, 199, 221, 222, 228, 231, 254; claims for animal magnetism, xi-xii; his role in history of psychology, 3; early life, 6-8; dissertation, 7-9; medical practice, 8; and Mozart, 8-9; dispute with Maximilian Hell, 9-10; develops theory of animal magnetism, 9-10; performs for Bavarian court, 10; spurned by medical and academic world, 10-11; treats Maria-Theresa von Paradies, 11; moves to Paris, 10-11; publishes first *Mémoire*, 12; seeks official endorsement, 12-13, 16-17; treats patients in Paris, 13-16; mounts defense of theories, 18-19; establishes Society of Universal Harmony, 19; denounced as fraud, 20-24; returns to Vienna, 24-25; last years, 25; addresses issue of sixth sense, 45; eulogized by Justinus Kerner, 76-77; enlists support of George

Mesmer, Franz Anton (*cont.*) Washington, 192; and *passim*
theory of animal magnetism: traditions out of which it developed, 4-6; scientific foundations of, 5-6; occult features of, 6; derivative nature of, 14, 54; significance of crisis, 15-16, 29; meets with hostility of academic world, 16-17; investigated by royal commission, 21-23; investigated by Royal Society of Medicine (Paris), 23; satirized, 23-24; rôle of magnetic fluid, 29-30; traditional features of, 48-49; and *passim*
Mesmer, Maria Anna von Bosch, 8
mesmerism, *see* Mesmer: theory of animal magnetism
Miko, Stephen J., *Toward "Women in Love,"* 252n
Milner, Max, on Balzac, 180n
Milton, John, 179
Mimosa pudica, 53
Mitchell, Silas Weir, 36
Moby Dick, *see* Melville, Herman
Morris, Max, *Heinrich von Kleists Reise nach Würzburg*, 104n
Moynahan, Julian, *The Deed of Life*, 250n
Mozart, Wolfgang Amadeus, *Bastien und Bastienne*, 8; *Così fan tutte*, 9; *Don Giovanni*, 129, 130
Mühlher, Robert, on Hoffmann, 138n, 139n, 147
Müller, Adam, 104, 105n
Müller, Helmut, on Hoffmann, 140
Müller-Seidel, Walter, *Versehen und Erkennen*, 83n, 102n, 103n
Murray, Peter, on *The Blithedale Romance*, 220n
Murry, John Middleton, *Son of Woman*, 245n
Musschenbroek, Pieter van, 51
Musset, Alfred de, 156

Nabokov, Vladimir, xi, 243
Nancy, University of, 33
Nancy school, *see* Liébeault, Ambroise Auguste, and Bernheim, Hippolyte Marie
Naturphilosophie, 105; and Schelling, 69-73; and Schubert, 73-74
Negus, Kenneth, on Hoffmann, 139n
Nerval, Gérard de, 270; *Aurélia*, 268-69
Neubauer, John, on Brown and German Romanticism, 56n; *Bifocal Vision*, 57n
neurypnology, 31
Newton, Sir Isaac, 8, 43, 55, 63; and subtle fluids, 49
Night Watches of Bonaventura, The, 79
Nollet, Abbé Jean-Antoine, 51
nous, 69
Novalis [Friedrich von Hardenberg], 80, 81, 121, 269; on sensory perception, 46, 73-74; "The Novices of Sais," 46, 68; on a moral sense, 47; on John Brown, 56-57, 58n; views on galvanism, 63-69; Klingsohr's *Märchen (Heinrich von Ofterdingen)*, 64-67, 144; concept of golden age, 67-68; on Schelling, 70; on oxygen, 71n
"Novices of Sais, The," *see* Novalis
Nyomarkay, Joseph, on Hitler, 266n

Ochsner, Karl, *E.T.A. Hoffmann*

als Dichter des Unbewussten, 122n
O'Connor, William Van, on *The Blithedale Romance*, 223n
O'key, Elizabeth and Jane, 189
Oliver, Clinton, on *The Bostonians*, 242n
Oppeln-Bronikowski, Friedrich von, *David Ferdinand Koreff*, 123n
Opticks, see Newton, Sir Isaac
organe moral, see Hemsterhuis, Frans
Ossian, 56

Paracelsus, Philippus Aureolus [Theophrastus Bombastus von Hohenheim], 5, 61
Paradies, Maria-Theresa von, 11
Pascal, Roy, on Kleist, 117n, 118n
Pattie, Frank A., on Mesmer's dissertation, 7n
Penthesilea, see Kleist, Heinrich von
Peters, Diane Stone, on Hoffmann, 126n
Petersen, Julius, *Die Sehnsucht nach dem Dritten Reich in deutscher Sage und Dichtung*, 67n
Petetin, Jacques-Henri-Désirée, 25, 27; aligns himself with animists, 26
Pétigny, Jules de, on Balzac, 154
Pierre, see Melville, Herman
Pikulik, Lothar, on Hoffmann, 143
Pinel, Philippe, 35
Podmore, Frank, *Modern Spiritualism*, 195n
Poe, Edgar Allan, x, 92, 191, 196; views on mesmerism, 197-98; "Mesmeric Revelation," 198; "The Facts in the Case of M. Valdemar," 198; *Eureka*, 198-99; "Tale of the Ragged Mountains," 199-200
Pollin, Burton R., on *Frankenstein*, 61n
Pomme, Pierre, *Traité des affections vaporeuses*, 15n
Poughkeepsie Seer, *see* Davis, Andrew Jackson
Poulet, Georges, *Etudes sur le temps humain*, 169n
Poyen, Charles, 194, 195; tours New England, 192; *Progress of Animal Magnetism in New England*, 193n
Praz, Mario, *The Romantic Agony*, 180n
pressure technique, 41
Priestley, Joseph, 51, 70n
Prince Friedrich of Homburg, see Kleist, Heinrich von
Pritchett, V. S., *Balzac*, 184n
"Professor Fargo," *see* James, Henry
Prometheus, 63
Pryse, James M., *The Apocalypse Unsealed*, 254
Psychiatric Society (Vienna), 37
Psychoanalysis and the Unconscious, see Lawrence, D. H.
psychoanalytic approaches to literature, ix
Psychological Association (Vienna), 37
Pushkin, Aleksandr, *Eugene Onegin*, xi
Putt, S. Gorley, *A Reader's Guide to Henry James*, 233n
Puységur, Armand-Marie-Jacques de Chastenet (Marquis de), 25, 40, 42, 134, 159, 176; sponsors electromagnetic fluid, 27; treats

Puységur, A.-M.-J. (*cont.*)
Victor Race, 27-28; stresses role of trance, 29-30
Pyrrhus of Epirus, 4

Quimby, Phineas Parkhurst, 193-94
Quisling, Vidkun, 267

Race, Victor (Puységur's patient), 27-28, 39
Radet, Jean Baptiste, *Les Docteurs modernes*, 23, 24n, 157
Rauschning, Hermann, *Gespräche mit Hitler*, 267n
Reil, Johann Christian, 105n, 107; *Rhapsodieen*, 107n
Reni, Guido, 206
resistance, 42
Reske, Hermann, *Traum und Wirklichkeit im Werk Heinrich von Kleists*, 83n
rest cure, 36
Richards, David B., on Schiller and mesmerism, 76n
Richter, Johann Paul Friedrich, *see* Jean Paul
Rieff, Philip, on Lawrence, 244n
Rieger, James, on *Frankenstein*, 61n
Ringe, Donald A., on Hawthorne, 217n, 218n
Risse, Günter B., on John Brown, 56
Ritter, Gerhard, on Hitler, 266n
Ritter, Johann Wilhelm, 69, 70, 75; on an internal sense, 46; on an electrical sense, 48; on the universe as an *All-Tier*, 59; views on galvanism, 59-60
Ritterbush, Philip C., *Overtures to Biology*, 52n, 53n, 54n
Ritzler, Paula, on Kleist, 100n
Roazen, Paul, *Freud*, 42n
Röschlaub, Andreas, 57n, 105n
Rosicrucianism, 156
Rougemont, Denis de, 271; *Love in the Western World*, 271n
Rousseau, Jean-Jacques, xii
royal commission, 41; refutes claims of animal magnetism, 4; investigates animal magnetism, 21-23
Royal Society of Medicine (Paris), 12, 17n; petitioned by Mesmer, 16-17; investigates animal magnetism, 23
royal touch, *see* "King's Evil"
Ryan, Lawrence, on Kleist, 117n

Sainte-Beuve, Charles-Augustin, on Balzac, 152-53
Saint-Martin, Louis-Claude, 184
Salpêtrière, *see* Charcot, Jean-Martin
Samuel, Richard, *Heinrich von Kleist: Prinz Friedrich von Homburg*, 116n
Saussure, R. de, *Naissance du psychanalyste de Mesmer à Freud*, 44n
Savigny, Friedrich Karl von, 75
Scarlet Letter, The, *see* Hawthorne, Nathaniel
Scheele, Karl Wilhelm, 70n
Schelling, Friedrich Wilhelm Joseph von, 67, 74, 75; Brown's influence on, 57; views on nature, 69-70; reception of his work, 70-71, 74; basic premises of *Naturphilosophie*, 71-73
Schenk, H. G., *The Mind of the European Romantics*, 70n
Schiller, Johann Christoph Friedrich von, 67, 75, 76n
Schlegel, Caroline, 57n
Schlegel, Friedrich, 71, 76

Schleiermacher, Friedrich Ernst Daniel, 75
Schneck, Jerome M., on Browning and mesmerism, 191n
Schneider, Emil, *Der animale Magnetismus*, 4n, 7n
Schopenhauer, Arthur, *The World as Will and Idea*, 175; philosophical views, 175-76; animal magnetism and human will, 176-77
Schorer, Mark, on *Women in Love*, 248n, 251n
Schrenck-Notzing, Albert Freiherr von, 255-56; *Materialisations-Phänomene*, 255, 256n
Schubert, Gotthilf Heinrich, 107; on anatomical polarity, 73-74; influence on Kleist, 104-106; *Views on the Nocturnal Aspect of Natural Science*, 105, 107n, 110n; autobiography, 105n; influence on Hoffmann, 122-23, 128
Schuckmann, Dietrich, on *Mario and the Magician*, 258n
Schürer-Waldheim, F., *Anton Mesmer*, 7n
scrofula, 4
Seeress of Prevorst, The, see Kerner, Justinus von
Seligmann, Siegfried, 131
Senger, Hans Joachim, *Der bildliche Ausdruck in den Werken Heinrich von Kleists*, 101n
sensibility, 55
Serapionsbund, 122, 125
Serapiontic Principle, 125
Shaftesbury, Anthony Ashley Cooper, third earl of, on a moral sense, 47
Shakers, 192
Shakespeare, 77, 159
Shelley, Mary, *Frankenstein*, 60-63
Shelley, Percy Bysshe, and genesis of *Frankenstein*, 62-63; "Magnetic Lady to Her Patient," 190; "A Defence of Poetry," 269-70
Sierke, Eugen, on Mesmer, 7n
Simon, Gustave, on Victor Hugo, 159n
Singer, Herbert, on Kleist, 109n
Slessarev, Helga, on Hoffmann, 123n
Snelders, H.A.M., on *Naturphilosophie*, 71n
Société Harmonique des Amis Réunis, 29
Society of Universal Harmony, 27, 157, 192; founded in Paris, 19
Socrates, 159, 269
Solger, Karl Wilhelm Ferdinand, 75
Sophocles, 77
Soulié, Frédéric, *Le Magnétiseur*, 157
Speyer, Friedrich, 148
spiritualism, xiii, 4, 6, 26, 31, 254; in Germany, 75-77; in France, 155-60; in America, 195-96; and Thomas Mann, 255-57
Starobinski, Jean, *La Relation critique*, 44n
Stendhal [Henri Beyle], 156
Stern, J. P., *Hitler*, 258n
Stern, Martin, on Kleist, 101n, 102n
Stewart, Walter A., *Psychoanalysis*, 35n
sthenic diseases, 56, 57. *See also* Brown, John
Stransky, Christine von, 76
Stubbs, John Caldwell, *The Pursuit of Form*, 214n, 219n

Studies on Hysteria, see Breuer, Josef, and Freud, Sigmund
subtle fluids, xiii, 43, 55, 69; and animal magnetism, 5; as agents of second sight, 48; as animating agents, 49-50; as unifying forces, 73-74; Goethe's views on, 79; Balzac's views on, 162, 166-68
Sucher, Paul, *Les Sources du merveilleux chez E.T.A. Hoffmann*, 122n
suggestion, 5, 40; early medical use of, 4-5; and animal magnetism, 15, 22, 29; and hypnosis, 32, 42; Charcot's use of, 34-35; Freud's use of, 38-40; Freud's views on, 262-63
Sulzer, Johann Georg, 10n
Svengali (character in du Maurier's *Trilby*), x, 270
Swedenborg, Emmanuel, 184
Swedenborgianism, 156, 162
sympathy, 48; Hawthorne's concept of, 221-22
synesthesia, 46

talking cure, 29, 39
Taylor, James, 190
Tennyson, Alfred, Lord, 190
Thackeray, William Makepeace, 190
Thomas, Ursula, on Kleist and Schubert, 105n
Tieck, *Der blonde Eckbert*, 99
Tindall, William York, 253; *D. H. Lawrence & Susan His Cow*, 254n
Tischner, Rudolf, *Mesmer und sein Problem*, 7n; *Franz Anton Mesmer*, 7n
Todorov, Tzvetan, 231; *The Fantastic*, 136n, 137n, 231n
Townshend, Reverend Chauncy Hare, 198; *Facts in Mesmerism*, 191, 197
transference, 22, 42
Trilby, see du Maurier, George
Trilling, Lionel, on *The Bostonians*, 242n
Tropp, Martin, *Mary Shelley's Monster*, 61n
Turk, Horst, *Dramensprache als gesprochene Sprache*, 90n
Twain, Mark, *Christian Science*, 194n; *The Adventures of Huckleberry Finn*, 196

Univercoelum, 195

vapeurs, 15
Vautrin, *see* Balzac, Honoré de
Veaumorel, Caullet de, *Aphorismes de M. Mesmer*, 45n
Veith, Ilza, *Hysteria*, 7n
Viatte, Auguste, *Les Sources occultes du romantisme*, 155n; *Victor Hugo et les Illuminés de son temps*, 159n
Vienna, University of, xi, 7, 9
Villiers de l'Isle-Adam, Auguste de, *L'Eve future*, 63
Vinchon, Jean, *Mesmer et son secret*, 7n
Virchow, Rudolf, on John Brown, 56
Volta, Alessandro, refutes concept of animal electricity, 59
Voltaire [François-Marie Arouet], 12
Vordtriede, Werner, *Novalis und die französischen Symbolisten*, 77n

Waggoner, Hyatt H., *Hawthorne*, 219n
Walmsley, D. M., *Anton Mesmer*, 7n

Washington, George, 192
Webb, R. K., *Harriet Martineau*, 191n
Weigand, Hermann J., on Kleist, 109n; *Thomas Mann's Novel "Der Zauberberg,"* 257n
Weikard, M. A., 56
Wellek, René, on Hoffmann, 140n
Weltseele, see Schelling, Friedrich Wilhelm Joseph von
Werdet, Edmond, on Balzac, 152, 153n
Werner, Hans-Georg, *E.T.A. Hoffmann*, 122n
Wetzels, Walter D., on natural science in German Romanticism, 59n; *Johann Wilhelm Ritter*, 60n; on Klingsohr's *Märchen*, 64n, 65n, 66n
Wiene, Robert, 265
Wilson, Edmund, on *The Bostonians*, 235n
Wizard of Menlo Park, *see* Edison, Thomas Alva
Wolf, A., *A History of Science, Technology, and Philosophy in the Eighteenth Century*, 51n
Wolfart, Karl Christian, 45, 75
Wolff, Robert Lee, *Strange Stories*, 190n, 191n
Wollheim, Richard, *Sigmund Freud*, 35n
Wöllner, Günter, *E.T.A. Hoffmann und Franz Kafka*, 139n
Women in Love, see Lawrence, D. H.
Wukadinović, Spiridion, *Kleist-Studien*, 104n

Yoga, 254

Zenge, Wilhelmine von, 85-86
Zoist, 190
Zola, Emile, on Balzac, 154
Zweig, Stefan, *Die Heilung durch den Geist*, 7n, 193n

LIBRARY OF CONGRESS CATALOGING
IN PUBLICATION DATA

Tatar, Maria M. 1945-
Spellbound: studies on mesmerism and literature.

Includes index.
1. Mesmerism in literature. I. Title.
PN56.M52T3 809'.933'1 78-51199
ISBN 0-691-06377-X